Praise for
MISSION READY

"Space missions fail for human reasons—and succeed because of them. With a great selection of space-flight stories and grounded research, Elkins-Tanton delivers a model for leadership that shows how clarity, kindness, and courage lead to mission success for any team."

—Bob Smith, former CEO, Blue Origin

"*Mission Ready* is a powerful guide to building teams that thrive under pressure. Elkins-Tanton shows that when individuals are empowered, culture is thoughtfully built, and leadership is grounded in trust and transparency, teams can accomplish extraordinary things—even in the most challenging environments."

—Adena Friedman, chair and CEO, Nasdaq

"I've been hanging out in high-performance innovation ecosystems for fifty years now—Boston, Silicon Valley, Austin. High-performance teams make the right things happen. One of their key skills is being able to take conversations up a level, to talk about what they are talking about. The good news from Professor Elkins-Tanton is that NASA teams of rocket scientists aren't much different. *Mission Ready* is a how-to book about how to practice what she calls 'metacognition.' Read it, then send a copy to all your team members."

—Bob Metcalfe, Ethernet inventor and Turing Laureate

"Elkins-Tanton's book reminds us of something we know but keep forgetting—that it is not technology alone that moves us forward. People in teams need to make things happen, from small startups to monumental undertakings like the NASA Psyche mission. *Mission Ready* is a practical guide—with checklists, surveys, and actionable advice—but the real experiences and examples chronicled by Elkins-Tanton are what bring these valuable lessons to life."

—Deepak Kamra, general partner, Canaan Partners

MISSION
READY

MISSION READY

READY

How to Build Teams
That Perform Under Pressure

LINDY ELKINS-TANTON

BASIC

VENTURE

New York

Copyright © 2026 by Lindy Elkins-Tanton

Cover design by Kapo Ng
Cover image © VKA / Shutterstock.com
Cover copyright © 2026 by Hachette Book Group, Inc.

Basic Venture
Hachette Book Group
1290 Avenue of the Americas, New York, NY 10104
www.basic-venture.com

Printed in the United States of America

First Edition: April 2026

Published by Basic Venture, an imprint of Hachette Book Group, Inc. The Basic Venture name and logo is a registered trademark of the Hachette Book Group.

The Hachette Speakers Bureau provides a wide range of authors for speaking events. To find out more, go to hachettespeakersbureau.com or email HachetteSpeakers@hbgusa.com.

Basic Venture books may be purchased in bulk for business, educational, or promotional use. For more information, please contact your local bookseller or the Hachette Book Group Special Markets Department at special.markets@hbgusa.com.

The publisher is not responsible for websites (or their content) that are not owned by the publisher.

Print book interior design by Bart Dawson.

Library of Congress Cataloging-in-Publication Data
Names: Elkins-Tanton, Lindy author
Title: Mission ready : how to build teams that perform under pressure /
    Lindy Elkins-Tanton.
Description: First edition. | New York : Basic Venture, 2026. | Includes index.
Identifiers: LCCN 2025042950 (print) | LCCN 2025042951 (ebook) | ISBN
    9781541706033 hardcover | ISBN 9781541706057 ebook
Subjects: LCSH: Teams in the workplace | Teams in the workplace—Management |
    Leadership
Classification: LCC HD66 .E423 2026 (print) | LCC HD66 (ebook)
LC record available at https://lccn.loc.gov/2025042950
LC ebook record available at https://lccn.loc.gov/2025042951

ISBNs: 9781541706033 (hardcover), 9781541706057 (ebook)

LSC-C

Printing 1, 2026

To the NASA Psyche mission team

CONTENTS

CONTENTS

INTRODUCTION

The room around me was dark, and my husband was snoring gently beside me. Outside, the night birds and crickets of Merritt Island, right next to Kennedy Space Center, were calling in the moonless night. I, however, was sitting up in bed with my laptop on the quilt in front of me, AirPods in, listening to an intense conversation happening on Webex with people in Florida; Washington, DC; and Pasadena, California. It was 2:00 a.m. in Florida in 2023, and there were seventy people online.

We were all looking at a graph that showed how quickly temperature rose after a particular little mechanism called a cold-gas thruster was turned on. Our beautiful $1.2 billion mission and its spacecraft, scheduled to launch in twelve days, after twelve *years* of work, needed these thrusters. While the thrusters are not the main propulsion of the spacecraft, they, among other things, rotate the spacecraft so that the main antenna can point toward and communicate with Earth. The cold-gas thrusters are indispensable. And we had just discovered that they could fail shortly after launch. Catastrophic, mission ending.

Despite multiple careful levels of review and parts-acceptance policies, mistakes had been made and details missed down in the miles-deep ecosystem of subcontractors and parts manufacturers and inventory control systems. But the expert checks and reviews by the National Aeronautics and Space Administration (NASA) and Jet Propulsion Laboratory (JPL) had caught the problem. Thank all the gods.

We had to be ready to launch at some point within the next month, or we would run past the time period when a launch could allow the spacecraft to follow its planned path through space and, after years in cruise, intersect with the special, metal-rich asteroid that was our target.

Missing this launch period would be, at worst, a mission-canceling catastrophe, and, at best, would require an extension of the mission timeline, costing perhaps tens or even hundreds of millions of dollars. Missing this launch period would also be a terrible blot on the reputations of all the organizations involved. The stakes were very, very high. And as the leader of the NASA Psyche mission, this megaproject, I held the ultimate responsibility. I felt a tremendous pressure to push us all to succeed. But pushing was not what the team needed . . . the team needed calm and confidence. We all needed to take a breath and think steadily and carefully.

At a moment like this, a team really shows its heart and soul. Stress on this level, where personal and institutional reputations are on the line, budgetary costs are potentially so high as to be ruinous, and the world's press is watching, can break individuals and teams. And our team had already been under intense stress for years: We had built the spacecraft during COVID and then had not been able to complete software testing in time for our original launch period, which had slipped by over a year under intense scrutiny from NASA headquarters and the aerospace community. Now, just when we thought we could heave a sigh of relief, watch our rocket recede into the clouds, and have a party, came a clear death threat to the whole project.

People could have opted out. They could have said, "Too much stress; I'm done." People who were still in could have reacted at 2:00 a.m. with anger, passive-aggressiveness, and pessimism, and they could have derailed the critical and delicate problem-solving process.

And this was indeed a delicate and complicated problem-solving process, requiring not just the full commitment and positive, responsible attention and participation of all individuals involved, but also the synergy of the ways they worked together, communicating the most relevant information and finding their way, like trackers in a jungle, to the best path to solutions.

I was observing how each of the team members was fulfilling their role. There was hardly a misstep. Everyone listened, everyone made suggestions, everyone joined one or more subteams testing every potential solution, working around the clock.

Never has there been a time when I was prouder of the excellence of this team.

People say to me sometimes, "Building that space hardware must be so difficult!" To many, the spacecraft and the rocket, the physical manifestations of space exploration, seem like the miracles. Other people, more experienced in space exploration, will say, "It's always the software." Hardware is difficult, but you can see and touch it. Software is much harder to assess. But I've found that the humans, the people themselves, are both the most miraculous and the most devastating part of every story. Science and engineering are the structure of what I am doing, but people are the way it gets done.

I've had career-long intersectional experience with teams across the private sector, in government, in academia. I worked for years as a management consultant and then as an independent business-plan writer working with tech start-ups, as the cofounder of an education tech startup, as the director of two of the top Earth and planetary science research departments in the country and of a major lab producing spaceflight hardware, as an adviser to tech companies and venture capital firms, and as the originator and leader of the Psyche mission. These projects have been at all stages—in development, in production, and with teams that needed change and those that were purring along. I specialize in developing and supporting teams when the pressure is on and the stakes are high.

The Psyche project began with just five people and an idea. We convinced the Jet Propulsion Laboratory in Pasadena, California, to manage the mission. We interviewed and selected industry partners, particularly the spacecraft chassis builder Maxar. I led the grueling three-year process of NASA competition against twenty-seven other mission concepts. When we won in 2017, I became the second woman in the world to win a competed space mission. The team has had almost three thousand people work on it over time, from partner and subcontractor organizations across the country and around the world, and we've had more than two thousand college students participate in our student collaborations programs. I've been asked to speak about team culture at organizations as varied as Apple, Unilever, Honeybee Robotics, Amazon, and Stanford University. People are the way it gets done.

Now, I want to show other people how do to this. *Mission Ready* is a guide to creating the best possible teams, and the way to do that is with these elements: the individual, the team, and the leadership. Teams produce the greatest miracles of our advanced species, but they work only if they are made up of people who understand the team's vision and are capable of carrying it out. The only enabler of understanding and carrying out vision is culture, team culture.

I have come to see these three elements of a team—the individual (thinking inwardly, about one's own capabilities and effects on others) networking into a team (thinking outwardly, creating connections and building a team) and leadership (thinking from above, the aerial view of strategy, culture, leadership, and progress)—as essential for successful teams.

Though leadership has its own section in this book, in a real sense every one of us can be a leader. To be a leader, you need a vision and a positive influence on your team (you don't need people reporting to you officially—that makes you a manager, a good but different role). This book, then, is written for *every* person. Each of us can become more individually successful, better networked into a team, and more of a leader.

The cold-gas thruster crisis that opened this introduction illustrates the ways in which teams become great. First, at the foundational level, each individual had crafted themselves into a great team member: They were aware of how their actions and even their tones of voice enabled or disabled others from effective work, and they had already developed their own sense of quality and responsibility. Then, the team members networked themselves into a team with a functional culture that promoted progress. Finally, team leadership guided the team most effectively toward success and sheltered the members from drama from the outside.

Starting with yourself as an individual is critical: Advancing your vision, the vision of your team, or even your vision for society requires making yourself better at working in and building teams. Each of you can improve your personal efficacy, your cultural interactions, your contributions to the team, and your strategic thinking, and thus be seen as a leader.

Part I of *Mission Ready* shows how you can build five key attributes that will greatly increase your ability as an individual to problemsolve, communicate, and continuously improve. These five attributes—attributes that are seldom taught in school—include how to communicate clearly and calmly even in the most difficult circumstances, how to recognize problems and act, how to not give up, how to develop a strong sense of quality, and how to recognize the importance of process through strategic thinking and metacognition. In the age of AI, these are robot-proofing, success-creating, even happiness-creating attributes.

Metacognition is a concept worth underlining here. It's the process of standing to one side, so to speak, examining more objectively your own thinking, your own actions and processes, and their effects on others. It's becoming self-aware. If you can analyze objectively what you are doing and how well it is working, you can both improve everything you do and progress in that lifelong pursuit of moving your ego out of the way and seeing your team and the world more clearly.

Next, you need to connect with others until together you form a team. In Part II, I show how every organization, every team, every community consists of a network of one-on-one relationships, which I call dyads, your primary contacts. To coalesce into a real team, you need to move beyond the individuals you know best and create a common team experience. After cultivating your dyads and networking into a team, the team needs to set its culture, deciding on the ways people will interact and get the work done. Then the team is ready for the empowering practices of continuous, transparent communications, delegating authority, and structuring decision-making and follow-through so that everyone understands what will happen next.

The dyad is a central concept. We might talk about team loyalty and team cohesion, or team conflict or miscommunication, but in the end, every action that seems to be about a whole team is actually happening on the level of one person to another. Your team is not loyal to you; the individuals on the team are loyal to you. Your statement did not confuse a whole team; it confused some number of individuals on the team, each one in a slightly different way. Every group experience is actually a collection of one-on-one human experiences, the experiences of dyads.

Part III of *Mission Ready* looks at teams from above, from the vantage point of leadership. Ironically, people do not often perform or behave their best without leadership. Just as humans are naturally creatures of a networked community—a village—so also do we expect in our primitive brain stems that there will be a leader.

Successful teams need leaders who understand and practice culture building, communications, delegation, respect, and clear decision-making. Looking at a team from above, the leadership can use these practices—lead by example, keep teams from losing the recipe, excel at using margins and metrics, develop better assessments and rewards, and build your partner ecosystem—to guide, measure, and reward the team to keep both performance and happiness strong.

In successful teams, each member of the team is a problem-solver, a leader in their actions if not in their title. You may not be a leader by job function yet, but you need to be thinking like a leader now. Further, thinking like a leader, flourishing as a team member, and being your most effective individual self all rely upon one central concept:

autonomy. Ironic, isn't it? But the greatest teams are made up of people who know how to think for themselves and who are accorded the respect of being given the right level of autonomy in their decision-making on the job. Autonomy—and its flip side from the point of view of others, respect—is the top characteristic of a job that most people wish for.

Throughout the book I will introduce specific tools and techniques that teams and individuals can use for improvement, including the following:

- A formal risk list for your project using a structure that the Jet Propulsion Lab has used (Chapter 1).
- A series of steps to help a new team member (or yourself) execute tasks and develop solutions to meet desired outcomes (Chapter 2).
- A table for moving from problem statement to best solutions (Chapter 2).
- A process for thinking about new ideas (metacognition) to ensure they are as objectively supported and unbiased as possible and to gauge their use (Chapter 5).
- A system for thinking about processes (also metacognition, like the above) to ensure they are taking you to your goal and that your goal is the right one (Chapter 5).
- A workshop for getting even the most skeptical team member to discuss process and relational work, and to set some common expectations for interactions (Chapter 7).
- A tool NASA uses (science traceability matrix) to get from questions to solutions to implementations (Chapter 10).
- A visualization exercise to anticipate how key presentations and meetings will go and to be ready for reactions and questions before they come (Chapter 10).
- A checklist for leading by example (Chapter 11).
- A list of actions for changing a bad culture (Chapter 11).

- A checklist for leading during a crisis (Chapter 11).
- A survey to help you measure the functioning and satisfaction of your team (Chapter 14).
- A checklist to follow the minute one of your partner organizations begins to slip on delivering to you (Chapter 15).

Feeling pressured to use new concepts and new processes can reduce the joy of progress and even the efficacy of learning while you read this book. I'd suggest picking one new idea from the book and applying it once per week or once per day. These practices will add up over time and infuse into the way you work every day.

Leadership and teamwork are amorphous concepts and can mean many things—each of us is many things at once, with different roles in response to different people, in different projects, in different organizations. Everything is relative, and so everything is contained inside each of us, and each of us is capable of everything.

You may not be launching a rocket into outer space, but the lessons in *Mission Ready* are applicable to you, no matter where you sit in your organization, no matter what the size of your project. This book is not just about the mechanics of team success. It's about understanding that you can create the world you want to live in—in your organization and outside it. You can make the culture of the groups you are part of. You can help people rise on their merits and enjoy their working days. How you treat others, and how they treat you in turn, is not separate from having a project goal or a team vision—it's integral to that goal or vision. This book is not just about how to get to your goal faster in the current system, but also how to have the courage to create a better system.

And that's exactly what happened on the Psyche mission. The rocket roared, the shocking cracks of sonic booms followed, and our spacecraft disappeared into the clouds. Sixty-two minutes later, the spacecraft separated from the rocket, the cold-gas thrusters oriented the spacecraft (and they did not overheat), the spacecraft locked on communications with Earth, and we were on our way.

PART I

INWARD

How an Individual Becomes
a Great Team Member

That's nice in *theory*," said the first engineer, "but we don't actually believe the modeling. If you had let us build the other design from the beginning, we wouldn't be where we are today."

The Psyche mission, which launched in October 2023, is a spacecraft journeying to a metal-rich asteroid—named (16) Psyche—that is orbiting the Sun between Mercury and Jupiter. And what's more important on a spacecraft headed to a new kind of solar system object than a camera? But that day, we were discussing the news that the design of the cameras that would take photographs during the mission was making them almost impossible to focus. Bad, bad news, which had taken some months of work to uncover. We had gotten to the point of having daily meetings, and people's nerves were frayed.

I sighed inwardly, and I could see the same reaction in the eyes of Lucas, a second engineer. He and I had talked about this kind of defensiveness and passive aggression frequently, helping to immunize ourselves against its aggravation.

Lucas replied, "Let's talk about the modeling. Tell me more about what you're skeptical of."

Lucas was demonstrating his ability to sidestep emotional responses that would not drive the conversation forward. He could have said, "You know perfectly well why we decided not to proceed with the other design at that time." Or "OK, then what do *you* suggest?" But neither of those responses would have moved toward a solution, which is what we needed. Lucas's relentless calm, steering toward a solution, is a big part of what finally carried us through to success. Self-awareness and the communication style of an individual are all important, both for their own success and effectiveness and for those of their team.

Another way to think about this is how we spend the hours of our days. We need to be happy with what and whom we see when we open our eyes in the morning, and we need to enjoy and value the people we spend our working hours with. For this reward, we each need to rise above being a passive cog in the machine, and we need to relinquish working just for our own fame and success.

We need to become members of a team improv troupe: We need to say "yes, and . . ." instead of "no" and to work for the common good. A win for all is the goal. People who manage themselves and their own projects, and who create synergies with others, create success for the project as well as satisfaction and even joy in the workplace.

In Part I, readers will be introduced to the five key practices that allow anyone to be more effective and therefore raise their own success and the success of their team. These five practices for individuals, each with its own chapter, are as follows:

- Speak Clearly, Calmly, and on Topic
- Recognize Problems and Take Action
- Do Not Give Up
- Create Quality in All You Do
- Become an Expert Thinker: Metacognition[1]

A common thread among these skills is that you no longer reflex-ively accept the world you are in, but instead think about how to improve the content, the issues, the process, and especially the effects of your own behavior and speech. That's the key: *being self-regulating*, which requires you to be self-aware, to metacognate. Monitor your tone when you are speaking, harness your agency to solve relevant problems, and develop your metacognition. Throughout, you are becoming more self-aware, gaining a better understanding of how your speech and actions affect others and therefore of your own efficacy. We can all improve, all the time.

Being a great team member is central to life as a human, in many ways. You'll be more effective in your family and friend groups, and you'll be a major force in your workplace. Even if you are a senior experi-enced strategist and leader, these skills can help you counter the dangers of protracted possession of power and maintain your humility. And you can use these ideas in your mentorship and team training.

Together, these skills keep your output as optimized as possible, and your communication clear, useful, and without hubris. Who wouldn't want to work with you?

1

SPEAK CLEARLY, CALMLY, AND ON TOPIC

The first email hit my inbox: "The toilets in the lab building are clogged again." It came from the head of facilities, and I was the director in charge of the campus, so it was sent to me, with a copy to a dozen or more other people on campus. "We're going to have to close the bathrooms and dig for the pipes; we can't clear them from inside. Lindy, we can't let this go on. The women have got to stop flushing anything except toilet paper down the toilet."

That last line gave me a shock. And then another email popped up in my inbox. Then another. Then many. I started checking in with some of the personnel, and both women and men from the building denied flushing anything inappropriate. They started arguing about the several times that this had happened in the past, and they electronically pointed fingers.

While clogged toilets may seem like an unusual case study for a book about teams, I use it here because it is such a clear example of dysfunctional team culture. At the time, I could only wonder whether plumbing could really be my life as director of this department. I was sitting in the back of the room at a board meeting being held out of town, wearing a serious suit, with my serious face, and my inbox was filling with enraged emails about clogged toilets. It was the Great Toilet War.

Adjudicating the disputes of this furious crowd via email is impossible. And that day the individuals on the email chain were getting angrier and angrier. Each email contained a new accusation. Since I was not on campus, I called a meeting for later in the week when I would be back, and I let everyone know that facilities was moving ahead to fix the problem. I also made a rule: If you cannot leave history and emotion out of your emails, then you are *only* allowed to send your email to me. All emails to the group will be civil, focused only on the facts of the current situation, and aimed at providing information.

Weirdly, this rule did work. Maybe people took a deep breath and agreed to wait for in-person conversation, or maybe my rule just made them so incandescently angry that they could no longer type. But my intention was to remind everyone how critical a professional tone is to actually reach an understanding of, and solution to, a problem. When people are filled with anger, there is no capacity for progressing down a logical, fact-based pathway.

When we finally gathered in our new, calmer, and conversational setting, we were able to determine that the clog was actually caused by paper towels the cleaning staff were forced to use because the facility manager was unwilling to purchase proper cleaning tools for them. The irony. Bringing back transparent civil discourse allowed us to uncover this unfortunate practice, to equip the cleaning crew correctly, to fix the toilets once and for all, and to cut down on the incidence of empty accusations and needless insults. So, in a way, having the Toilet War was a gift because it made these destructive practices so obvious that we were able to work on solving them.

HOW IMPORTANT IS IT, REALLY, TO BE
CALM IN A CRISIS?

What was it, exactly, that turned this small facilities problem into a war? What was it, precisely, that triggered anger and retaliation on the parts of the hearers, rather than patience in the face of the inconvenience? Looking back, it's clear the very first email from the head of facilities, which immediately blamed the women in the building (baselessly, as it happens), set people off. The fact that he also made the problem into a kind of ultimatum—this can't go on—without suggesting any solutions or even steps toward a solution made the situation even more fraught.

I can hardly overemphasize the importance of maintaining an even temperament in the face of crisis, especially because almost any other crisis is more important than the Toilet War. Think of the beautiful, convincing writing of Patrick O'Brian in his novels about the Napoleonic Wars: In the midst of ship-of-the-line battles with cannon and boarding parties with scimitars, the captain will still address his crew as "Mister Smith" and "Mister Brown." The façade of civility is a reminder of civilization, of correct behavior, of the persistence of structure. The tone and respect keep everyone aimed toward achieving the goal of the group, rather than reeling into emotional reactions, or worse, circling their wagons, so to speak, and shooting inward.

Calmness is contagious. If your teammates see you reacting with calm, especially if you are in a position of leadership, they will immediately be more likely to respond in the same manner. If everyone is calm, then everyone can feel that prevailing beyond the current emergency is inevitable, and then your team will succeed.

Even polar explorer Ernest Shackleton recognized that while a person's technical expertise is very important, it is not the essential thing. The essential thing is how a person communicates and how they affect their teammates. When Shackleton prepared for his intended cross-Antarctica expedition in 1914, he thought about the qualities of the people he needed to recruit. He wrote, "First, optimism; second, patience; third, physical endurance; fourth, idealism; fifth and last, courage." Note that none of these characteristics are technical skills; those came lower on the list.

A major point here is that each individual's technical knowledge is necessary, but *it's not enough*. Effective use of technical knowledge starts with common behaviors that allow people to communicate clearly with one another, to understand the problem at hand, and to make the right decisions.

Just one bad apple can drain the energy and positivity from a whole room. In the Toilet War, that bad apple was the head of facilities, with his blaming and shaming. The whole curlicue of finger-pointing and emotion threatened to consume all the energy of the team, when simply solving the problem would have used only a fraction of that mental and emotional energy.

The spreading of high, negative emotions is easy to see when it's as blatant as in that email, but more commonly, a person telegraphs their inner pain in more subtle ways. Some years ago, a project manager from another team joined us in a Psyche meeting and added sharp, passive-aggressive retorts to our conversation. Her comments, like little firecrackers, produced tiny flinches and moments of silence among members of our team. More thought was poured into managing her than was used on the topic of the meeting. Here was a clear example of how we are all attuned to the signals from each other, and how we can be either inspired by them or distracted by the need to manage them.

In contrast, listening to the calm, focused conversation in the meetings about the spacecraft-thruster problem just before launch, a casual observer would never have guessed the millions of dollars, reputations, and jobs that were on the line. Closer inspection would reveal the time (2:00 a.m.), the dark circles under the eyes of people supporting three shifts, and the twenty-four-hour-a-day work going on. Yet all the energy in the room was focused on supporting one another to find the best solution as quickly as possible.

Of course, every member of the team was feeling the stress and risk, even to almost debilitating levels. We were also doing our best to get on with the most effective behavior possible. Later, one of our leaders both acknowledged and assuaged the stress everyone was feeling with a show of humor, with a meme graphic stating: "I survived the great cold gas thruster crisis." The excellence of the team, in both their knowledge and their behavior, ensured success for the mission and the project, and some laughter along the way really helped.

NOT SURE I CAN BE CALM FOREVER

In the thruster problem meetings, a challenge we all faced was how *long* we could keep our outer calm and focus. We were all deeply feeling the stress, and we were all low on sleep. How long would our willpower to be our best selves last?

The lesson is that you need to avoid spreading whatever churn is within yourself and avoid getting swept along by the churn of others, if there is any. You need to take the high road, keep whatever anger someone's remark triggered in you to yourself, and avoid contaminating your environment with snap judgments, angry outbursts, sarcastic comments, passive-aggressive rejoinders—whatever your negative, personal emotion of choice is.

Personal pain and anger can often shut people up or prompt them to send the same emotion right back at you. Is that really what you want? If you want someone to think about your message, and not end up on the path of inaction because of some emotional overload, how can you focus less on yourself and more on the purpose of the group? By staying on the topic, by not venting.[1]

That can be hard to do, so before you speak reflexively, take a quick note: Are you feeling a wave of anger, frustration, or cynicism? Pause, and think about what you want the result from this conversation to be. Sending out strong emotions in your words will likely distract your listeners from the words themselves, may divert the conversation from the topic at hand, and may even reduce your colleagues' trust and respect.

Instead, focus on the outcome you want for the project and the team—and the secret here is that being your most effective self on behalf of the project will also lead to better outcomes for you personally. Add something to the discussion that moves it in the right direction and carries with it your best expertise and manner. Create an emotional tone around yourself that allows others to also be calm, to make the right decisions themselves, and to have faith that all is going to be OK.

Self-regulating emotions is the work of a lifetime for many of us. Staying calm and focused when exhausted, irritated, or impassioned: This is the key to communicating clearly, earning respect, and winning negotiations. You may feel like you have less self-control at the end of a long, hard day or when you are otherwise exhausted. You may feel like you lose your temper more easily when stressed or exhausted, or that staying calm while making decisions gets harder as the week wears on. But a team at Stanford University has demonstrated that thinking you have less self-control when stressed is, well, all in your mind.

That team—Veronika Job and her colleagues Carol Dweck and Gregory Walton—found that people who thought that self-control was *not* a limited resource did not lose control as their exhaustion rose.[2] In other words, if you *think* you're going to lose your self-control after using it all day, you probably will, and if you don't think you will, then you'll be just as controlled at the end of a series of exhausting emergencies as you are at the beginning. In fact, the study found that people with nonlimited mind-sets performed even better on the day after a particularly draining day. Think of that: You have one of the most exhausting days of your life at work, making a million decisions and discussing things with people who are upset, and the next day, you are even better.

CALMNESS AND KINDNESS SHOW STRENGTH

If calmness in communication can keep a group of people on track, then kindness and optimism can take each person's work to the next level. Demonstrate your dedication to the topic at hand by asking questions rather than asserting your knowledge. Imagine and act as if you respect everyone in the room at the same high level.

I've heard, and maybe you have too, that kindness can be seen as softness. People who are kind sometimes use kindness to avoid conflict. So make sure you use kindness for, well, to be kind. And if you need to be strong in a conversation to stick to your principles, do that, too, but you can still do it in a kind, correct, clear way. Being kind to others does not turn off your brain from being able to see what you think is right, detect flaws in work, or act decisively. See kindness as one strength among many.

Along with calmness and kindness, optimism is critical for anyone on any team. Cynical disbelief poisons the conversation fast, and if the cynical person does not believe in what is being done, why are they even there? Adlai Stevenson said, "Pessimism in a statesman is like cowardice in a soldier." This applies to anyone working toward a goal, as much as it does to a statesman.

No matter your personal stance on political and social matters, Ruth Bader Ginsburg is a great role model in the long path toward successful change. The former US Supreme Court justice understood that the only way to move forward is to encourage others to join in. Ginsburg said, "Fight for the things you care about, but do it in a way that will lead others to join you."

Now that you are a master of tone, speaking calmly and optimistically, how do you stay right on topic? One of the most distracting things in a meeting is to hear comments that are interesting but not on point for where the meeting is going. So the next superpower you must master is self-editing: Learn to say only the most important things that are most on topic.

Think about what the purpose of the meeting is and where the conversation has come so far. Does the path need to be steered back to the meeting topic? Do you have an important point to make? First, make sure that your contribution is important and that it has not been said before by someone else in that same meeting. Second, make sure it fits in the flow. Always acknowledge and build upon the previous statement, or check, simply by asking out loud, if the group is ready to change direction. Focus on outcomes, using specifics and facts. Now, speak up!

Speaking up is critical because your ideas—each person's ideas—need to be in the mix to achieve the team's best outcomes. Speaking up is also critical because you need to do so to be seen. If you are going to conferences, ask questions of the speaker. If you meet new colleagues, add your ideas to the conversation. And in key work meetings, make sure you contribute. Speak with assertion, but don't be arrogant. Leaving room for other people's perspectives is a fantastic, unexpected strength in speaking.

Adam Grant, professor at the Wharton School of Business at the University of Pennsylvania and prolific author and thought leader, wrote in a *New York Times* opinion essay that "it turns out that women who use weak language when they ask for raises are more likely to get them. In one experiment, experienced managers watched videos of people negotiating for higher pay and weighed in on whether the request should be granted. The participants were more willing to support a salary bump for women—and said they would be more eager to work with them—if the request sounded tentative."

The women were given a script that included "I don't know how typical it is for people at my level to negotiate, but I'm hopeful you'll see my skill at negotiating as something important that I bring to the job." Those softeners—*I don't know* and *I hope*—apparently helped avoid the impression of arrogance and improved their chances of a raise. If men used that script, however, their chance of a raise was neither improved nor diminished.

So both speaking up *and* leaving room for others in the conversation are key strengths, no matter who you are. Yet the same language can have different results when used by a man or by a woman; this has long been recognized. Unconscious bias has us—all of us, men and women—interpreting the same words differently depending upon who says them. In this case, women benefit by using more permissive language and therefore not offending the hearer with a sense of arrogance.

OFFER SPECIFIC FACTS AND WAYS TO MOVE FORWARD

Speaking up is especially important if you might be overlooked because of bias about sex, race, disability, or background. Visible, irrelevant reasons, such as looking like you are the most junior person in the room, being female, or having brown skin, may lead some in your organization to have lower expectations of you. To be included, you need to show your value. You need to speak up with specific, insightful, actionable information.

Stick to the facts and their importance. Let's imagine that there is a problem with the browser page your team is coding: A particular user keeps getting blocked from opening the first video. You've put forward your idea about what happened. Another person could say to you, "You're wrong when you say it's because of the code's ability to run on the Chrome browser. What really happened was a problem with the user trying it on her iPhone." By starting with "You are wrong," the other person may have made you feel defensive. Their statement was ad hominem, to borrow a handy Latin phrase: The statement was about the person, you, and not about the conversation topic.

That person—and you and I, every time we speak—would be better served to have said something like, "I see what you are saying, but because of the way the problem so far only happens to that one user, I wonder if the cause of the problem might not be more related to the platform, since we don't have other smartphone testers that I know of. Let's see if we can get her to try it on another platform, and let's all test on our smartphones now." Now the speaker is bringing alternative ideas to play in a way that includes the old idea, does not alienate its originator, and suggests a productive path forward.

You may have something to say that is right on topic, maybe even the brilliant breakthrough the conversation needs. You are a little breathless with excitement. Take that breath! You need to set up your idea carefully so that people immediately see how it fits in with the conversation and the direction people are thinking in. If it's too far away from the conversational stream, people will not be able to hear it.

As neurologist and author Oliver Sacks puts it: "[The] process of accommodation, of spaciousness of mind . . . is crucial in determining whether a new idea or discovery will take hold and bear fruit, or whether it will be forgotten, fade, and die without issue. We have spoken of discoveries or ideas so premature as to be almost without connection or context, hence unintelligible or ignored at the time."[3]

Make sure the people in the room have spaciousness of mind and the ability to accommodate your new idea—lead them to it in a few steps to make sure your idea will have the best chance of being heard fully.

KEEP A RISK LIST

You can take a page from how the Jet Propulsion Lab words its risk statements. Every time a key issue, challenge, or risk is identified in your project, formalize it and track it (keep a record of it and check in regularly on progress). JPL uses formal language to describe a risk to mission success that someone on the team has identified and wants to explain to others. The risk statement is structured like this:

"IF this happens [problem] DUE TO [cause], THEN this will happen [consequence]."

Here's an example: IF the cold-gas thruster stops functioning DUE TO overheating, THEN we may be unable to turn the spacecraft to communicate with Earth or orient the solar panels to the Sun.

You don't say, "If Joe's screwup with the temperatures causes the thrusters to overheat . . ." Instead, the clear, focused, impersonal statement allows the team to calmly look at the issue at hand and discuss possible solutions.

Ask yourself before you speak, "Does my approach offer both concrete ideas and suggestions for moving forward?" If so, you are helping yourself and your team make progress. If you pose a problem and offer no path forward, you are acting like you have only problems and no ideas, and the recipient of your statement may feel like you're trying to dump your problems in their lap. Even the most powerful leader can feel empowered by concrete solutions from coworkers and disempowered by a set of challenging problems presented with anger or frustration.

Finally, try this exercise: Practice imagining how an upcoming conversation or meeting will go before you are in it. Anticipate—that is, imagine—what key people will say in response to the points you want to make. Adjust your presentation to answer their anticipated questions. Then, identify in your own mind what your desired outcome of the conversation is, what decision needs to be made or action taken, and speak to those right at the beginning as the purpose of the conversation so that everyone will be aligned from the start. These are effective actions you can take no matter your seniority. You don't need to be leading the meeting to add comments that guide the meeting to where you hope it will go. Then, as your strategic thinking speeds up, you can make these guiding comments in real time if you see the discussion straying, because you have already imagined where you want the discussion to go.

The Toilet War was resolved in a positive and constructive way, even though it did not start this way. After we changed our email habits and a few days had passed, we had calm conversations both over email and in person. In the end, everyone spoke up well; most importantly, those who normally had no voice in leadership, the cleaning crew, were heard. Before the final meeting, I and others spoke to each member of the crew in one-on-one sessions and heard what had really happened. And then, with no public shaming even for those responsible, everyone came to know why the toilets had clogged and how the problem was resolved. Our cleaning crew's job was better organized and supported, and everyone knew a little more about how to make their job better. Clarity was reached, the wrongs were righted, and even the plumbing was fixed.

So that is the first and most important practice for each of us: Speak calmly, clearly, and on topic. Simply practicing these ideas sharpens and clarifies your thinking about what the topic at hand really is and what will be productive to discuss. Then, take the next step and work on being a best-in-class identifier and solver of problems. In many ways, this is the top skill of a lifetime, and the next chapter walks us through it.

2

RECOGNIZE PROBLEMS
AND TAKE ACTION

Do you know what happened this week?" my colleague Tim asked, sharply. "The administration announced that the Tuesday and Thursday study halls were library study only."

"Yeah," I said, "I was thinking that seemed reasonable since I heard that a lot of the kids were goofing off and need some more structure. Maybe they'll get their homework done during the day and get to sleep more! That would be great for these teenagers."

"No, it's not fine," said Tim, who had taught music at the school for decades and was a very fine classical organist. In a dark and sardonic tone, he explained: "Those were two of the very few hours left to give music students private lessons. It drives me crazy. The school wants beautiful concerts but won't make it possible for the students to attain excellence. Do they think concerts happen without practice? This kind of erosion has been going on for years! We get less and less."

"Wow, if it's been going on for years, what kinds of actions and conversations have you had to try to stop the decay? Why's it still happening?" I asked.

Tim looked at me blankly. "Well, no," he said, "I haven't actually taken any actions."

In that moment, my husband invented this motto: "No Whining Without Action." You can complain and vent your frustrations, absolutely! But then, you must do something to try to make the situation better. All too often people get stuck in their complaints. You probably have coworkers who complain, and they might even resist change that might fix the problem (I surely hope this isn't you—a good moment for a self-check).

Why does it not immediately occur to people to go beyond complaining to the next step, trying to fix things? In his book *The Elephant's Dilemma*, Jon Bostock, CEO of Kodak Alaris and venture investor, writes about captive elephants, brilliantly smart and immensely strong, who are chained by the leg to an immovable object when they are first in captivity. After fighting and failing to free themselves for enough time, they give up fighting and can be tethered with only a light rope, and they won't try to escape.[1] This acceptance is called learned helplessness. We're not born with it but most of us learn it. Where do most people get infected with learned helplessness?

Think of your own experiences sitting in a schoolroom, the kind with all the desks in rows. To best succeed there, you may have learned to accept the information the teacher gave you, do the problems the way you were told to do them, and then perform exactly as you'd been taught on tests. You accepted the information the teacher provided, and you did not challenge it. You learned not to disagree with the teacher or even ask too many questions.

Some students come to think that questions directed to them are to be feared because the questions are really tests—the teacher already knows the answers. Questions that the students themselves ask are liable to showcase their own ignorance. We are taught that all answers are already known. The answers are in the book. This is learned helplessness.

But in real life, for peak effectiveness, you need to be constantly questioning and looking for opportunities for improvement. You need to overcome your learned helplessness and find the best ways to take action to solve the problems you perceive. Problem-solving makes a leader.

Think of our friend Tim, who had a long-standing complaint with the scheduling decisions of the school administrators but who had never taken a step toward fixing the problem. Tim felt that he was not accountable, not responsible for flaws in the running of the school. It's easy to notice—and correct to say—that it *was* his responsibility in some part to take action, but it's equally true that many people just don't see their own responsibility.

Perhaps this lack of accountability comes in part from learned helplessness. If someone else is always the one who decides what we learn, how we learn it, when we learn it, it's hard to change back to being a person who has an opinion on every step, is willing to help improve the whole process, and even has some ideas on how to do that.

By examining the world around you—your world, your country, your town, your team, your family, and especially yourself—you begin to move from not being accountable, to having ideas for improvement, to being determined to make a difference and knowing that you can.

Perhaps you are thinking, "But I am already a spectacular problem-solver and active thinker." Excellent, then this chapter offers some more tools for your kit. If you are less in the habit of problem identification and solution finding, you'll find here that there are many places to start. And even if you have worked on your skills for years and excel as a tactical thinker—solving the immediate steps ahead of you—you can now work on considering your projects and goals on another, higher level, a level of structure and strategy, and problem-solve there.

START WITH A QUESTION

It's often a question that brings a whole conversation or investigation to a new and fruitful level or direction, or that reveals a region of ignorance that no one had yet noticed (it's amazing how caverns of ignorance can be obscured by a community's blind acceptance of an untested "fact"). Starting with questions also leaves the solution undetermined, which is critical at early stages of any project. Bringing in solutions too soon tends to cut off critical research and discussion that might offer better paths. Questions are the key to recognizing unsolved problems. This is the first step: Increase your awareness of unsolved problems, note them, and collect them in preparation for finding solutions.

How many times have you been in a meeting and, when considering some barrier or problem, one person speaks up using a voice of assurance and states what has to be done? Sometimes this is a power play: The person wants to be the one who came up with the solution. Sometimes it's just a normal leap to solution. No matter the person's motivation, though, the effect is both to create risk and to waste time.

Risk is created by the momentum the meeting suddenly has in the direction of this first possible solution, without having worked on the whole range of possible solutions and considering which is best. And the time waste is the time needed to walk the group back to considering the range of possible solutions while still keeping a feeling of energy and momentum. Instead of asserting knowledge prematurely, pose problems as questions.

Discover the power of saying "I don't know." Welcome discovering gaps in your knowledge. Encourage your colleagues to be comfortable saying "I don't know" too. Then, once you have filled in those gaps with real information, everyone will feel more secure in searching for solutions.

Posing problems as questions keeps the solution space open. When identifying problems and seeking solutions, we each need to keep our mind open and not leap to solutions. Start simply, by defining the problem as a question: "How might we improve our product quality?" (not, at least not yet, by saying "We have a problem with our plastics subcontractor") or "Can our students have higher success finding internships?" (too soon to jump to "Our students don't interview well"). And then work systematically toward possible solutions.

Here's one place where brainstorming can really help. You may have heard, or experienced, that brainstorming solutions actually can be really *un*helpful, in that it encourages groupthink, can narrow rather than broaden people's thinking, and rushes people to solutions that feel good rather than to what may be the best solutions—all because brainstorming completely skips the information-gathering steps that inform the best solutions.

Questions, however, are a great topic for brainstorming! Go ahead and brainstorm all the questions you have around the issue you are discussing, and that will help you create a solution space.

Two other notes about brainstorming: Northwestern University psychologists Brian Lucas and Loran Nordgren report that the initial ideas people generate while brainstorming are the most conventional. After those initial, more ordinary ideas are out of the way, the rest of the ideas brought forth are the most unusual and innovative.[2] In addition, people do influence one another's thinking while brainstorming, so asking participants to think of ideas individually and silently first, before sharing them with the group, can lead to more interesting and useful results.

BE A DIPLOMAT

Being both a problem-identifier and a problem-solver is a strength that comes with both power and the need for diplomacy. You've identified problems, which on its own can threaten other people who either didn't notice or didn't take action, or who feel they might be blamed for the problems. You want to strengthen your team, not make yourself out to be a superstar on your own.

Start by thinking of all the stakeholders who are involved in a problem and how they might think the problem affects them personally.

- If you have a product quality issue, then all the people immediately involved in creating the product probably feel pretty sensitive about having this problem raised. Talk to them individually and see if you can get them on board with helping to solve—and thereby get credit for solving—the problem.
- Anyone you report to probably does not want to be surprised, so discuss with them well in advance of taking any actions.
- Your peers on other projects always want to know what you are doing, and it's great teamwork to share with them challenges and solutions whenever possible, opening communications and building even more trust.

The goal of all these individual and side meetings is to lower any high emotions and get everyone on board with finding solutions. The goal of these meetings is *not* to demonstrate how you are the clever person who discovered the problem and now owns the solution to it.

Sometimes this process is called socializing a problem. Talk to people individually, listen to their concerns, and use their ideas to improve what you are doing. Then speak to small groups. Finally, when no one is going to be surprised, talk with everyone together if that's necessary. It's a community effort, removing blame, encouraging input, making sure no one is surprised, and keeping the tone light.

TAKE RESPONSIBILITY FOR THE PROBLEMS YOU IDENTIFY

During the early phase of the Psyche project, everyone owned their own swim lane, so to speak, and communicated easily across the lines of buoys. What I mean by this is that the person who was in charge of the science instruments knew what they were managing (their swim lane) and also worked closely with the person in the swim lane next door who was working out the details of the power system, for example. But as we moved into development and issues cropped up with parts availability, or system interactions, or unintended software issues, the swim lanes seemed to diverge a bit, and new areas of need appeared like open water in between them. When problems occurred in those new no-man's lands, who was responsible for solving them?

Maybe you see a problem and it's not in your job description, so you assume it belongs to someone else. With your new awareness of learned helplessness and the constant need for more problem-solvers in our world, you may now realize it's unlikely others have picked it up. So you need to pick up that problem and hold it and take responsibility for it until you find its proper owner.

MOVING FROM QUESTION TO SOLUTION: FRAME YOUR PROBLEM FIRST

Not so fast! As noted earlier, it's tempting to spring to the first appealing solution, but chances are if it's at all a complex problem, you don't really know enough yet to select the best solution. Take your time here to learn more about the problem and work on keeping the solution space open for as long as possible. Leaping to the solution can be as unhelpful as not seeing the problem in the first place. Here's an example.

We've got a problem question in front of us: How might we improve our product quality? First, you need to *frame* the problem by taking these steps:

1. Research and analyze the problem's scope, causes, and effects.
   - How do you know the product quality is low? Did you hear that from customers? What, specifically, is deficient? Do you see it yourself? What is your evidence?

31

- Based on that evidence, where specifically is the problem? Is it a material or workmanship defect? Or is it due to customer expectations or customer service?
- What is the scope of this problem? How big is it? What percentage of the product has low quality, or how troubling is the quality level?
- What problems are these quality issues causing for your organization, for your customers, and for other stakeholders?

2. State why the problem needs to be solved.
    - What are the outcomes you want that you don't now have?
    - What would happen if you did nothing?

Now you have a framed problem, and you can move on to thinking about solutions.

NOW LET YOUR PROBLEM INCUBATE

You've framed your problem, and you're ready to dive in to finding solutions, but I'm going to suggest you pause and allow the problem to incubate. During incubation the problem is settled in your mind, but you are not actively thinking about it all the time. I'm absolutely fascinated by this fact: Our unconscious minds can solve problems for us while we think of other things. Our unconscious mind is often better at solving things than our conscious mind! Here's the history and science of this phenomenon and how to harness it in your life.

Experts say problem-solving has four stages: preparation, incubation, illumination, and verification. There are many, many possible preparation steps. We went through one above, with framing the problem. You could also write down everything this problem reminds you of, make a drawing of the parts of the problem, and find some reference books or websites that discuss similar problems.

But the strategy that may be the best of all is to write down the problem clearly and then go do something else and stop thinking about the problem. Incubate it unconsciously.

Though there is not a solid scientific explanation for how the brain solves problems unconsciously, scientific studies demonstrate that it absolutely does so. How and whether problem incubation works has fascinated people for centuries, and well over two hundred scientific studies trying to understand whether this is a real effect or a kind of mind trick we are playing on ourselves have been conducted. A research study led by Ut Na Sio and Thomas C. Ormerod from Lancaster University in the United Kingdom investigated more than a hundred studies on problem incubation and found that a strong majority of them, over 73 percent, indicate that incubation does help solve problems.[3]

Kenneth J. Gilhooly, emeritus professor of psychology at the University of Hertfordshire in the United Kingdom, has made a career of investigating the incubation phenomenon. Gilhooly's 2019 book offers a plethora of examples from history, firsthand accounts of moments of discovery that were germinated by walking, sleeping, or being distracted from the problem. The most effective way to use incubation is what Gilhooly calls immediate incubation: Read or otherwise understand the problem at hand, and then immediately, without working consciously on the problem at all, spend some time (minutes or hours) doing something unrelated. If your problem is about writing, spend your time doing something mathematical, or cooking, or playing a sport, or sleeping. Then return to the problem.[4]

The incubation phenomenon implies that people whose minds wander may be more creative problem-solvers than those who stay focused. People diagnosed with ADHD have more of a tendency to mind-wander, according to several researchers (for example, Joseph Biederman from the Massachusetts General Hospital in Boston),[5] and they also tend to score higher on tests of creativity.

Conversely, people who are strong practitioners of mindfulness— that is, staying mentally present—generally score better on rigid analytical problems but worse on solutions needing sudden insight or creativity, according to work and reviews of the field done by Claire M. Zedelius and Jonathan W. Schooler of the Psychological and Brain Sciences program at the University of California Santa Barbara.[6] I find this ironic, since I feel like being mentally present is emotionally associated with creativity in the pop conversations of today, but the studies tell us a wandering mind is more creative!

Walking is a spectacular way to boost creativity for solutions that require unconventional thinking. Marily Oppezzo and Daniel Schwartz, faculty at Stanford University, noticed how productive their own walking laboratory meetings were, and then conducted a series of experiments to measure the effects of walking. When asked to think of solutions to a problem while just sitting, compared to sitting to read the question and then walking to incubate it, the walkers produced on average twice the number of solutions.[7]

You might even try keeping a list of active problems that need solving in your life or work. Choose one each night, write it out in detail, read it over, and then release it from your mind and go to sleep. Or do the same writing and reading exercise just before a long walk. Load up your brain with problems that need solving and then leave it to your unconscious mind to work on them for you.

In summary, follow these steps within the time span of an hour or so:

- **Frame the problem.** What is the problem? How big is it? Whom does it effect? What might be causing it?
- **State why the problem needs to be solved.** What are the outcomes you want that the problem is preventing? What would happen if you did nothing?
- **Incubate the problem.** Without working any more on the problem, stop thinking about it and do something entirely unrelated: go for a walk, do unrelated work, go to bed and sleep on it.

Now, start work on solutions.

ANALYZING SOLUTIONS WITH THE OTHER
STAKEHOLDERS AND PICKING THE BEST ONE

Tracy Drain, a lead systems engineer, called a team meeting. The team, working on a deep-space mission we'll call Planetary Probe 1, had just discovered that there was an issue with the power system of the spacecraft: As one part of the team had begun work on details of the orbital plan once the spacecraft got to its target, they realized that the power system was not perfectly designed for their needs, and changes to it had to be made.

Some tempers were already high. These were all highly knowledgeable experts, all with high intelligence and drive, all used to making hard decisions every day. Some were power-system experts; others came from a wide range of other areas relevant to space missions. Everyone had many urgent tasks on their to-do lists, and the urgency and the exact nature of this new problem wasn't yet clear. And for everyone, it's always deeply frustrating to find a big problem late in the game, even though, at the same time, it happens regularly. Every mission is a custom job, and every one comes with surprises.

All this can make it tempting for people to want a problem to get solved by changing something that seems "easy"; for example, people who are most familiar with the complications that come with changing hardware might wish that a software fix would solve the problem. People most familiar with the complications of changing or writing new software might wish that a hardware fix would solve the problem.

Some people felt that the orbital trajectory and implications for the power system should have been known and communicated more clearly before the power design was completed. Some felt that those factors had been understood well enough but guidelines and restrictions that went into the power system design weren't communicated broadly enough to spot the disconnect. Some folks were defensive, some anxious. But most were also just glad the issue was being caught now.

Tracy stood at the whiteboard, relaxed, a slight smile on her face. Her posture and expression said "calm." She began by drawing a table and then seeded it with the suggestions made by the people in the room. The group focused on the task, and the energy level went up; everyone was ready to work on something productive.

She kept the team focused on the board, away from what happened in the past, and toward what could be done about it. Personal feelings became less relevant as everyone pitched in to help define the problem and work up a set of potential solutions. After an hour, they had some good options on the board, and everyone had assignments to flesh out the pros and cons that would help make the final decision. The energy that had been directed at one another was now directed at solving the problem.

Afterward, Tracy shared with me these principles:

- Work at being genuinely curious about why people think the things they think and say the things they say. If you're only listening to quickly bounce ideas off your own perspective and jumping straight to "yep, nope, yep, nope," you'll wind up dismissing too many things too quickly and missing opportunities to learn and to perhaps ultimately land on a better path forward. Being curious leads you to ask deeper questions, explore those other perspectives more thoroughly. When people can tell you are curious and listening, they loosen up and find it easier to listen to you later too.
- Work at always asking yourself, "How do I help this group of folks work our way through this?" instead of "How do I convince these people to do what I want them to do?" No one person ever has all the right answers; doing this can help draw out the best ideas.

- Always assume people are saying and doing things with the best of intentions. I can't stress this enough: Assuming people dismiss your ideas because they are out to get you or to one-up you is the easiest way to completely miss the real underlying idea the other person has, which might be a winning solution.

- As a corollary, never assume you truly know what others' intentions are even when you assume they are good. You actually have to inquire of people to know what they are thinking. I find it useful to say, "I think you're trying to achieve [blah, blah, blah], but help me understand. How would you describe in your own words what your proposed solution is going to achieve?" I guarantee if you thought they had a bad motivation, you'll be pleasantly surprised at what they have to say.

- Then once you understand it, repeat it back and let them know you got it and are happy about that goal (if you are), and you can point out any unintended consequences you see. Not in a "OK, but your idea is terrible because" kind of way but by giving them the benefit of the doubt that they've considered the downside and don't think it is a problem because of some legitimate reason. For instance, "OK, I get it. But I'd worry about this side effect, which none of us want. If you've thought about that, how do you see avoiding that? Or if you haven't, can we talk a little and see if we could work out how to avoid that?" That can show them you're not dismissing their idea out of hand, and that even if you see difficulties with it that they missed, you are open to together seeing if their idea could be modified to handle those difficulties.

- Make sure that everyone is heard, their options are included, their pros and cons are noted, and they are paying attention to and helping assess the other options. This is a way to quell arguments if someone is initially overly attached to a specific idea.

37

- Keep firm milestones in front of the team. When do we need to have a solution in place? With that in mind, when would we have to start implementing each option, and if the options differ in timeline, when do we have to make decisions on which path to take? This helps ease tension too, if people understand how much time they have to flesh out an idea and get it implemented.

In the end, the solution Tracy and her team came up with solved the initial problem and even left the spacecraft with better operations than it would have had. It was a big win.

ASSEMBLE THE TEAM TO EXAMINE SOLUTIONS TOGETHER

You have incubated—you've slept on it, you've stashed it in your subconscious and gone for a walk or a run, you've had flashes of intuition while in the shower or bath—and now you have a list of ideas that might be solutions. This is a good time to bring in the key stakeholders to discuss the range of possible solutions. I'd suggest you welcome to this meeting anyone who wants to join. Why not?

Make it clear to everyone that this meeting is to lay out possible solutions and then do an analysis to discover which is best. This meeting cannot be allowed to devolve into an "I know best" kind of confrontation; everything about it is going to be analytical and impersonal, and every person attending is invited to bring forward ideas. The final decision will not be made in this meeting.

Why am I talking about bringing in stakeholders and how to run meetings in this section that's focused on what you can do specifically within yourself to become a great team member? Because *you* are the problem finder here, and *you* are the person who is causing change to happen. So it's you who has to know how to do this critical work, which is often threatening to others.

Make a table of possible solutions on a whiteboard or somewhere else that everyone can see. The goals here are to get everyone to a common understanding of the problem and to agree upon the right ways to assess potential solutions, and then to list everyone's proposed solutions and analyze them all in the same way to select the best one.

List the possible solutions in the "Candidate solutions" row, as shown in this example:

SEEKING A SOLUTION TO THE PROBLEM			
Problem statement: The well-framed question that requires a solution.			
What are the option spaces for solutions? For example, can we change hardware, software, or only how we operate the machine? Can we retrain only our own people, or can we expect change from the end user too?			
Candidate solutions: Write down as many as you can think of, each in its own column, and then analyze each using the rows below to find the best option.	Candidate A:	Candidate B:	Etc.
Data needed: What needs to be known to guide us toward the most effective solution.			
Analysis: What are the pros of each solution?			
Analysis: What are the cons of each solution, including specific risks?			

The table here is a pretty simple one, and it might be just what you need. You can also consider adding rows for any of the following, if they are relevant to the problem you are solving:

- Does the proposed solution completely address the core problem and its key elements?
- Are the technical requirements of the solution realistic and achievable with existing budget, time, and personnel limitations?
- Does the solution include contingency plans or check-in points to manage unforeseen issues?
- What impacts upon each stakeholder would this solution have?
- Will the solution have lasting benefits?
- What long-term negative consequences might this solution have?
- Can the solution be expanded or adapted for larger contexts or different purposes?

You want to encourage divergent thinking in this meeting. If everyone converges on one idea right away, they may just be reacting to peer pressure or not really thinking. You want people in the room who don't think like you do, and you want to gather as many different ideas as possible. The best solution might be the most surprising, or it may be a combination of several of the proposed ideas.

IMPLEMENTING YOUR SOLUTION

Deciding on the solution might in fact be done at the end of the meeting where you fill in the possible solution table (above), or the decision might be made by the same group after a day's pause to think things over, or the decision might be made by a leadership group after they have digested that table.

Once the solution is selected, working through another table will help make sure that no steps are missed and everyone understands what's to be done and by whom. The more systematic and logical you can be in finding problems and suggesting solutions, the better for yourself and your team.

IMPLEMENTING YOUR SOLUTION	
Problem statement: The well-framed question that requires a solution.	
Selected solution	
Who is leading?	
Who else is involved in producing the solution, and what are their roles?	
What are the milestones and deadlines in creating this solution?	
What is the definition of success, and what can we measure to show we have succeeded?	
When will success be assessed, and by whom?	

Now you have the whole process of problem identification and solution:

- Constantly scan for unsolved problems.
- Think about all the stakeholders involved in the problem you identify.
- Take responsibility for the problem until you find its right owner.
- Pose the problem as a question and frame it so you understand it better.
- Use some strategies to think of possible solutions: Incubation and the solution table shown above are good choices.

The skills used in this process are so central to being effective in work and life that I can't stress them too much. This is the way you grow in agency and effectiveness, become invaluable to your coworkers, earn autonomy, and become a leader, whether you have that title or not.

Even in small doses, these problem-solving techniques can have big effects. I had an inadvertent effect on someone, apparently spurring them to become a better problem-solver, at a particularly high-tension moment. A leader for one of the Psyche mission subteams came into my office and, with high emotion, started explaining that the subcontractor building a key part of the subsystem was just not producing. She'd been to visit them, and it was apparent to her that the subcontractor's team was too thin in personnel to reliably deliver.

With high stress in her voice, she said, "You *have* to do something! We are already behind schedule! This is never going to work!"

At that moment, I was not in the steadiest state myself, and her entreaty sparked bright anger in me. I should not have responded this way. I was violating my own principle of speaking clearly and calmly. But I was on topic.

I said, with anger in my voice, something like, "Delivering on this subsystem is *your* job. If you come with this kind of crisis, you need to come with some ideas about how to move forward. You can't just come and throw the problem at me and back away. What are you suggesting?"

The conversation luckily became more productive at that point, and we thought through some good steps forward: increase the cadence of meetings, work on the schedule to see what might be possible, and, most importantly, start looking for other subcontractors who might deliver.

A couple of years later, when she'd succeeded in her job on Psyche and moved on to another project, her new project manager happened to run into me in the hallway and remarked on how well she was performing on the new project, what a gift and a joy she was to work with.

The project manager commented, "One of her very best points is how she always comes with smart ideas for how to move forward when we are faced with problems."

Sometimes a focus on problems seems depressing; sometimes we'd like to imagine we've reached a steady state of good functioning and high spirits. A different, freeing way to think about it is that change is a constant, so seeking better ways and focusing on special projects is a gift. Seeing challenges as a gift is another way to never give up.

3

DO NOT GIVE UP

A week after that 2:00 a.m. meeting about the cold-gas thrusters and their problem with overheating, I stood at Kennedy Space Center in front of the Psyche team, which was still deep in crisis. I needed to make a statement that would remind us of our excellence, as well as being honest about our situation. When is it the right time to sugarcoat? Never, I would say.

I looked up and said, "We're right up against this incredible deadline. We need to be able to launch this spacecraft and have those thrusters work autonomously from the moment after separation from the rocket. We all know this; they must be fixed before we launch. We have four more days to complete the testing and update the parameters.

"We're almost there, and we are going to make it. We're going to make it because through all the challenges of the last seven years, through COVID and all its dread and isolation, and the closures of the labs, and through reviews and budgets and schedules being cut and shortened, no one has given up.

"It would have taken only 20 percent of us to say, 'This is too hard, I'm done, I'm going somewhere else,' and the whole project would have failed. People on this project are hard to replace! You are the people who really understand our spacecraft. You are uniquely critical. We are here, succeeding, solving our latest mountain of a challenge because every individual cares and shows up. That is our greatness."

Here are a few of the many moments in life and work when a person might give up: You found a problem with something at work and suggested a solution, and your boss said something dismissive, and you've heard no more. You've been working toward an advanced degree for a few years, but the thesis step feels impossible and the timeline is lengthening and your money is tight. You've been leading a big project at work for some years, and it hit a huge problem that will delay the conclusion of the project for ten more months at significant cost; you are being blamed.

Now let's vote. In which of these cases should you give up? I vote: none of them.

When *should* you give up on what you are working on? Almost never. Instead, own the responsibility, find a path forward that you can see as progress, dismiss the concept of failure. Acknowledge your mistakes but hold your head up and move forward. Persisting means you are responsible, determined, reliable, and undaunted—all of which are critical to your own success, as well as the success of the team.

Jack Ma, the billionaire founder of Alibaba, famously started out poor and struggling and overcame ridiculous numbers of disappointments and rejections along the way. He applied to Harvard *ten times* and never got in. Another time, he was the sole person out of twenty-four applicants in a group interview who was not hired. He made huge mistakes (and admitted them!) and persisted with his company, Alibaba, through dark times.

Look around and think about public figures who have suffered big setbacks and yet are still active afterward. I'll bet none of them gave up. Though they might have felt defeated inside, they held up their heads and kept marching; they were the optimistic determined leaders through the whole mess. That's how to succeed in the end.

BUT WHAT IS SUCCESS?

It's popular, particularly with public figures, social media influencers, and television stars, to say that success is fame. Fame in the form of many followers and high name recognition. They and others might also say that success is money or power (and money often is power). I have academic friends for whom success is winning the big prizes in their field. But one thing that many of these people have in common is that those kinds of success do not bring happiness. In 2007 the psychologist Tal Ben-Shahar invented the term *arrival fallacy* to describe the idea that reaching a goal will bring lasting contentment or fulfillment, when in fact the burst of happiness is brief and the void that follows it is deep. What's the next prize? It's just a big anticlimax.

Along with the determination never to give up comes an invitation to think about what success is to you. Could it be doing the best you can with dignity and calmness? Could it be following the path to quality or justice or kindness or wisdom without needing a lot of ego? I hope that whatever kind of success you choose, it comes along with being kind and watching out for others.

Brad Stulberg, who is a clinical assistant professor at the School of Public Health at the University of Michigan as well as a speaker, coach, and writer, has spent a decade interviewing top performers in athletics, science, art, medicine, business, and education. Their lasting success and satisfaction, as he wrote in *The New York Times* in 2024, came down to how they answered these five questions: Did they give their pursuit their all? Did they live in alignment with their values? Were they patient and present? Did they embrace their own vulnerability? And did they build meaningful and mutually respectful relationships along the way?[1]

Keeping your head up and walking forward in the face of problems need not be hubris. In fact, it had better not be—our world needs a lot more humility and a lot less hubris. What I'm suggesting is that there's a nice middle ground where you know that you're continuing to do your best, you have more to offer, a setback is not the end, and you can be relied on not to make yourself the starring victim of the story. This should never be about your ego. This should be about being a good partner, a good teammate.

AND SO, WHAT IS FAILURE?

There's only one sure way to fail and that is by giving up. Giving up means both accepting all the blame and saying you can't fix the problem. Giving up, just like failing to recognize and take action on problems or complaining about others instead of coming up with ideas for paths forward, is a signal to yourself and to your colleagues that you see yourself as powerless, maybe even as a victim. Not only do others not want a victim on their team, but some people also like to attack a victim. You don't want to be that limping antelope when the lions are closing in!

If you still feel like giving up, spend some time analyzing why. Sometimes the project actually does seem impossible, but often it's because a bad actor is making your work unpleasant or blocking a path to success. Think about your emotion as a problem to be solved. What's the issue? What's causing this? Maybe you should revisit the last chapter on problem-solving and see if you can tease out what the root cause is.

MOVING FORWARD

Quality in our actions and products, and an appreciation for quality, comes with the necessity of personal accountability. Each person remembers what they have done and said, and if it needs correcting or retracting, they do that. If something has to be done, the individual has to own it, track it, and make sure it is done, rather than assume someone else on the team is on it and it's out of their hands.

When your project encounters challenges, acknowledge your responsibility and any errors you've made without bowing out. Be transparent and accountable, no matter how frightening that is. Then, carry on.

What if you are facing a challenge, and you don't know what to do next, despite your efforts at problem framing, incubation, and finding a solution? Now you need to signal to the rest of the team that you are still on board and accountable and that you need more people to gather round and help solve.

From the beginning of the Psyche mission, I have had the strategy to be transparent with our sponsors at NASA and earn trust over time by never giving them a marketing presentation but instead always showing where we really are with our progress. Individuals can and should follow the same trust and ownership paths with their own teams. Show your progress and your wins and then spend more time discussing the challenges you are still facing. Describe the steps you yourself have taken so far (*always* do analysis and work on your own before bringing challenges to others) and invite the group to help find solutions. You have not given up. In fact, you have driven the project forward with your analysis and framing, and you have discussed the problem with your colleagues from a position of strength.

On the Psyche project, long before the cold-gas thruster crisis, when we realized that due to issues during COVID and with software testing that we would not be ready to launch on our original date in August 2022 and the launch would slip at least a year, the team was in such a fragile state from not knowing the path forward that we knew we had to do more experimentation with communication. We were not sure what kinds of communication would be most effective or most welcomed by the team, so we tried a number of methods, and we watched for feedback. We started having all-team virtual meetings for a half hour twice a week, during which we would update rapidly on all topics. We tried following these up with a summary email. We tried updating on what had happened that week and on what was coming up. Some of these methods failed because they confused people (what had already happened, and what was about to happen?), and some failed because people did not retain the information (emails, though emailing was necessary to reach those people who preferred not to join the online meetings). Each of these failures was a way to learn.

Along your way, develop the skill of experimentation. Experiment in small ways to gain information about how to move forward. The skill of experimentation, as Turner Bohlen, my son and business partner, says, requires a willingness to fail in the short term, meaning the organization must cheer on some failing experiments as important for progress. That is, the organization needs to demonstrate publicly that failure is not just acceptable but an important part of learning and making progress. You have to fail intelligently and learn from the failures and then take a big leap toward success in your next experiment. Simply floundering in experiments and failing over and over is not a form of progress.

Thinking of your project as an informed experiment allows you to reframe a failed step or a sense of failure into a learning experience and an opportunity to pivot in a new direction.

Being transparent, keeping your head up, and marching forward, bravely experimenting and pivoting when needed, are closely connected to the concept of a growth mind-set, as researched and described by Carol Dweck. Dweck got her PhD in psychology at Yale in 1972 and spent the next fifteen years or so at the University of Illinois studying children's learning patterns. Most of her work focused on learned helplessness, and then she moved to studying intelligence in children and the role of motivation. Who was motivated, and why? And why did motivation actually appear to increase intelligence over time?

Dweck describes people as having either a growth mind-set (that is, believing that their abilities can improve through effort and persistence) or a fixed mind-set (that is, believing that their abilities are innate and cannot be changed). People with a growth mind-set are less discouraged by failure because they see it as a learning and growth experience and as temporary.[2] Which mind-set—growth or fixed—would you want in your teammates? Which would you rather have?

Finally, if the project you are working on just isn't going to have the outcome you need, and you've tried all the reasonable pathways, the rational choice, as you balance time spent, cost, risk, and reward, may be to end the project. This is not the same as giving up: This is a rational decision and a path forward. And it's a big learning experience that will stand you in good stead in the future.

In 2023, two weeks into the cold-gas thruster crisis that came just before our launch, the whole spacecraft team was utterly exhausted. We had been staffing three shifts (working around the clock) testing several possible solutions, including changing either hardware or software.

On September 27 we were directed by NASA headquarters to reschedule from October 5, our original date, to an October 12 launch. But there was nothing official yet. The spacecraft was not yet encapsulated in the fairing, as was necessary to put it on the rocket.

The team had been ruling out solution options, one after the other. We had only one possible solution left, which involved operating the thrusters differently than we had originally planned. We had begun thousands of computer simulations of the whole spacecraft trajectory to see if the new plan would work. Fifteen days before launch.

And of course, we made it. The team did exceptional, exemplary work, work that included many experiments and very tight timelines, and the simulations worked, and the spacecraft worked, and we solved the problem.

That work was the work of people obsessed with quality. They were concerned with the quality of the overall project, the quality of their own work, and the quality of the way the team communicated and organized. That quality carried us through and reinforced our determination: Just don't ever simply give up.

4

CREATE QUALITY IN ALL YOU DO

We were feeling good, right on schedule with building the radio communications system for an Earth-orbiting weather satellite. But sitting around the table for the morning "stand-up" meeting, where each of us gave a quick update on what we'd done the day before and what we were planning for the day, Steph, the lead engineer on the radio system, looked worried.

"Today, I was going to install the transponder for the radio system," she began, "and so I went to the parts storage yesterday to get the brackets and the housing, which were marked as having been received and checked in six months ago. But I'm sorry to say, they were not made right. The width of the space for the transponder is too small, and we can't use them."

"Oh my God," I breathed, half laughing at the outrageousness of this problem, "you mean they were not built to our requirements?"

"Not just that," she replied, "but the parts-acceptance people checked them in without measuring them to make sure they were made right. And it takes at least six months to get new ones, so suddenly as of this minute, we are six months behind schedule."

We think of quality in terms of craftsmanship. We accuse the parts provider of poor quality when they don't make the parts to spec. We criticize the quality of the installation of a stove, or the seams on our T-shirt, or the texture of a cookie. But while our team hadn't made the bracket, it failed to check whether the parts were right—we were guilty of a lack of quality too.

Quality results from the combination of all the characteristics of the item, event, or idea being considered. Quality is the best content (the most perfect stove installation, the best conversation, T-shirt, cookie, or essay), delivered in the best way, with the best schedule, and, especially, with the best human interaction—clear communications, calm, respect, cooperation. With those bad brackets for the radio system, we had a poor-quality piece of hardware, poor execution by the parts-acceptance people, and nonexistent communication. Quality is what allows us to compare one object or event or idea to another.

I think we've all heard that old joke. Quality, schedule, cost: Pick two. Except it's not really a joke, of course. You can't prioritize everything at once. In business, schedule and cost are often the drivers, and quality gets optimized as best it can within those other constraints. Or, more often, quality is just as good as we can get by with. It's a kind of least common denominator—just as small as it can be. Ugh. Is that the kind of world we really want to live in?

This kind of prioritization happens in every aspect of human endeavor, really. Sometimes we create the best thing we can in the limited time we have, and as long as it works a little bit, that's enough. Other times, budget pressures drive us to sell more, to write more grant applications, to fill the lecture hall with more students, to cut corners on materials. All the pressures end up diminishing quality.

However, under any set of constraints, it's still possible to care about the quality of what you are making and make it the best it can be.

The truth is, everything we do in life, even how we think, can be judged for its quality. Robert Pirsig wrote beautifully about this in *Zen and the Art of Motorcycle Maintenance*: "Quality," he said, "is an integration of the intellectual and the emotional, an internal state."[1]

HOW HAVE PEOPLE THOUGHT ABOUT IMPROVING QUALITY?

Humans have thought of various ways to improve quality, with varying success. For example, the Six Sigma process can help teams and organizations achieve quality. Six Sigma is customer focused and data driven and applies best to organizations with mass production of some sort. The phrase *six sigma* refers to driving errors down until they are six standard deviations away from the norm—that is, having fewer than 3.4 errors per one million units or opportunities to make errors. Statistical quality is the easiest to measure, and the repetitive processes that underlie it are easiest to analyze and improve over time.

Here, however, we are talking about quality not just in the work product but also in everyday work and life activities. We are talking about quality produced by one individual, you, and the effects that quality—or the lack of it—has on you and on those around you and how they perceive you.

Some institutions and organizations that are judged as the most excellent in the world (think top-ranked universities) have created quality through exclusion. If only people who are already excellent are accepted—say, the top 4 percent of all applicants—then the excellence of the organization is assured. Most of those excellent people are already by definition driven by an internal system of judgment of excellence and will create a culture around themselves that expects and values excellence. Quality by definition.

Leaders in business, on sports teams, and in the classroom have also attempted to force high quality through punishment or fear—for example, the fear of failing or the threat of being fired. The "get it right or I'll hit your hand with a ruler" kind of learning. But this kind of learning is entirely outward focused: To avoid the punishment (being fired, getting an F), you are trying to guess exactly what the manager, teacher, or parent (God forbid) wants. It's almost the opposite of what we are trying to create here, which is the deep, authentic, thoughtful pursuit of your own internal determiner of quality—what you, in your gut, know is better and truer.

We want a world where quality is driven from within and does not need intimidation, threats, or exclusion. Each of us can create quality. This chapter argues for and outlines steps and processes for creating an internal, personal sense of quality in all the things you do.

HOW YOU CAN WORK ON QUALITY

The simplest scenario to consider is attempting to achieve greater quality when you are building something, such as a part in the Six Sigma process. First, you need to meet the specifications or requirements of the thing you are creating by meeting certain measurements—the part you make needs to be so wide and so thick and no thicker, or the training you are designing has to hit the ten major learning objectives for the subject. In most cases, these are simple metrics, and the requirements may come from someone else, your manager, or your customer, though you might have the luxury of setting them yourself.

A deeper way to think about meeting requirements is by being more detail oriented. Pay attention to each step, measurement, and outcome. Think about what would go wrong if you were not accurate or skipped something. And write down what you are doing and how it turns out, each step of the way. Imagine, each time you are doing something, that you are *practicing*, practicing to do it better the next time.

You might be thinking, "This is way beneath me. I'm a much more sophisticated thinker than this." But you might be surprised. Try it sometime. Keep a lab notebook of your actions as you create something that you want to be of quality. Maybe it's an object you are building, or an event you are planning, or advice you are giving. Write down your steps and how each turned out.

Later, read them over. Could you have done better? Anything out of order? Did something end up imperfect, and can you go back and see where you could have prevented that mistake? This is all part of our perpetual attempt to get things right the first time and better each time.

And then, an even more critical step is to work on an ever higher inner measure for quality: What improvement could I suggest? What are the inherent weaknesses or unexpected outcomes of the steps I have taken? How can I think ahead to the experience of the user, the student, the theatergoer, or the reader, to anticipate and make this product better still?

In general, we know when something is done or made badly. All of us are pretty good at being critics. It's especially easy to critique something that someone else made, so start with that little mental fiction: The thing or idea in front of you was actually made by someone else, and you are there to critique it. Go through the process of experiencing or using the thing you have made, and think of ways to make it better. Perhaps the instructions are vague, such as a long, ugly sentence starting with "it" that leaves the reader wondering what the sentence is about. Maybe a plastic part is weak or a solder joint is not well bonded on both sides.

Even considering what might be the best quality for most of the things you do may be unfamiliar. All too often people are rewarded just for completing something, even if it's not very good, or even just for showing up. You can do better; everyone can. So think beyond that. What could make this thing the highest quality? How could the whole concept be improved? Could there be a scale going from bad to normal to excellent to exceptional? You've just moved your own thing from bad to normal or normal to excellent, perhaps, but what would make it exceptional?

Imagine an expert in your field looking at your work. What would they say? This is a kind of metacognition, thinking about thinking, breaking out of your experience of the moment and analyzing it from outside. Metacognition is one of our superpowers, and I'll talk a lot more about it in the next chapter, but here is an example: Think about your creation from the outside. Think of a productive critic in your life, someone who can pick out what needs to be fixed and then let you know it in a constructive, helpful way. Imagine they are there looking at your creation. What would they tell you to improve?

Part of quality is always asking: How have people solved this before? Which of their ideas has been shown to be effective? What are the key differences between those ideas and the problems they solved and your idea?

One tool for improving one's sense of quality is to seek, or imagine, exemplars of the highest quality of the kind of thing you are doing. It's sometimes hard to think of how to improve the thing in front of you unless you have an idea of what an even better version might be. The most beautifully written sentence, the most convincing essay, the longest-lasting tire, the most productive meeting. The space between what you have done or made and the best one you can find or imagine is the space where quality grows.

Almost everything we ever do has been done by someone else before. Learn from history and then improve upon it. Stand upon the shoulders of giants. Find something so good that there is space between what you have made and it, and then think about what it would take to traverse that space and exceed it. You can find a best of its kind for each thing you do or create, and you can aspire to that quality.

FIND AN EXEMPLAR

Finding or imagining the exemplars of highest quality can be hard, harder even than raising the quality of what you are doing. How can you know what a great negotiation is like if you've never been in a great negotiation?

Finding an exemplar can be a journey in itself. Searching online is an obvious first step, but you'll likely find cheap, mass-produced things, no matter what you are looking for. So search on specialist sites for things that are handmade, craftsman-made, or made as single pieces by obsessive hobbyists. If you are seeking examples of writing, try using generative AI as a starting point: Ask AI to write an example. If you can afford to and you're building physical objects, buy some examples and look at them in person. Here are some more ideas for finding exemplars:

• Interview experts in the field of the thing you are creating.
• Have friends experience what you have made (read the essay, use the tool, etc.) and give you feedback.
• Read about the history of what you are creating. How has that thing advanced over time? How has its style, materials, or use changed?
• Find examples of similar things that are not exactly what you are making or doing. If you are making part of a smartphone app for learning math, for example, look for smartphone apps teaching other things to a similar group of people and discover which were really successful and why. Was their success linked to quality? What aspects?
• Seek exemplars of what you are making at their source. If it's software, look on GitHub; if it's writing, read the best in your genre; if it's art, go to a gallery or museum with similar work in it.

Once you have one or more exemplars, describe to yourself the attributes that combine to produce exceptional quality. Measure the distance between what you have done and the exemplar. See if you want to close that difference, or if you have thought of an even greater or more desirable quality you want to move toward instead.

The beauty of an exemplar is that you have now defined the playing field beyond where you are standing now. You can move toward your exemplar, or you can move away from it in a new, better direction.

WHAT CAN HAPPEN WITHOUT AN EXEMPLAR—
AN EXTREME BUT ILLUSTRATIVE CASE

Uh-oh, I think, as I start to read the email. "Dear Dr. Elkins-Tanton, I have found the explanation for why Earth has continents with seas between them, and why these relationships have changed over time. Geologists have misunderstood the nature of Earth all along, but I have discovered the answer by carefully studying nature over many years."

I look up and sigh. This person is not a scientist trained at a university; I can tell. The fundamental problem he is approaching is too large (everything all at once about the formation and evolution of continents and oceans), and his immediate dismissal of all of known geology has me worried.

I read on. This person is likening the crust of Earth to the coarse, brittle bark of a tree. This is a metaphor I have heard before, but like every metaphor and every toy model used in science, it is useful only for the most superficial comparison, and anything deeper quickly goes wrong.

He explains that as the planet grows (uh-oh, Earth is not growing from within, so that's a problem), the "bark" cracks, forming continents, and Earth's interior wells up, making the floors of the oceans in between.

It's a gorgeous metaphor, I have to admit. But it's not science, and it's not defensible as anything other than an imaginary scenario. If this person is really aiming at getting the attention of the science community, he needs to be his own critic and then find exemplars. Here are the steps he missed toward reaching a quality he aspires to:

- Use his own internal critic first. He should ask himself, "Where are the weak spots in my idea? What might I immediately expect other people to critique?"
- Compare his theory to other hypotheses for continental formation (exemplars) and notice that the others are backed by dozens of scientific studies investigating each part of the hypothesis. In his case, these would be, to begin with: What evidence is there that Earth is changing in size? What evidence is there that the crust grew all at once? What evidence is there that the oceans have increased in size over time? If all this were true on Earth, why did it not happen the same way on the other rocky planets? In other words, what evidence must be shown for scientists to take my idea seriously? Lesson for us all: Before you stray too far from what others are expecting your product to be like, prepare them and yourself to defend it and explain it.
- Approach possible experts with an open mind, asking sincerely for feedback and taking it seriously. This person did listen to some of what I suggested, but in general, the people who send me these "manifestos," as I call them, are not looking for feedback but for buy-in and help getting published. Invite your possible critics into the process and learn from them.

The many manifestos that have come my way over the years are almost always extreme extensions of simple ideas: a misunderstood visual metaphor (like a growing tree standing for a planet or a water whirlpool being the same as a black hole) or an exciting but oversimplified or incorrect numerical calculation that is extended beyond any possible meaningfulness.

I don't think any product you or I make—whether it's writing an essay, running a meeting, or writing some code—can be as far off the mark as those of these good-willed people attempting to prove scientific hypotheses without data. But the extremity of their need for recalibration surely makes them good examples for how to achieve greater quality.

For everyone, you and me alike, quality is attained through iteration. It need not be ten thousand hours of practice, but some mindful practice along the lines of the above advice will improve quality over time. Progress, that's what we are after—constant progress.

DECIDE ON YOUR VALUES

Everything that makes a team great is created by the members of the team. To be your best self, to control your fast reactions and moderate how you interact with people, to make key decisions, to direct your career, to be a great leader, you need to know your gut-level fundamental values.

Think about a person who really inspired you, whom you would want to work with or even be. What are their most compelling attributes? Write them down.

Then, think about what your top two or three values for life are, the ones you think are nonnegotiable, the ones you most strongly aspire to. Give it a good, hard try until you have some words you could sign your name to.

Then, look at the list of values below. This list was compiled from several workshops I've led on value setting; you can find other lists online. Anything there leap out at you as critical, something you might have overlooked? Anything make you frown, or that you reflexively reject?

Keep these top values, along with the ones you don't want to promote, and check in on them as you make decisions. Do your plans for the future serve those values?

LIST OF VALUES			
Boldness	Freedom	Justice	Self-awareness
Courage	Fun	Love	Self-questioning
Courtesy	Generosity	Mutual respect	Self-reliance
Creativity	Good citizenship	Optimism	Socialization
Critical thinking	Graciousness	Patience	Spirituality
Decision-making	Gratitude	Perseverance	Stability
Determination	Honesty	Perspective	Striving for quality
Directness	Humbleness	Persuasiveness	Tolerance
Empathy	Humility	Pleasure	Tradition
Equality	Humor	Power	Transparency
Fairness	Improvisation	Quality	Trustworthiness
Fame	Inclusivity	Respect	Willingness to take action
Fearlessness	Influence	Respect for others	

WHAT'S THE IMPACT OF YOUR QUALITY?

A sense of quality is required for people who work in a risk-tolerant, innovative organization. An organization can only tolerate risk, as Gary Pisano, professor of business administration at the Harvard Business School, points out, when it also has an intolerance for incompetence. Even when failures are an accepted and even encouraged part of learning in an organization, no organization can afford an infinite number of failures. An organization can be sunk by personnel who cause too many failures simply out of ignorance or preventable mistakes and who fail to learn from their mistakes fast enough. Risk and failure are effective at driving innovation only when they lead rapidly to learning and success.

As in the previous chapter where I linked experimentation to not giving up, here a sense of quality will keep you learning and improving and limit the failure cycle as learning accelerates. Experimentation requires a tolerance for short-term failure and a sense of quality, along with the ability to analyze dispassionately what can improve quality; all these attributes will move you more quickly to success.

As Gary Pisano says about a risk-tolerating, innovative organization: "These cultures are not all fun and games. Many people will be excited about the prospects of having more freedom to experiment, fail, collaborate, speak up, and make decisions. But they also have to recognize that with these freedoms come some tough responsibilities. [As a leader it's] better to be up-front from the outset than to risk fomenting cynicism later when the rules appear to change midstream."[2]

So a sense of quality and the ability to rapidly improve will raise your effectiveness at experimenting and innovating. You'll reach a good-quality outcome faster. What else does quality do for you? First, let me talk about what *not* having quality does to you.

Part of always thinking about the quality of what you do and make in your life is having a sense of pride in yourself and respect for others around you. If you consistently create poor-quality work—whether it's keeping incomplete notes on what happened in your meeting, making too many mistakes in your work, or being unreliable at walking your dog or getting groceries for you and your partner—you are degrading your own life and devaluing yourself to others.

As you work on quality, you will develop a gut feeling about where improvements can be made. You'll become less tolerant of inefficient processes and mistakes in others—this is a double-edged sword! You'll need to work on patience and on constructive ways to help others. But you'll also see many places in your own work and life where you can do better.

Quality is not just conforming to manufacturing requirements—and it's not just about things. Each of us should have a determination to move toward excellence and listen carefully to our itchy feeling of dissatisfaction when what we witness or what we produce could be better.

And what does having a sense of quality do for you? Well, first of all, it makes you so much more employable. In fact, it can make you irreplaceable. You are dependable (your qualities include reaching deadlines and communicating clearly about challenges), and you push your team to greater outcomes just by being an example of quality yourself.

A pursuit of quality can help your whole life become a work of art for you. It's a place where striving to be better is never misplaced. Many Buddhists believe that their everyday work reflects the divine, and thus, they aim constantly for quality and beauty. Everyday activities are a kind of meditation when done with awareness and intention. What a culture this creates! Quality everywhere. The Shakers, a Protestant sect founded in England in the late eighteenth century, also believed that the quality of their work was an act of worship. They saw God present in the meticulous details of their craftsmanship. Today, their beautifully simple furniture and architecture are widely seen as of exceptionally high quality.

I don't mean to imply that one must link spiritual belief and quality. Personally, I do not. But these examples show how profound a personal meaning the search for quality can have. Demonstrate your sense of quality with every product you make, including every email, every report, every essay, every meeting. Your work is speaking for you.

Listen to what that work is saying. Stand back and look objectively at what you have made and how you made it. That's the ultimate superpower skill, examining our actions and learning from that examination. Metacognition is what it's called, and the next chapter is all about it.

5

BECOME AN EXPERT THINKER: METACOGNITION

You may always have been aware, on some level, that to be your most effective, you need to master the behaviors we've talked about so far: speaking calmly, never giving up, pursuing the answers to problems, and seeking to achieve the highest quality in everything you do.

The critical part of all this is that no matter how aware of these you have been previously, every one of us—no matter how sophisticated and successful—can profitably spend more time thinking strategically about these and other aspects of our performance and behavior. We can be more self-aware.

This chapter is about the many ways we can examine how we think and how we learn in order to learn faster, think more effectively, lose our biases, and develop insights. This is metacognition: becoming more and more aware of what we believe and know and why, and how to use this understanding to learn faster and plan better.

Metacognition is thinking about thinking; that is, your knowledge of your own thinking processes. The difference between regular thinking (cognition) and metacognition is in its goal: Cognition seeks to acquire and use knowledge for some purpose, while metacognition seeks to analyze, craft, and improve the knowledge-acquisition process and outcome. Cognition learns for and does the task. Metacognition plans, monitors, and evaluates.

You can gradually become a better and clearer thinker and problem-solver if you think about thinking on two levels: ordinary cognition and the upper level of monitoring, analyzing, and strategizing. Rising above the work and thinking about your process and the future fosters leadership traits in you and also helps you to be a better team member.

We all get a little lazy, go on autopilot. Or we have completely overlooked whole areas where doing things better will make an outsize difference to us. Every day you walk down well-worn mental trails, processes that you've done over and over. The process might be organizing a meeting, your own mental practice of identifying and solving problems, or the act of reading to learn something. Applying metacognition to these well-worn trails means thinking about how and why you do them and how they can be better.

Metacognition can boost your effectiveness more than perhaps anything else in this section of the book. These cognitive skills enable you to purposefully and systematically think ahead and make better plans, analyze the course of a meeting conversation and make the suggestion that turns it in the right direction, and understand so much more as you learn.

This chapter is about thinking metacognitively, starting with analyzing the effectiveness of your thinking and learning (including discovering biases) and then creating strategies and planning the tactics to carry out your objectives, whatever they might be: a big new project, a problem that needs solving, or simply having a better, smoother day.

METACOGNITION AS A WAY OF LIFE

Deanna Kuhn, a faculty member at Columbia University, describes metacognition as the slow replacement of less-efficient thinking strategies with more-effective processes to become a better and better thinker. It's a mental self-improvement program that reaches into every aspect of your life.

Kuhn points out that children start their lives without metacognition and that it develops slowly over time. Your expertise in metacognition can be virtually unbounded. It's your job to make sure your metacognitive development never stalls. [1]

David Perkins, a professor of education at Harvard University, defined four levels of metacognition:[2]

1. *Tacit learners* are unaware of their metacognitive knowledge. Without further analysis, they accept learning as it comes to them. (More about tacit learning and tacit knowledge—knowledge that you possess but that you are not conscious of—later.)
2. *Aware learners* use some metacognitive techniques, such as finding evidence in service of a new idea they have generated, but they are not necessarily conscious and deliberate about their metacognition.
3. *Strategic learners* consciously organize their thinking by using metacognitive techniques such as classifying knowledge, organizing knowledge mentally, and seeking to fill in gaps to speed their learning and make it more effective.
4. *Reflective learners* are strategic about their learning, and they also reflect upon the process of their learning while it is happening, assessing the effectiveness of their strategies and changing them for best effect.

Metacognition connects strongly with quality. In music, sports, and other fields, teachers often encourage "deliberative practice," practice in which you are thinking carefully and focusing on the thing you want to improve. Normal practice might be working on a skill by repeating it over and over until it becomes automatic, in contrast to deliberative practice in which you stay highly focused on your activity, thinking about whether you are improving. You are being metacognitive about your practice.

The key to successful deliberative practice, or metacognitive practice as we might call it, is to identify aspects of what you are doing that can be assessed objectively and compared from one instance to another. Then, focus on those aspects and consider how well you are doing, and whether you are improving over time. Analyze why you are or are not improving. Examples might be as follows:

- You decide to focus on improving your participation in meetings by asking prepared, strategic questions in each meeting and assessing how people respond.
- You think critically about how you bring new people onto your team: Are you telling them the most important things? Can you assess whether they remember the messages?

BECOMING A MASTER LEARNER

The process of learning is a key place for metacognition. Learning itself is a learned behavior! Think about it: There are people who are not in the habit of learning. They don't immediately become alert when a contradiction crosses their path or the effort they are making is turning in an undesirable direction.

If you consciously think about the way you are learning, you become a better learner. You can learn through memorization or repetition of a task, or you could instead learn through the analysis of not only how you are learning but also what you are doing with your learning and how you could learn better.

For example, imagine you want to learn how to make a great cup of coffee. (I know, you are already an expert in coffee. But bear with me, it's an example.) A naive learner, a tacit learner, might find a source online and read it carefully end to end. A more sophisticated learner will immediately start questioning whether this is the best source, or whether it is biased in some way, and will seek a number of sources to compare. Then, this more metacognitive learner might try several of the processes, with different beans, to see what aspects of the process make the biggest difference.

The first learner was effectively memorizing one source. The second was learning with context and analysis. The difference between memorization and learning with context and meaning is similar to the difference between familiarity and understanding. You may be familiar with a given process, like organizing a meeting, and be able to reproduce it. But have you thought about how well it works and whether it's the best process to do? That's the path to understanding.

Familiarity is not the same as understanding, as my brilliant mathematician husband, James Tanton, has often said. It's metacognition that points out to us that we don't completely understand something but only find it familiar or are following familiar steps that are standardized and therefore unquestioned but are not necessarily optimal or even correct.

There are tools to help you improve your metacognition. You should be striving to think in layers, from a passive layer, where you learn and attend to what is in front of you, up to a metacognitive layer, where you are deploying metacognitive strategies to improve your thinking in your passive layer, and finally to a reflective layer, where you are analyzing the effectiveness of your metacognition. Here are some prompts for mentally stepping up into the second metacognitive layer and the layer above that, where you analyze your metacognitive thinking.

- In the simplest case, for young or new learners, practice metacognition by setting goals and deadlines and measuring yourself against them as you are learning.
- Organize what you know on a given topic into a mind map and look at connections and gaps; criticize the knowledge you write

down (Is it correct? Is it relevant?); connect the map at its borders to other topics you know.

- Articulate your process of thinking out loud to someone else and discover in that way your own gaps.

- Imagine what a top expert would say if you explained to them your plans (it's amazing how our mind can take on the other voice and point out weak spots!).

- Tell someone else about what you just learned to test whether you actually did learn it. (For example, if you sometimes tell friends at dinner about something you just read, you are testing your ability to learn and remember. Check, after you get home, whether you got it right. If you didn't, send a quick email of thanks and a correction to your friends.)

- As you are learning something new (for example, reading a book), imagine you are about to teach that to someone else and review in your mind whether you are taking in what you are reading clearly enough to be able to teach it. This is a higher level of metacognition than the prompt just above. In this case, rather than actually teaching what you learned, just imagine you are.

- When you are learning something new, push yourself deep into your learning zone, where you are a little uncomfortable and compelled to concentrate deeply on serious reading or analysis or practice. Don't push into what Noel Tichy, professor at the University of Michigan business school and the former chief of General Electric's management development center, calls the "panic zone." That's past optimal learning and too far into stress.

- When faced with a piece of information, something asserted to you by another person or in writing, ask yourself (or them!), "Why?" Why, for example, do you say it's best to keep the printed circuit board at 220°F for one minute before continuing to heat it up? "Because that's how my mentor Kate did it; she said it allowed gases to be released and avoided making bubbles in the solder." But why were there gases to be released? Well, it turns out in the end that Kate was referring to an old kind of solder not in use anymore, and this step is unnecessary. I can't tell you how often the "common knowledge" on the Psyche mission turned out to be wrong or outdated when tested with a series of *why* questions—in the most polite and respectful way, of course.

ANALYZING FOR BIASES

When we were planning the Psyche spacecraft, way back in 2011 and 2012, one of our big decisions was which instruments to fly on the spacecraft to collect our science data. Most of the instruments we were interested in had versions made by several organizations around the world. As we were discussing one key instrument, one person in the room said we should use the version made by a particular university, that there was no better one for us. After a few clear agreements from others in the room and a brief discussion of capabilities, that version of the instrument ended up on our list. And it stayed.

Years later, when that university just could not deliver the instrument, we had to do the in-depth research to look for other possible vendors, praying we would find them. And we did. And we could have chosen them way back and not had that crisis and U-turn in the middle of the project. We had been victims of common knowledge. Everyone just knew the group we went with first was the right group. But no one had really done their homework.

On the other hand, there were many people who said we should go with one of the standard NASA prime contractors to build the basic structure of our spacecraft. These companies absolutely know what they are doing, and they have had success after success. That was the common knowledge, *and* it is true. But in our case we didn't accept the common knowledge. We researched, ran scenarios, and looked at risks, and we selected Maxar, not the common knowledge answer. Maxar turned out to be the right choice for *this* mission.

"Common knowledge" is a form of bias: If everyone says something is so, I feel compelled to also agree. It feels safe to agree. Common knowledge is especially comforting and easy to agree with when a senior person with a lot of success in their past asserts something is true. Who's going to check? They already know. If you follow their advice and accept what they say, they will approve of your actions.

When someone senior asserts something to you, though, remind yourself that one of the dangers of being a respected, senior person is that one stops fully questioning oneself. The respected senior person develops a little extra respect for, well, themselves. Find ways to check, gently, anything that's just asserted to be true without supporting evidence.

Part of examining what you know and how you know it is understanding the ways your knowledge is influenced by external sources. Sometimes that external source is someone trusted whom you'd be inclined to accept information from without question. Other times, information comes to you from someone you don't know or trust. Is the information from one really more likely to be correct than from the other? I'd say, we have no way to judge that. All we can do is take information as it comes to us and then question it. It's your responsibility to always ask yourself, "How do I know this?" And to speak only with the level of confidence your information supports.

In the 1950s economists and social scientists started trying to explain in a new way how people think and what our limitations are. They described, and therefore made more visible to us, the ways in which our motivations, previous experiences, and unarticulated emotions affect our ability to think clearly and make good decisions.

Herbert Simon, an economist and cognitive psychologist, began it all by coining the word *heuristics* to describe how we take mental shortcuts to arrive at decisions. By shining a light on these shortcuts, Simon effectively showed us all how there was a limit on our ability to be rational. Then Daniel Kahneman (later famous for his popular book *Thinking, Fast and Slow*) teamed with Amos Tversky to describe the ways that people do not make rational decisions in finance and economy—for example, people hate losing money much more than they love gaining money, so we make irrational decisions to avoid loss—and changed the field of economic forecasting.[3]

Kahneman and Tversky described a whole series of heuristic models, that is, models that our brains use to make judgments and decisions, even if the models are flawed or misleading. Their work was built upon by a generation of researchers, and now we have a rich list of heuristics that we can take from our subconscious and bring into conscious thought and even arrange and assess, using our metacognitive skills. Biases, heuristics, and schema are the *cognitive* structures that you use to organize your knowledge. *Metacognition* is your awareness and control over these structures that allow you to arrange, assess, and use your knowledge effectively.

Have you ever found yourself amazed by something you learned online and eager to share it with your friends? Did you immediately accept it as true? It turns out that having a strong emotional reaction to a piece of information—believing that the information must be either true or false—is a big flashing warning sign that you are not being critical enough, as Turner Bohlen pointed out to me. It's a sign of confirmation bias. All people are highly resistant to believing things that don't agree with their (flawed! biased!) existing internal ideas. So every time you are deeply satisfied with some new piece of information, stop and do some analysis. You might even pick some piece of knowledge that you feel especially emotional about—either happy about it or angry and sure that it's wrong—and do some broad, unbiased research to determine whether your emotion is justified or not.

Now, not all heuristics are biases and not all heuristics lead us down wrong paths; our brains use heuristics as shortcuts to best answers, especially when information is incomplete. But as usual, being more aware and metacognitive allows you to be more effective when using heuristics.

Some Specific Biases to Watch Out For

Many kinds of biases have been described and named. Becoming consciously aware of some of them is greatly helpful in clear thinking. Again, it's metacognition: If you are aware of common biases, then you can be constantly analyzing your thinking and checking whether any of the biases are at work. Here are a few examples.

Apophenia

The tendency we have to imagine meaningful connections between unrelated things is called apophenia. One simple example of apophenia is the morning when your neighbor listened to a radio news piece about spiders and then found a spider in his car. The spider in his car was not caused by the news, but his awareness of spiders was heightened by the news.

Another example of apophenia is a tendency to focus on and overestimate clusters or runs of repeats or patterns in large data samples. We are captured by patterns and encouraged by repeated numbers—they stand out to us. In fact, people commonly think that clusters of the same number in data means the data is *not* random, that it has structure and an underlying cause. In truth, clusters and runs and streaks are actually the very hallmark of random data. If you flip a perfect coin over and over, you should expect to get some sequences where it's just heads for a while, and others where it's just tails, over and over. Similarly, if a few big newsworthy earthquakes happen somewhere in the world all within a given month, someone is sure to start looking for some alarming underlying cause. But if you look at earthquake data over many decades, you'll see that clusters of larger earthquakes spread over Earth (not all in one place, which is a different story) are common.

Availability Heuristic

We tend to think recent or especially memorable events (those that are more available in our memories) are more likely to recur. This bias toward memorable events is called availability heuristic. An example of this is when we hear of a lightning strike that caused an injury at a soccer game, we overestimate the chance that the rain shower over our game will bring a lightning strike to the field (though the caution and safety that result from that overestimation of risk is only a good thing).

Our bias toward the likelihood of highly available events in our own memories also leads us to use human-centered analogies to explain less familiar and possibly entirely unrelated events. I see this all the time in science. People commonly use cooking metaphors to explain processes in geology, like melting rock into magma. We are so used to heating things up on the stove and having them melt (think, melting butter) that it seems obvious that's how rocks melt, too, by heating. In truth, most of the melting of magma on Earth is produced by hot rock moving upward inside Earth, closer to the surface, and thereby experiencing lower pressure that allows melting, and not by heating at all.

Another example of the availability heuristic is that once you have noticed something, then you tend to notice every subsequent incidence of that thing, leading you to the belief that it occurs at a high frequency. Have you noticed that when you learn a new word, you then see it again somewhere soon after? That word has not become more common; you just overlooked it before.

Overall, the availability heuristic causes us to use our most memorable experiences as examples of what we think happens most often, and which explains other similar experiences. Neither of those may be true.

Implicit Association

Finally, a subconscious "tell" on what we really think: *implicit association*. We associate words with each other according to whether they fit our unconscious biases, even if in our conscious mind we deny having these biases. Project Implicit, led by Dr. Tony Greenwald from the University of Washington, Dr. Mahzarin Banaji from Harvard University, and Dr. Brian Nosek from the University of Virginia, offers an online implicit bias test that reveals these associations.[4]

This test identifies your implicit biases by tracking how quickly you are able to sort words. For example, your screen might show a Black person and a white person, and you might first be asked to sort words associated with badness to the white person's side, and words associated with goodness to the Black person's side. Later, you might be asked to sort words associated with badness to the Black person's side and goodness to the white person's side (the test alternates which associations come first to each person taking the test). If you more easily associate "goodness" with "Black," then you will be able to sort those words faster, and associating "goodness" with "white" may cause a little lag in your reaction as your mind takes a moment to follow the rule and overcome your unconscious bias.

You can take online tests to examine your own biases about people, and more importantly, you can ask yourself when you are making decisions about hiring, promotion, or even listening with care whether you are taking these actions with equal attention to merit and respect, no matter to whom you are speaking or referring.

An Example of Bias at Work: The #8 Screw

On the Psyche mission, on an inauspicious day in 2022 during the year-long launch slip, we received some unwelcome news. Upon a routine spacecraft inspection after the spacecraft had been shipped to Kennedy Space Center, the team had noticed that two #8 screws were missing. Immediately, an extensive search was begun: in the area around the spacecraft, in places the spacecraft had previously been, and throughout every nook and cranny of the spacecraft that could be seen with eyes or an endoscope, looking around corners and into tight spaces.

In our project meetings and with the Jet Propulsion Lab leadership, these two #8 screws became quite a topic of conversation and concern. They were easily replaced—that wasn't the problem. The problem was this: Could they be lodged somewhere in the spacecraft, perhaps fallen there during transport or while in vibration testing, and cause problems later? In one meeting we spent about forty-five minutes talking about the two screws and only fifteen minutes on all the rest of the risks the mission was facing: software not yet tested, team morale, organizational challenges. These risks were far greater than the screws but much harder to talk about.

I think this #8 screw fixation was a kind of availability heuristic. We all had experience with screws, knew what they looked like, how to search for them, and what they could do to the spacecraft. Understanding the problems with a line of code or how to motivate hundreds of stressed people called to mind no clear memories and inspired no obvious paths in our minds. The screws were so much more available to our memories and experiences. And we never did find those screws!

Being aware of mental biases and heuristics helps you learn and make decisions. Everything you hear or read you need to contend with and accept or reject from within some context. If you make that context more logical and clearer, you'll over time build a much more useful internal knowledge base, freer of biases.

As the great writer and neurologist Oliver Sacks wrote in his book *River of Consciousness*: "To get something in a flash, the mind must be able to accommodate it, to retain it. The first barrier lies in allowing oneself to encounter new ideas, to create a mental space, a category with potential connection, and then to bring these ideas into full and stable consciousness, to give them conceptual form, holding them in mind even if they contradict one's existing concepts, beliefs, or categories."

What a great summary of thinking clearly: Create a mental space for new information, think about how it might link with other information, and weigh the merits while trying to eliminate biases. In fact, cognitive scientists say that the best way to remember new information is to network it into things you already know.

Here are some steps summarized from the chapter:

- If you have a strong emotion about some information, view your decision about it with special skepticism and make sure to check it more carefully.
- Notice when something is "common knowledge," and check on its truth. Sometimes common knowledge is called out by someone: "Three tests are enough; everyone does it this way." But a more dangerous form of common knowledge is the unquestioned and unstated process or belief. Watch out for those!
- Organize your information into maps and graphs and look for gaps.
- Familiarity is not the same as understanding.
- Check your decisions and ideas for bias.

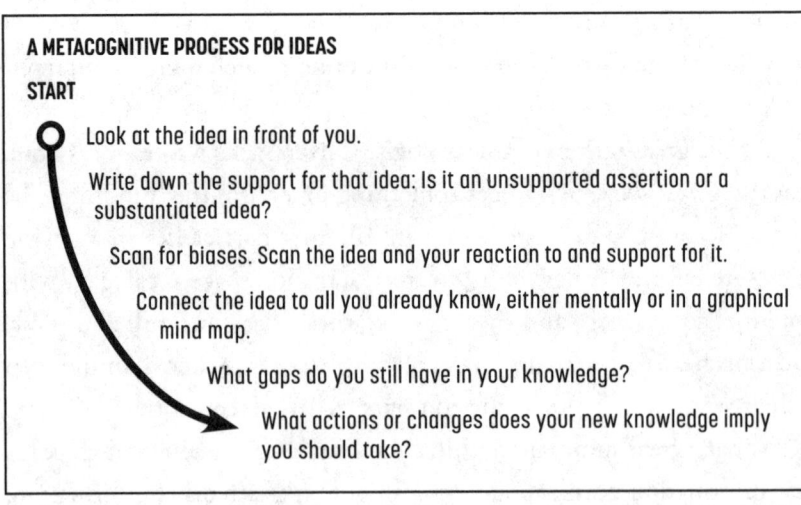

A METACOGNITIVE PROCESS FOR IDEAS

START

Look at the idea in front of you.

Write down the support for that idea: Is it an unsupported assertion or a substantiated idea?

Scan for biases. Scan the idea and your reaction to and support for it.

Connect the idea to all you already know, either mentally or in a graphical mind map.

What gaps do you still have in your knowledge?

What actions or changes does your new knowledge imply you should take?

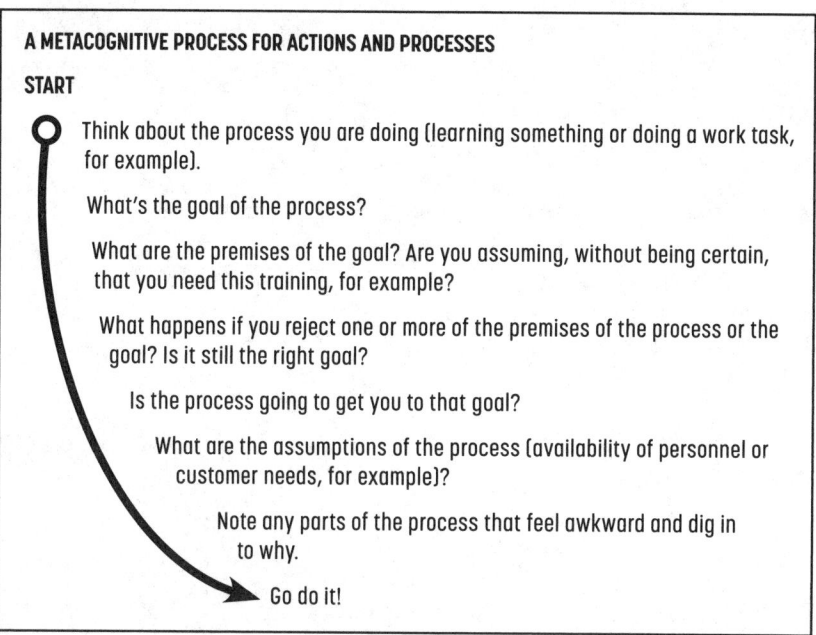

A METACOGNITIVE PROCESS FOR ACTIONS AND PROCESSES

START

Think about the process you are doing (learning something or doing a work task, for example).

What's the goal of the process?

What are the premises of the goal? Are you assuming, without being certain, that you need this training, for example?

What happens if you reject one or more of the premises of the process or the goal? Is it still the right goal?

Is the process going to get you to that goal?

What are the assumptions of the process (availability of personnel or customer needs, for example)?

Note any parts of the process that feel awkward and dig in to why.

Go do it!

When you encounter a new idea or a start a new process, these steps can form a template, or a kind of warning system, to wake you up when you feel confident in your knowledge but perhaps need to think more deeply.

Finally, monitor what happens as you practice metacognition. Track your efficacy and learn from it. Work your new information back into your metacognitive skills by using it to update your knowledge and remove biases. Having the clearest, best-supported knowledge, the ability to detect biases, and the tool set for creating and carrying out strategies makes you the most valuable player, every time.

PART II

OUTWARD

How Individuals Connect into Networked Teams

When I was trained at MIT to be a scientist, I learned that my innovations should be in how I *thought* about the natural processes that I was observing. I didn't get to change or affect those processes, just measure and interpret.

And then I took a job at a management consulting firm where one of my first assignments was to help a big aerospace company fix its manufacturing process. The manufacturing team had an overly complicated, slow, and confusing way to organize its parts, allocate the parts to people on the line who needed them, and make sure the parts were ready for use on time. With the consulting team, we first imagined how the processes should go to solve the problems the manufacturing team was having: We redesigned how people should work together, in our imaginations. We thought about how they should interact, how to track the parts, how to ask for information, and how to ensure the parts were ready on time. This is not radical. We can all imagine how processes *should* go.

But then a miracle happened: We explained our new ideas to the manufacturing team, and once we had convinced them to work that way, they did. In science, you don't imagine how you wish something would happen, and then it starts working that way. But with humans, if you can imagine a new team process vividly enough, you can make it happen in the real world. Each of us can have immediate successes in making ourself more effective, and then we can spread our ideas on how to work more effectively together. Teams are built from what we imagine is possible, human by human.

And it's not just the processes of how the work is carried out; we also need to work on the social ways people interact while doing the work. Teams work together under a suite of common, but often unspoken, assumptions, norms, and values that together create their team culture. A rude team culture predicts poorer outcomes, and a positive culture predicts team success, creates resilience in the face of adversity, and can create contentment for individuals, and thus lowers turnover and can increase diversity.

You can think of culture within a huge space mission team, or you can think of it within your office group, study group, or family. Team culture is not, as I've been told sometimes in the past, about unnecessary emotions or time wasted supporting the weaker people. Team culture is a common understanding of how we treat each other so that we can all succeed to the best of our abilities. Shows of anger or passive aggression stop others from speaking. Pointing out your own excellence (status signaling) causes newer team members to either stand up and beat their own chests in turn or retreat into silence. All those behaviors distract from the work at hand and also silence people whose voices need to be heard for the team to create the best outcomes.

A good team culture should be fostered because it is ethically the right thing to do and because it brings greater joy and success to the team members and leads to better work and higher productivity.

We are working toward a world where gender and other demographic characteristics do not influence or constrain one's career trajectory and opportunities. Not least, a good team culture is a goal because it helps you win—in our case, win a deep-space mission.

The success of a team should be measured not just in the success of the project it is undertaking but also in the success of each individual to stretch and to rise on their merits. Both kinds of success are critical in today's world, where traditional career paths seem to have been erased, the world is changing, education is broken, and some people feel disenfranchised. You need your organizations to succeed, and you need individuals to succeed as well.

A team's culture consists of how the team members treat one another. Teams are created by individuals, each member coming together with other members in dyads or pairs of people with their own working relationship, and then into a team. Even if we like to think of a team as a single unit with a lot of commonalities among the members, the truth is every action, success, failure, emotion, and misunderstanding boils down to a relationship between two people, a dyad. Think of it this way: Your speech didn't inspire the team as a unit; your speech inspired Chris in one way, which is dependent upon Chris's relationship with you. Your speech inspired Alex in another way because you have a different relationship with Alex. Everything depends upon the dyads each person builds; they are the building blocks, the only building blocks, of a team.

Building on the individual skills developed in Part I, Part II will cover these topics:

- Build Your Dyads
- Discuss Culture Together and Practice It Consciously
- Enable Continuous Communications to Flow
- Distribute Authority
- Work Together on Decision-Making, Tactics, and Strategy

Learn to notice who is silent, and don't just listen to the loud voices. Encourage the quiet and always engage the silent. Stop rudeness when you see it: Rudeness will silence even more people, removing even more diversity from the innovation and problem-solving resources of your team. The goals of all these ideas are to create success not just for the team but for every person on the team.

Networking into teams requires each member to take on characteristics of all the traditional organizational roles: junior member, peer, leader, facilitator, administrator. Becoming conscious of the many ways people interact and what helps people perform best is part of creating a great team.

All these efforts—from getting to know team members, to creating a culture that allows work to flow, to communicating copiously, to sharing decision-making and planning—are aimed at creating a team where each person takes responsibility and has respect for the others. This is a team in which great work happens, innovation is natural, and individuals thrive. Success, ethics, fairness, loyalty, retention—that is why.

6

BUILD YOUR DYADS

A couple of weeks after a new person joins my team at the university, I have them give a presentation at our Monday all-team meeting. They are encouraged to introduce themselves in whatever way feels comfortable and authentic. This has included descriptions of coaching their kids' hockey teams, a childhood in India, and the importance of a family's dogs. This way, we learn to respect and appreciate the individual.

Then we ask them to explain their job and its responsibilities. This allows the engineer to understand more about how the finances are controlled, and the distracted senior leader sees the undergrad intern as a whole person with a variety of skills.

Collaboration, trust, and culture begin with how people interact with each other one-on-one, so creating relationships is how a team begins to create its network. These pairs of people who know each other, called dyads, are the building blocks of trust in a team or an organization. Knowing every person's discipline and thus their critical value to the team should be central to your normal functioning as a team member.

To build the trust and create the beautiful team synergy that is possible, everyone has to become a person who is pleased to see others succeed. Taking conscious and visible pleasure in the success of another person is seldom what's rewarded at work. Instead, we are out there promoting ourselves, fighting to win. If the goal is always personal and selfish, the team will suffer, but if each person knows and respects every other person, then they can ask for, accept, and offer help more easily. They will listen more carefully. And they will celebrate one another's wins and forgive and work with less friction when the pressure is on. Celebrating someone else's win with genuine emotion not only bonds you to each other but actually raises your own appearance of leadership and desirability. The easiest way to help people care about what happens to each other, and to cheer each other on, is to help each team member make a genuine personal connection with every other team member.

Over and over, studies of what brings people satisfaction at work find that it's not money or power but respect and connection. "For top performers, a great workplace isn't about a lavish office, a beautiful gym, or a free sushi lunch," says Reed Hastings, Netflix CEO, in his book *No Rules Rules*. "It's about the joy of being surrounded by people who are both talented and collaborative. People who can help you be better. When every member is excellent, performance spirals upward as employees learn from and motivate each other."[1]

MATTERING AND ANTI-MATTERING

But unlike Reed Hastings, who leans heavily on firing low performers, I know that we can create excellence in our teams by influence, example, and training. Simply firing the underperformers and weeding people out until only the excellent remain, though some of that happens inevitably everywhere, is not the only or even the main way to achieve excellence. We can all *become* excellent together.

Part of connecting in dyads and coming to know people as people is gifting each other with the feeling that you matter. Everyone wants to be seen, heard, and respected. If you spend all your time making sure they hear and know about you, then you are not spending enough time listening and learning about them. Do that part first: Listen and learn about the other person.

Years of being overlooked, unheard, and generally unrespected makes people bitter. We all know who they are: The people who immediately "Reply all" with a long email complaint about the announcement you just made, or who always seem to voice opposition in meetings. Often, in the organizations I've been in, these people feel sidelined and unrespected. Of course, their confrontational behavior, a result of feeling unrespected, only increases their colleagues' avoidance of them. It's a terrible reinforcing cycle.

A few times in my career I've instituted a policy that whenever someone has a significant concern or complaint, particularly one voiced to the whole group in person or in an email, I make an appointment for an hour-long meeting in their office to talk it over. In that hour we try to solve the problem or at least find some positive steps toward a solution. Two good things came from this policy. First, people who felt unheard got intensively listened to, problems were unearthed, and some were solved. Second, people who were complaining just for sport gave it up because they didn't want to have to meet with me again for an hour to talk about solutions.

Through these years I learned something important: As people become more senior and experienced, they do not always gain respect or have their opinions sought after more often. That can leave people feeling, as Gordon Flett, a professor in the faculty of health at York University named it, "anti-mattered."[2] Instead of mattering, they feel unvalued, unheard, irrelevant, and invisible. Anti-mattered.

Everyone, I think, understands immediately what it means to feel like you matter. People listen to you and show they care about what happens to you. Flett's research has demonstrated that when people feel they matter to others, they actually perform better (we rise to the level of expectation of those around us, as we'll discuss more later in this book). Mattering requires both that you add value and that you are perceived as valuable. How wonderful, then, that when you are perceived as valuable, you are actually more likely to add value!

And conversely, if you feel anti-mattered, you are less likely to speak up, less likely to engage, less likely to produce quality work. Not just our emotions but also our actual work quality depend upon the actions and validation of our colleagues. Now flip that: You can respect and listen to your colleagues and show them that they matter, and doing that will help them do better.

Zach Mercurio, an organizational strategist, summed up in *Harvard Business Review* several research studies on this phenomenon. In one study of two hundred thousand employees across more than seven hundred companies, the high performers who left their jobs listed compensation as the *last* reason for leaving. In a complementary Gallup study of seven hundred employees who had recently left their jobs, 42 percent said that had the managers acted differently, they would have remained in their jobs.

"When asked what their manager could have done to retain them," Mercurio reports, "employees said they wanted them to invest more in their well-being, engage in more positive interactions, and meaningfully recognize their unique contributions."[3]

Flett and his colleagues created a five-item inventory to measure the extent to which a person feels anti-mattered and a second five-item inventory about mattering. Do any of these resonate with you?

Anti-Mattering Scale

How much do you feel like you don't matter?	0.63
How often have you been treated in a way that makes you feel like you are insignificant?	0.73
To what extent have you been made to feel like you are invisible?	0.83
How much do you feel like you will never matter to certain people?	0.76
How often have you been made to feel by someone that they don't care what you think or what you have to say?	0.82

Mattering Scale

How important are you to others?	0.76
How much do others pay attention to you?	0.74
How much would you be missed if you went away?	0.80
How interested are others in what you have to say?	0.65
How much do other people depend upon you?	0.64

The numbers after each measure show, out of a maximum of 1, how important each measure is for indicating a feeling of anti-mattering or mattering.

The top two indicators of anti-mattering are the extent to which the person feels invisible and how frequently they were made to feel someone didn't care what they thought or had to say.

The top indicator of mattering was the person's feeling that they would be missed if they went away. Start helping your colleagues know they would be missed by recognizing specific things they do that are valuable. When your teammate runs a great meeting, thank them for doing so and highlight aspects they created that made it great: Did they explain something clearly and with great expertise? Did they defuse an escalating conversation by encouraging people to explain completely their concerns about the issue? Or ask your colleague a question. Ask them to explain something to you that you need to know and that they are more knowledgeable about.

THE DANGER OF STATUS

Where do I start. Reacting to perceived status is ingrained and reflexive in human communities (and perhaps in almost all animal communities), and it's almost never helpful when trying to establish clear, fearless communication or solve problems. Status judgments are triggered, among other things, by anything that indicates a difference between people. We define status through difference and simultaneously give one side value and power. Dividing a team into subteams immediately creates a feeling of us versus them. The minute there is a difference, or a boundary, there is a judgment about relative power and therefore status. For example, let's suppose person A manages more people than person B, so person A is more powerful in the organization. But let's suppose person B went to an Ivy League college, and person A didn't go to college, so person B is a fancier and more powerful person in that sense. But does person B actually know more than person A?

The existence of a status hierarchy in an organization or team is not in itself negative and nor, I would argue, is it possible to entirely get rid of status, even if we wanted to, because it is baked into our biology as primates. Status plays a role in how we interact with others, and status can create a power dynamic where one person is listened to more than another, as Cyndi Suarez points out in *The Power Manual: How to Master Complex Power Dynamics*. So you should be aware all the time of whether the power and status you hold, and that of others in your organization, is being used for clarity and guidance or for unmerited influence.

Suarez says that leaders often think that if they create new organizational structures, those structures alone will shift the way people in an organization interact. The lines on a new organizational chart, however, are far more likely to create competition and status signaling than they are to create positive communication. Focus instead on creating a collective understanding of how people are currently interacting and what their processes of work are and then create a collective understanding of how we desire people to interact.

TREAT ONE ANOTHER AS HUMANS

The lessons are the same from all these examples: Treat one another as humans, and take the time to interact, ask questions, and listen. Start with your own dyads, working on these personal connections with every team member. Think about whom you don't yet feel a personal connection with, and go have a chat with them to learn more about what they do. Don't stop: It's the work of a lifetime.

Here are some ways you can organically start to build and nurture these dyads:

- Listen first.
- Ask about their job, learn what works well for them and where the challenges are. You might be able to help, and you will certainly learn information that will help you navigate the organization.
- Respect the person, no matter your initial bias about their status, power, or value. Start with the assumption that they are there because they are needed and bring value and that they command your respect simply for being human.
- When people raise problems, don't spend time venting back; instead, calmly and rationally start investigating and seeing how they could be solved.
- Have a meal together. Eating together is a primal behavior that, I half jokingly tell my team, speaks to our reptilian hindbrain with the message that we are not enemies.

ONLY PEOPLE, AND NOT ORGANIZATIONS, HAVE LOYALTY

Have you heard anyone lament, as their career comes near to a close, that the organization owes them? On the face of it, that feels like an entirely legitimate plea. That person may have worked in the service of the organization for years or even decades. Perhaps they received some token of appreciation every five or ten years. It's easy to feel sympathy for the plight of the underappreciated worker, and very often, this sympathy is entirely justified.

But in many ways, organizations are imaginary constructs. Organizations produce things, and they are usually visibly populated with people. But organizations do not remember people or feel loyalty or care; organizations are legal entities. Organizations exist on paper.

Loyalty and emotional debts can be owed only between individuals; in fact, between the two people in a dyad. Your long-term rewards depend upon your long-term relationships with people in leadership in your organization. If the people in leadership you have relationships with leave, they take with them all but the most skeletal and legalistic sense of what you have done for the organization. New leaders will need to build their own sense of connection and obligation to you as you build your dyadic relationships with them.

Two conclusions may come from this: First, anything critical to your future in the organization should be in writing, and second, your own strength and efficacy and your reward structure depend upon the strength and efficacy of your dyads.

Take stock of which dyads in your team you have already created and which need work. Think through each person. When did I last speak with them individually? Do I know what they are working on right now?

Then, think across the organization: Whom should I know whom I don't at the moment? Invite them for a cup of coffee. Pay attention to who is making waves, who just had a big win, who is quietly efficient and effective. Talk with them with the intention of learning about them and how they do their work, more than telling them about yourself. Practice asking questions. Though building your dyads is presented here as key for making a great team, approach it as a human, for the joy and richness of knowing new people.

Remember this great quote: "People will forget what you said, people will forget what you did, but people will never forget how you made them feel." And apropos of the first line of the quote, its first use is attributed in 1971 to Carl Buehner, an official in the Church of Jesus

Christ of Latter-Day Saints, but has since more widely been assigned to Maya Angelou, activist and poet.

Along with giving credit where credit is due, there are a great many other standards to how we interact that do help people perform their best. That's where team culture comes in: Once you have networked yourself into a team, then the team will develop its working habits, its culture. Make that culture explicit and communicated because, whether you do or don't talk about it, there *will* be a culture, maybe just not the one you want.

7

DISCUSS CULTURE TOGETHER AND PRACTICE IT CONSCIOUSLY

Before NASA gave the green light to the Psyche mission, our team took part in a three-year competition against twenty-seven other proposal teams to win a NASA contract and the chance to fly. During that process, there was one absolutely critical day of presentations to the professional NASA review board. And on that day, we purposefully arranged the room so that when any member of the review board was looking at the speaker, they would see behind the speaker both the screen and just to its side the seats of some of the team leadership.

We asked the leaders to remember they were always in the background of the review panel members' view but gave no further instructions. It was just our nature to nod in agreement from time to time and show support. Some review panelists later told us how great it was to see the leadership nodding and smiling in support of the presenters' words. They said, to our shock, that they often saw, in other teams, teammates who sat back, arms crossed, frowning, or even rolling their eyes or shaking their heads while their teammates spoke.

We were demonstrating the team culture we wanted to have— collaborative, positive, respectful of others' expertise—and it really

97

showed. But it only worked because the culture was genuine. We really did allow the expert on the team, no matter how junior, to answer questions on their topic from the review board; we really did support each other to give good presentations.

Once, when we were facing a significant challenge on the Psyche project, a new friend commented, "Oh, it must be the hardware. It's so difficult to get hardware to work in space." But a more experienced person standing nearby commented, "I'll bet it's the people. Helping people succeed is always the hardest part."

Now that you have worked on your dyads within and outside your teams, it's time to get together and set your culture. I view culture in three dimensions, just like the structure of this book: the culture I follow as an individual, the culture we expect within team interactions, and the culture that the leaders follow. Many of these cultural aspects are the same, but some differ. For example, as an individual you are responsible for maintaining the highest quality of your own work.

The challenge of creating productive, positive values and social norms within each team, and of uniting them at the organizational level, is the topic of this chapter.

TASK AND CULTURE: WHAT WE DO AND HOW WE DO IT

The word *culture* has been applied to organizations for fewer than one hundred years. It's a relatively new way to view our world. The first person to study the workplace through the lens of an anthropologist—viewing the organization's culture as a shared set of beliefs, identities, rituals, and myths—was Andrew Pettigrew. Now professor of strategy and organization at the Saïd Business School at the University of Oxford, Pettigrew began a study of a school in the early 1970s, just after he completed his PhD. In this study he identified a series of social dramas critical to the development of the school (retirement of the first head of school, a restructuring of the school, and so forth), and he used anthropological techniques for studying what happened and the effects they had.

Specifically, Pettigrew pressed researchers to stop studying a person in isolation, and instead, study them in the context of their organization or society. All that we do while working, no matter what we are working on, can be divided into two categories:

- Task: Technical and task topics = The work that we do
- Culture: Process and relational topics = How we do the work

How we do it is often the harder part to get right, harder than the task itself; how we do it is controlled by the people and how we interact with and treat each other. How we do it is inside each person and their sense of quality and kindness and clarity of speech. How we do it is also the most important part. The huge Project Aristotle at Google,[1] which studied team effectiveness across the whole organization, concluded that *who* is on a team mattered less for team effectiveness than *how* the team works together.

Adam Grant, professor at the Wharton School whom we met in Chapter 1, moved the discussion of organizational culture from the competitive, zero-sum game of the past (this is oversimplified, of course) to the evidence-based understanding of today: Success is highly dependent upon *how* we interact. Grant describes people as takers, matchers, or givers. People who give without expecting an equal return often experience a far higher level of success than those who take, or expect, an equal match. Giving behavior creates trust, strengthens dyadic bonds, and raises the game of the whole team. It's culture.[2]

As Erin Meyer, professor at INSEAD Business School in Fontaine-bleau, France, related in an essay about organizational culture: "At the beginning of my career, I worked for the health-care-software specialist HBOC. One day, a woman from human resources came into the cafeteria with a roll of tape and began sticking posters on the walls. They proclaimed in royal blue the company's values: 'Transparency, Respect, Integrity, Honesty.' The next day we received wallet-sized plastic cards with the same words and were asked to memorize them so that we could incorporate them into our actions. The following year, when management was indicted on 17 counts of conspiracy and fraud, we learned what the company's values really were."[3]

Let's think for a moment about what "corporate values" really are. Values are always held by and acted upon by individuals, not by organizations. Do the individuals within the corporation really hold the values they are told to hold? Are corporate values a command or a suggestion? Who decides what they are?

Culture is the common understanding and practice, whether stated explicitly or not, of how we conduct our work and behave together. It's not necessarily what leadership says we do, or what is written in a corporate statement; it's not having a Ping-Pong table or breakfast cereal at work. It's how we actually interact, the tones of our voices, the ways and the rates at which we communicate in the everyday.

Every team within an organization has a culture. If the team members are relaxed and motivated enough to care about one another's performances and support one another, then they may be demonstrating a value of believing in one another's merit. If the team is toxic and each member is suspicious of the others, the team may have a common value of individual competition and individual success. Culture is baked in by the nature of humans being together. And it's not created by assertions from above.

Benefits of a Good Culture

When I was on the faculty at MIT years ago, I was talking to an older colleague about conversations we were having in my lab group about our group culture.[4] The topic of culture was a surprise to many within and outside my lab group: Lab groups traditionally read scientific journal articles together or discuss each other's work or the functioning of the instruments in the lab. My colleague told me that if we had to talk about how we felt (his interpretation of "culture"), we were too weak to be in serious science research.

I know—extreme, unacceptable, possibly sexist. And certainly the exception, but also indicative of a pervasive suspicion about discussion of culture, norms, behaviors, and the like in tech teams and STEM-oriented academics. A common feeling is: Let us get on with the work. This other kind of discussion is extra.

After the NASA reviewers told us that one of the reasons we won with the Psyche mission was that we worked well together, I could say that a good culture is literally worth, in our final contract budget total, over a billion dollars. A billion dollars, employment for hundreds of people over a decade or more, and a chance to change the textbooks about our understanding of how planets form. That's what good culture can create—one where we feel safe to bring forward problems, where we feel safe to ask for help, where we are not prejudged based on irrelevant (irrelevant to work) qualities like gender, race, or religion, is critical for teams.

First, this culture creates a team where people rise on their merits in a more ethical and a more enjoyable atmosphere. You learn the value of the people on the team and can raise up everyone to a higher level of excellence. With a positive team culture you also will have taken a big step toward minimizing the surprisingly damaging effects of the unconscious bias we all have toward each other (examples are a pervasive sense that women's work is not as good as men's, or Black people's is not as good as white people's, etc.). Reinforcing and living the principle of looking at the work and not judging the person can reduce biases over time.

A culture of bullying or harassment or simply of rudeness is a culture that will likely never be diverse, for this reason: If a person is without a peer support group (and Rosabeth Moss Kanter, the original researcher of this phenomenon, discovered it takes about 30 percent of the team to be like you before you stop feeling alone and tokenized), then they may be more likely to cut their losses and leave in the face of harassment or rudeness, thinking that they will have a better chance of success elsewhere.[5] Being rude or judgmental or harassing people literally reduces diversity on teams.

Second, a good culture where the person closest to the work is encouraged to speak up is a risk reducer because the manager and the manager's manager do not know what is actually happening with the soldering iron or the line of code; we need people to be able to speak up when they see something concerning. On the Psyche mission we say the best news is bad news brought early. You want people to bring up the problems, without fear, in time to fix them. Having a culture of respectful listening is literally a route to success.

A good culture, then, one where people are heard and respected for the content they bring, no matter who they are in the organization, is a direct contributor to risk reduction and project success. And beautifully, this kind of good culture is also best for individual growth and reduction of implicit bias. It's the best kind of win-win.

Finally, a good culture becomes effortless and therefore almost invisible to the participants; it's the unconscious way we normally interact. Process and relational practices, which we call team norms, help the *how we do the work* become transparent and effortless, and the *work that we do* become the point on which every person focuses their thought and effort. This is how good teams become great.

I suggest making cultural decisions consciously and explicit. This starts with talking about them, working on them, and setting them together—as a team.

Sometimes Discussing Culture and Norms Is Hard for Tech Teams

Norms are often the hardest things to discuss in technical and academic teams. As expressed by that faculty member at MIT, cultural norms are often seen as a luxury or a distraction. Academics, especially in science and engineering, may be among the most resistant to discussion of culture. I think it's because of the way we are trained to do the following:

- Have our own ideas.
- Make them important.
- Advertise them in the community to become a thought leader.
- Defend them.
- Make sure our students move away from our ideas to their own ideas but still reflect glory on us.
- Critique everything we read or hear as part of a process of understanding it deeply.
- Expect to be intellectually attacked, and be ready to fight.

Some of these skills are antithetical to what is needed to make a supportive team culture where everyone can rise on their merits. One of the top characteristics of a modern leader is joy at others' successes. That is often not what academics are taught to feel.

Discussing civility, norms, and culture can feel irrelevant because it seems so removed from our work product. I don't know if this would bear up under study, but I have a hypothesis that the more the work product of a team has to do with culture, the more the team will be willing to work on its team culture. A theater group, for example, is likely to be more willing to do this work on culture because its work product, a play, obviously relies on human relationships and how communication works—that is, culture. For a tech team, norms and culture may seem completely unrelated to or, as we nerds might say, orthogonal to the work it's producing. It's not so, though. No matter what our work is, how we work together is absolutely critical to the success of the work, the success of the individual, and the resiliency of the team during challenges.

So it takes special effort to make academics into team players: You have to change the incentives, talk about values, move some people out, and enlist the whole culture-change tool kit.

If there is one commonality among tech teams, it's the inevitability of challenges, deadlines, and crises. Any complex development project will have these aspects, and to meet them it's most critical that how we work together is so practiced that it is invisible, like the air we breathe.

START WITH CIVILITY

Professor Vicki Magley at the University of Connecticut has deeply studied civility and its positive effects on teams and, of course, the converse, what happens to teams with uncivil behavior. Here's how Magley and her colleagues define incivility: "Rude, condescending, and ostracizing acts that violate workplace norms of respect, but otherwise appear mundane. These routine slights and indignities are not motivated by overt malice." Civility, then, fundamentally means making use of your awareness of your own behavior and others' perceptions so as to treat others with respect.

Benjamin Walsh, a professor at Grand Valley State University, and Magley created a survey for teams that asks members about both uncivil and prosocial (positive) behaviors that team members have experienced. For example, the survey might ask:

Over the past six months, how many times has someone on your team displayed one of these behaviors?

- Shown you genuine concern and courtesy?
- Made jokes at your expense?
- Noticed when you did your best possible work?

The surveys ask questions about condescension and hostile looks, times when people did not consult you on a decision you should have been involved in or failed to give you information you needed to know about, as well as times people complimented you on your work and expressed interest in your work-related opinions.[6]

Of course, having the data from a team and thus being able to understand the positivity or negativity of the culture is valuable, but amazingly, even the act of asking these questions will likely improve the civility of the team.

Carl Wieman, emeritus professor of physics and education at Stanford University, has been thinking during his whole career about how to help people learn better. One topic he studied was how to help professors become better teachers; almost invariably, professors want to give lectures to their classes and teach much the way they themselves were taught. Astonishingly, though, lectures are an effective way to learn only for a very small percent of the population! But of course, almost all professors fall into that group, so it's hard to convince them to teach in different ways.

Wieman discovered that the most effective way to change how someone teaches is not to instruct them on how to do better, send them books on teaching, send someone to mentor them, or give them new requirements but, rather, just to give them surveys assessing their current teaching. In his surveys, Weiman would ask how many times in the last semester the professor allowed the students to direct class with their own questions, how many times the professor had the students do research in small groups and then report out to the whole class, and how many times the students were directed to teach one another a new topic. Those are all more effective teaching techniques than lecturing. By asking whether the professors had done these techniques, the survey implied that the professors should be doing them and put these ideas in their minds.

This may seem a little subtle as a way to change behavior, but in controlled tests, simply administering these surveys was shown to be the *most effective way to change* how a professor taught. In fact, even if the professor knew that no one else was even going to see the responses to the survey, this was the most effective way to change teaching. Simply by giving your teammates a survey on civility and incivility, your team will likely improve its behavior and relations.

RUDENESS: IT'S ASTONISHINGLY DAMAGING

In 2015 Dr. Arieh Riskin from Bnai Zion Medical Center, Israel Institute of Technology, started an audacious study.[7] He and his research team formed twenty-four neonatal intensive care teams and gave each of them a simulated health emergency in which a preterm infant's condition was rapidly deteriorating. Knowing that rudeness can poison a workplace, he instructed the expert leaders of some teams to be mildly rude and state that they had observed other infant care teams and were unimpressed by the quality of medical care in the country and suggest that the team members "wouldn't last a week" in their department. The other teams heard no rude comments from their expert leaders.

Sharing information and asking for help are critical to good health care. The teams with the rude leaders shared less information and asked for help less often than the teams without a rude expert leader. The result: Team members who had rude leaders made exceptionally serious errors, including giving the wrong diagnosis, resuscitating improperly, and giving the wrong medication. Some of the errors that the teams with rude leaders made would have been fatal for the patient.

Before Riskin and his team did their study, other psychologists had shown that rudeness toward a person lessens the clarity of their thinking. With this study, Riskin and his team showed that rudeness significantly impaired both diagnosis and the ability to correctly execute medical procedures, leading to poorer patient outcomes and even to life-threatening mistakes. The significant negative effects of even mild rudeness in this study have been duplicated in studies across several different fields.

When leaders purposely choose to be rude, rather than being gratuitously rude, as in the Riskin study, they may be attempting to make a point and send a clear and final message. A leader may think that a harsh, simple statement said with anger will emphasize the message, and the team will finally understand the importance of whatever the leader is concerned about. The team does indeed get the message: Speaking up is dangerous. The boss is judgmental. We'd better keep our heads down.

And the boss thinks we are pretty clueless; we only understand and get motivated when we're yelled at. The rudeness of the leader tells the team members that they are not highly trusted or highly valued and need a reprimand. In a high-functioning team, members are assumed to come with best intentions, are allowed to ask for help, and are known to be valuable; rude leadership violates all these tenets.

What the leader may not realize is that by violating that trust with rudeness, a result may be that members stop sharing information or asking for help. The leader will suddenly be in an information desert, the only communications coming from people who carefully craft their message by leaving out nuance and bad news and reducing their own risk in the interchange with the boss. The long-term effects—uninformed decision-making, poor product outcomes—of what the leader will now *not* learn from their people can be devastating, without the leader ever knowing why they didn't get the information they needed.

Here was the big surprise for me. Riskin and other researchers who did follow-on studies found that rudeness had the same effect on patient care *no matter who was rude.* The next time you or someone you know is in the hospital, think of this astonishing fact: Rudeness on the part of an administrator, the doctor, another staff person, or even the patient has been shown to significantly reduce team information sharing and help seeking, and thus to lead to poorer outcomes for the patient.

When I was in my twenties, I used to think of workplace rudeness as an aggravation I could not alter, a kind of fact of life. I also knew that rudeness was a habit I could not indulge in—it was for people with more power than I had. In my thirties, I recognized that rudeness stopped other people from asking questions. That insight opened my eyes. Rudeness was more than an aggravation. Rudeness actually undermines team functioning and puts outcomes in jeopardy.

As Christine Porath, professor of business at Georgetown University, points out, incivility is the result of ignorance and seldom arises from malice. Since every one of us has blind spots and areas of ignorance, each of us may be rude at times. We each need to stay alert to the responses of people around us, listen to our own words with an inquiring mind, and strive to speak calmly, supportively, and on topic.

THE BAD APPLE VERSUS THE
PSYCHOLOGICAL SAFETY OFFICER

In the early 2000s Will Felps, then a graduate student at the University of Washington business school, set up an experiment to discover how "bad apples" affected team behavior. He organized forty test groups and gave them work tasks to carry out. Each group was also given, unbeknownst to them, a bad apple: an actor withholding effort, being negative, or violating important interpersonal norms (in short, the Slacker, the Downer, or the Jerk). The existence of a bad apple diminished team performance by 30–40 percent in thirty-nine out of the forty test groups. The other team members reacted with anxiety, withdrawal, anger, and even fear. As we've already seen in the Riskin study, and as I've seen in my own experience, the other team members also stopped communicating and asking for help.

But in one single group, the bad apple caused no diminishment of work. That team worked effectively despite its bad apple. The key to that team's success seemed to be a person called Jonathan. "Over and over Felps examines the video of Jonathan's moves, analyzing them as if they were a tennis serve or a dance step," Daniel Coyle reports in his book *The Culture Code*.[8] "They follow a pattern: [The bad apple] behaves like a jerk, and Jonathan reacts instantly with warmth, deflecting the negativity and making a potentially unstable situation feel solid and safe." Jonathan "succeeds without taking any of the actions we normally associate with a strong leader. He doesn't take charge or tell anyone what to do. He doesn't strategize, motivate, or lay out a vision. He doesn't perform so much as create conditions for others to perform, constructing an environment whose key feature is crystal clear: We are solidly connected."

What Felps found was that the bad apple was overcome not by direct confrontation but by what has come to be known as "signaling safety." Jonathan let the team know, over and over, that they were safe to keep communicating.[9] Safety here means psychological safety, as coined by psychologist Carl Rogers in the mid-1950s.[10] Rogers found that for a person to be free to be creative, they needed three things: a sense of individual worth, a lack of external evaluation, and empathy. Psychological safety, in the sense that we are using it here, was extended to teams by Amy Edmondson, a professor at the Harvard Business School: Psychological safety means that individuals can speak up with concerns, mistakes, or questions without risk of being judged, criticized, shamed, or devalued.[11]

A first step in creating psychological safety is reducing rudeness. One of the challenges to combating rudeness is that it is typically low intensity and sometimes quite subtle. The target of the rudeness often finds it difficult to know whether the rudeness was intentional, and the person who was rude commonly claims no malicious intent. So what to do?

First of all, work on your self-reflection so that you yourself are rude as little as you can manage. Then, we can all be Jonathans. Many researchers have tested ways to signal safety. Here are some of the most important:

- Sit in close proximity, often in circles.
- Maintain high amounts of eye contact.
- Engage in frequent humor and laughter.
- Engage in some physical touch (handshakes, fist bumps, hugs).
- Make regular use of intensive, active listening.
- Encourage lots of short, energetic exchanges (no long speeches).
- Encourage high levels of mixing: Everyone talks to everyone.

And Paul Axtell, a corporate trainer who writes occasionally for *Harvard Business Review*, adds more ideas on creating psychological safety during a meeting:[12]

- Ask the group to devote their full attention to each person who speaks (do this at the start of the meeting).
- Allow each person to take their time and complete their thoughts.
- Ask follow-up questions for clarity if necessary.
- Share what is valuable about someone's question or comment.
- Use people's names and refer back to earlier comments they've made.
- Invite people into the conversation who have not spoken.
- Answer questions truthfully.
- Summarize what you learned as the meeting comes to an end.
- Explain what actions you will take to put those insights to use, and ask your team members for their suggestions as well.
- Acknowledge the quality of the conversation and thank the group for it.

Each of us, then, no matter our position on a team, can counteract the effects of rudeness and other bad apple behaviors and keep our teams running well. We simply need to exercise the social cues of successful working teams from the above list.

Why is psychological safety critical? Psychological safety enables better decision-making because more ideas and problems will be shared and people will feel more able to disagree constructively with each other. The least helpful problem-solving group is one where few people raise ideas and few people disagree. Psychological safety also encourages learning and innovation because people can share their mistakes safely as well.

The more creative, collaborative, and unique or experimental the work you do is, the more important psychological safety is to your project outcomes. Psychological safety gives people confidence that their contributions will not be automatically rebuked or attacked, and it allows people to bring forward problems that need to be solved. The best news is bad news brought up early enough that it can be solved in time.

Those problems and challenges that remain undiscussed and unsolved, sometimes until it's almost too late to fix them, often cause enormous product failures, cost overruns, and delays or even stay unsolved forever and create disasters. As was noted in the Presidential Commission report on the *Challenger* space shuttle explosion, "the invisible and unacknowledged tend to remain undiagnosed and elude remedy."[13] This is why when anyone on the team has something to say, they must not be blocked or devalued.

Start by signaling safety in your team. Listen attentively when someone is speaking and accept what they have to say with an open mind. No one should scoff or snort and sit back with their arms crossed. Nod your head. Ask questions that are real questions, not disguised criticisms.

AN EXAMPLE OF BAD APPLE CONSEQUENCES

One of my first tasks on the Psyche mission was assembling the science team, which had to include the most respected and accomplished thought leaders in the fields for which the spacecraft was expected to collect data way down the road, years in the future; those leaders would then have to interpret the data and come to conclusions about what this mysterious asteroid is. And in the shorter term, they would help decide what instruments the spacecraft would fly and what data it would collect. The critical phrase here is "most respected and accomplished thought leaders." These people were used to being the biggest experts in the room, people whose opinions go unchallenged. Each one of them was used to that. Bring them together, and it was bound to get exciting.

One scientist, whom I'll call Kevin, was especially sure he was right. He and another scientist, whom I'll call Keith, were both calculating some details of the possible interior structures of the asteroid. Their results differed. Kevin simply asserted, "Keith, your numbers are wrong. That's not the right way to calculate them. I've done it." Here, Kevin was rebutting, instead of replying. But we were not in a formal debate. We were trying to get to the truth, and so asking a question would have been more appropriate than offering a rebuttal.

Keith had the best possible response, which was a pleasant, relaxed smile and a calm request for Kevin to say more about his concerns. Unfortunately, Kevin was unwilling. He was angry and, I think, threatened. After the meeting, I sat down with him and asked him to please work with Keith before our next meeting and talk about the calculations to come to an understanding about each other's results so that we could all better understand the methods and implications. And again, unfortunately, Kevin was unwilling. Now I was sure he was feeling threatened. Despite my urging him several times, he was unwilling to resolve the issue. That refusal made him unsuited to be on a science team. We needed our team to focus on reaching the best understanding of our natural world. And so, Kevin became somewhat isolated on the team and out of leadership permanently. In this way, our team ended up protected from the negative effects of a bad apple, but the bad apple himself suffered. It's a good lesson to us all to swallow our pride and collaborate.

It's possible, however, to slide from psychological safety into a kind of ersatz universal approval. Can a culture be too safe?

Several teammates and I were in a Zoom meeting with another team that was considering using one of our education programs. We were doing a brief training that included prompts for the other team to give responses and ideas. Every prompt was met, without exception, with an "I agree" or "my point also" from the other team members. This kind of nonjudgmental, reflexive approval may be OK in a brainstorming session, where filters and criticism come later, but in the case of this team, the behavior was ubiquitous. They had confused criticism and questioning with disapproval. Being safe means opening the door to more ideas and clearer communication. Being safe does not mean stopping questioning or argumentation. Quite the opposite.

Psychological safety does not mean always agreeing; it means constantly arguing toward the best solution from among many different possibilities but without personal harm. Psychological safety makes space for candor. Feedback, argument, criticism, editing. These are all positive, necessary parts of team behavior leading to excellent outcomes. Part of the purpose of safety is, explicitly, to make these crucial behaviors safe but not to shield ourselves from alternative ideas.

WE NEED DISAGREEMENTS TOO

How many times have you heard someone describe themselves as "conflict averse"? How often have you thought, or even yelled at the television, *If you'd only had that difficult conversation and told them what you know, you wouldn't be in this fix now!* Fear of conflict is a big driver for our lack of communication.[14] I would assert, though, that fear of conflict is not the main problem. It's not the idea of a disagreement that raises blood pressure. The problem is fear of anger, disrespect, and the other painful emotions associated with having your ideas judged and possibly dismissed.

By separating the potentially frightening emotional fallout from speaking up in disagreement, from the simple fact of having differing views on offer, you can frame the issue this way: Differing views simply require discussion and civility to find a good answer. Conflict is just a state of nonagreement that takes some time and effort to resolve; it's an opportunity for learning and improving our work and for finding an even better third way forward.

Good decision-making, in fact, *requires* that people unearth and examine multiple options. If people are afraid to bring up opposing views, you'll never get to the best option. Peter Drucker in his classic book *The Effective Executive* explained that if everyone is in agreement before a topic has been fully discussed, then the topic is not well enough understood to have a good decision made.

Opposing views need create anxiety only when they are advocated in a personal way, or people's egos are deeply involved, or when the discussion becomes too emotional. Then, conflict arises that is hard to resolve.

Otherwise, opposing views are gold: They are the path toward good decisions and a stronger team. Conflict and disagreement, when handled productively, are actually the surest path forward to the best decisions.

Conflict over Tasks Versus Conflict over Processes

The conflict could be over specific tasks, such as the best way to solve a coding challenge or choosing which parts provider to use. Or the conflict could be over culture: How do we handle this process? Who gets invited to the conversation? How do we speak to each other and listen respectfully to each other's ideas? The latter is the more dangerous kind of conflict, the kind that feels personal quickly. From the early decades of research into workplace conflict, researchers have noticed that cultural conflict (including both process and relationship topics) is bad for teams. Cultural conflict creates personal rifts that are hard to heal.

Think about a conflict between two people on a team. If they're having a calm discussion of how best to perform a task, others on the team are likely to feel interested. But if it's an angry argument or one that becomes personal, then others will react with avoidance, or some may even take sides in the argument. Thus, the conflict between the two has spread: Conflict is contagious, as Karen Jehn, a professor at the University of Melbourne business school, has found. And that contagion can turn the whole culture of the team to negativity and noncommunication.

Through some clever analysis (see the box "An Exercise for a Team: Drawing Tree Diagrams" below), Jehn was able to tease out the emotions, actions, and outcomes that resulted from conflicts over tasks and those that came from conflicts over culture. This is the same division we discussed above:

- Task: Technical and task topics = The work that we do
- Culture: Process and relational topics = How we do the work

In one of the seminal papers on the topic, Jehn writes:

Summarily stated, relationship conflicts interfere with task-related effort because members focus on reducing threats, increasing power, and attempting to build cohesion rather than working on the task . . . relationship conflicts decrease goodwill and mutual understanding, which hinders the completion of organizational tasks. . . . The conflict causes members to be negative, irritable, suspicious, and resentful. To date, there has been no evidence of positive effects of relationship conflict on either performance or satisfaction.[15]

There you have it: Culture conflicts (about how we do the work) cause members to be negative and resentful.

On the Psyche mission, we noticed a difference in culture between the development team, which designs and builds the spacecraft and the flight software, and the operations team, which flies the spacecraft after launch. The development team had a terse, competitive edge. The team was racing through hardware decisions and trades on different risks that could be relatively quickly quantified and acted upon, and the operations team wanted to talk things out more thoroughly and calmly.

In contrast to development, as Tim Weise, our operations manager, observed, in operations there can be many solutions that would work, and people will tend to pick their personal preference. Then if the process is questioned, the choice can be perceived as a personal matter and not just a technical debate, and the risk of damage to team functioning is that much higher. Operation teams therefore speak more carefully sometimes and work harder to get at the real benefits and risks of different solution options.

Avoiding ad hominem conversations is critical. They are a slippery slope. When a disagreement is focused on the person instead of the topic or action at hand, when people take the conflict personally, then conflict can break a team.

Productive Versus Destructive Conflicts

One of the greatest risks to teams is conflict that leads not to an agreed-upon better direction or result but instead breaks personal relationships and harms team functioning.

Once you have this task-versus-culture conflict structure in your head, conflicts around you become much clearer. You understand that they can be approached with logic and dispassion, especially in the case of task conflicts, with outcomes that make all participants feel positive. Cultural conflicts, however, need to be avoided a priori. Cultural problems can be avoided through training the team and increasing its awareness, through encouraging team members to unite and act together, and through lengthy personal coaching of difficult individuals.

Teams with cultural norms that support task conflict do the best of all. Norms that support task conflict include welcoming people to speak up with other solutions or conundrums about the existing ideas and encouraging dispassionately consideration of more solutions. These norms and practices also help the team avoid succumbing to groupthink. By normalizing task conflict, much of the fear of disagreement is removed, and the team can work more effectively.

Kathleen Eisenhardt of the Stanford Technology Ventures Program at Stanford University has spent a career understanding how culture and behavior affect success in teams. She and her colleagues have identified six key characteristics of successful teams:

1. They work with more, rather than less, information.
2. They develop multiple alternatives to enrich debate.
3. They establish common goals.
4. They make an effort to inject humor into the workplace.
5. They maintain a balanced power structure.
6. They resolve issues without forcing a consensus.

Several of these characteristics are directly related to welcoming productive conflict and discussion: There's more information to consider, there are multiple alternatives, and this produces a more balanced power structure. Resolution cannot be reached without knowing the common goal the team is after. Humor is critical for avoiding negative emotional responses and deflecting ad hominem accusations. And that last one, resolving issues without forcing a consensus, will come up in Chapter 10, when we talk about each team member's responsibility to be able to disagree and still commit to the decision. The key takeaways about work conflict are as follows:

- Task conflict can be good for both team outcomes and team morale when it is encouraged through norms and handled dispassionately.
- Cultural conflict, whether about relationships or process, is generally bad for teams and can lead to unhealable rifts between team members.
- Norms that reduce emotionality and avoid finger-pointing but instead support dispassionate assessment of the task or topic lead to the best outcomes.

Ron Friedman, behavioral expert and founder of ignite80, a firm that trains leadership using evidence-based research, presented a study on high-performing teams in the *Harvard Business Review* in 2024. Friedman found that when launching a project, many teams follow a predictable two-step cadence: They assign tasks and then start working. High-performing teams, on the other hand, are more than three times likely to begin by first discussing *how* they will work together, creating better communications and fewer misunderstandings.[16] It takes practice to be ready when the hard challenges come. That's why we work on these topics. That's why every team should.

AN EXERCISE FOR A TEAM:
DRAWING TREE DIAGRAMS

Karen Jehn used a tree-diagram exercise to gather data on conflict in the workplace. This thinking-and-drawing exercise would be a clear, delimited, and revealing way to understand how your team is working.

Each person on the team will, in the end, draw their own tree diagram. Start by asking people on your team an initial question, perhaps, "What types of conflicts occur in our team?" They should respond in writing on their own, not sharing responses with other team members yet, and they should space their answers across the top of a piece of paper. Someone might write "problems related to the tasks we are doing, problems with other people, and broken equipment."

Then ask, "What are the ways you deal with these conflicts?" Ask the team members to write these ways to deal with the problems under each of the problems they wrote on their paper. Some of the possible responses are shown on the bottom row of the tree diagram shown here. In this example, task problems are delegated upward to the supervisor, and every other kind of problem results in negative emotions and damage to the team.

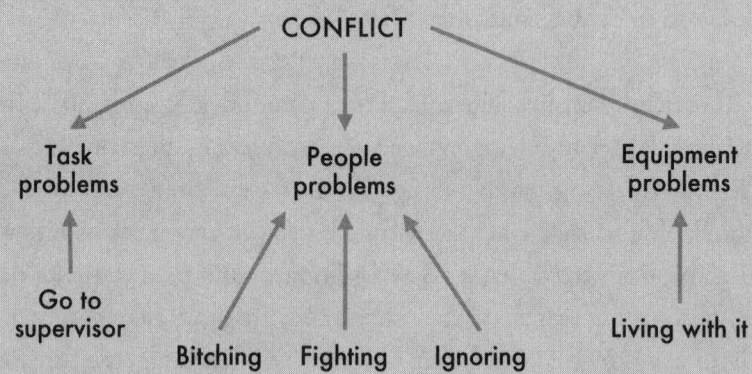

A common way that people think about conflict in the areas of task, relationship, and process is shown with this tree diagram, originally drawn by a person on a team being studied by Jehn for her 1997 paper. Norms of communication and behavior can help with all the needed solutions.

When Jehn ran the original experiments, she told the participants they could use any terms or categories they wanted and could continue branching until they could think of no more.

After each person draws their tree diagram, the drawings can be discussed by the team as a whole. Team members might also try drawing a tree diagram together, or you can gather the individual tree diagrams and make a hybrid one that everyone can discuss. This last idea preserves anonymity and may help people feel safer in the discussion.

Other questions for eliciting tree diagrams might be more helpful for your particular team (some questions are from Jehn):

- How are conflicts handled in your team?
- What things are frowned upon in your team? (This question and the previous one give insight into unwritten norms.)
- What problems occur in your team?
- What tensions are there in your team?
- What types of communication happen in your team each week?
- Whom do you communicate with to get your work done?

TEAM NORMS

Now it's time to zoom in on process and relational practices, which we call team norms. These make the *how we do the work* transparent and effortless, so that the *work that we do* becomes the focus of every person's thought and effort. Norms explain what is expected from group members, both what is acceptable and what is unacceptable. Norms thus allow you to anticipate what others will do and to better understand reactions to your own behaviors. In these ways, norms create psychological safety and, therefore, the opportunity for more innovation, problem-solving, and individual thriving.

Most importantly, norms prepare teams to act together productively in times of crisis. If you understand how you are expected to act and react day to day, then those behaviors are likely to persist in times of crisis, allowing you and your teammates to focus on the problem at hand and continue to function as a productive team rather than being distracted by unproductive behaviors.

At the end of this chapter, there's a description of a workshop you can run with your team to introduce the importance of norms and begin setting them together. For now, here are some examples of norms and what they might mean to a team.

Everyone Speaks Once Before Anyone Speaks Twice

One of my wishes in every group I work in is to avoid having one or two people dominate the conversation. When a few people dominate, we lose all the alternative ideas that everyone else has, and some of the quiet people feel disenfranchised. There's a Quaker business meeting policy that no one speaks twice before everyone has spoken once, and it's often strictly followed. In my meetings, I make this a recommendation rather than a rule, something to make us all think before we speak, and also to encourage quiet people.

Another version of this is: Every voice should be heard. But don't mistake this to mean *forcing* every voice to speak, since speaking is still optional (we don't want to reward irrelevant or repeated comments), nor that decisions will be made by consensus. Leaders listen and then make their own decisions. The correct application of this idea is that when someone has something to say, they feel free to say it.

The Best News Is Bad News Brought Early

This is one of our best norms on the Psyche team, and it's brought us far (though it has also failed at times). This norm means, implicitly, that people who bring forward problems should be respected, listened to, and even rewarded. If you don't know about a problem soon enough to fix it, then it's no longer a problem; it's a crisis or a tragedy. If you do know about a problem soon enough, it's a triumph.

Take Care of Yourself Physically, Mentally, and Emotionally

This is a different kind of norm, one that asks you to remember to be a whole person, to take responsibility for your life rather than sacrificing yourself as a martyr to your job: Do not fetishize busyness or burnout. This one came from Dustin Schroeder, a professor at Stanford University, from his list of team expectations (he doesn't call them norms). No team will succeed without functioning members. And this also reminds leadership not to expect people to work to burnout.

Reply to Email Within Forty-Eight Hours

This is a procedural norm, as opposed to a relational norm, as the others above are. This simple rule can remove a lot of doubt in communications. Did they get my email? Is it time for me to remind them, or will they be annoyed? So simple.

Believe That Others Come with Best Intentions

On the teams I worked with in my years at Arizona State University, this is one norm that keeps coming up. Believing that others come with good intentions is far harder than it might seem. Monitor yourself. If you are feeling a negative reaction to someone's words, think about whether you might react differently if you really believed the other person was trying their best to do the right thing—because they probably are. If you struggle with this, ask the person why they are doing what they are doing, and ask them to help you understand and relate their actions to your own ideas.

I recently had a big fail on believing others come with best intentions. I'd been hearing about a scientist I'll call Bern, who had some new scientific ideas that were shaking up the status quo. He was coming to give a lecture at my university, and so I arrived at the lecture hall on the allotted evening full of interest.

Now, I have a bit of an overreaction to hubris, after contending with so much over the years in academic science and space engineering. I am constantly trying to break through people's assertions to the content beneath. So when I heard Bern, while giving a lecture, assert that what he was doing was so much beyond what anyone else was even thinking about, the absolute answer to a huge question, both my skepticism and my annoyance kicked in. Why bother to assert you are best and have *the* answer? How demeaning to the audience of practitioners! Instead, just show us your ideas! I was deeply annoyed and turned off.

And then some months later, to my slight discomfort, I found myself at a lunch table with him at an interdisciplinary conference. We were each asked by the conference organizers to answer a question to help us know each other. The question was "When do you cry?"

What a question! The answers each of us gave, I thought, provided great insight into who we are. When it was my turn, I explained that though I used to, I now never really cry when faced with stress or fear or even, almost ever, with grief. Now, tears pour forth unasked when I see or experience acts of personal kindness. Those open my emotions all the way.

And then it was Bern's turn. He said, "I almost never cry, but I will tell you a story about crying that will give insight to who I am."

Bern continued: "Once I was in my office and a student came in, distressed, and I sat down to talk with her. I gave her some ideas on how to deal with her issue, and after a half hour, she left. A few minutes later my department chair came in. The chair said, 'Why didn't you do more for this student, bring her to me, walk her to counseling? Don't you realize she was sitting here crying for a half hour?' And I replied, 'I did not know she was crying. I thought she'd been out in the rain.'

"And the thing I learned that day was that when someone has water on their face, I need to ask them, 'Are you crying?'"

Bern fell silent.

I realized in that moment that I had completely misjudged Bern. He had deeply felt emotions, and he wanted to know what other people were feeling, but these were not simple problems for him. He had to consciously work at it. I realized my own preconceptions and biases had led my thinking about him. In the time since then, he and I have become good friends, and I can clearly see his care and connection. I had completely failed the test of "believe that others come with best intentions," and I had absolutely misunderstood the communications I was hearing.

Try to Say Yes

I was listening to one famous person from the rise of the computer industry, Sam, talk with another, Max. Sam said to Max, "You left Moon Microsystems at their peak, before the downturn of the company. Why did you make that decision, which looked strange at the time but in retrospect was a perfect choice?" (I have changed the names of the company and people for anonymity.)

Max answered, "I helped create Moon. I'd helped the company grow from under a hundred to over two thousand employees. Along the way, I experienced the highs of invention and fast movement and the incredible effectiveness of a great team. And then over time I saw the company change from a yes culture to a no culture. In the beginning, everyone was straining against the harness, trying to make things happen, shouting yes to great new ideas. Then people started pulling back and defending their space in the company and saying no to requests. Then I knew there was no future, and I left, before the company's fortunes began to fall. But I saw the writing on the wall when people started to say no."

Years later I experienced the same thing with a cranky head of facilities where I worked. He guarded his kingdom assiduously. The things he decided he and his team should do they executed well. When I or the staff asked him for something, though, we were generally met with no. As soon as I felt that resistance, I thought of Moon Microsystems.

I said to the facilities head, "Your job is to try to say yes. Unless the request is unsafe or way out of bounds, try to say yes." Even though I was his boss, he met this request with a cold eye; he was effectively saying

123

no again. I knew in that moment that his time in the job was probably limited.

The importance of yes was cemented for all time for me when we hired people in the Alan Alda School for Science Communications to train our postdoctoral scholars on how to give better talks. The trainers used improv techniques, and they stressed the importance of "yes, and . . ." as the way to bring people together and move forward, rather than to block them.

It's all too frequently that we hear, instead, some form of no in response to our efforts, or at best, "yes, but . . ." Work on saying "yes, and . . ."

Team Roles Differ in Their Responsibilities, Not in Their Value

A sense of hierarchy exists in almost every team. I don't just mean the standard seniority or leadership hierarchy; I mean a hierarchy in the value of people's roles. Often in tech teams, the engineers are the royalty. In most teams, administrative support roles are less valued. In truth, every single role is needed for the team to succeed—that is why those people are here! So value and respect each role, each person. This is a great topic to consider as you work on your dyads. Whom haven't you connected with?

A WORKSHOP FOR SETTING TEAM CULTURE

Each time I facilitate a norm-setting workshop, there's some surprising outcome, something unique to the group. At a summer science conference, I offered a similar norm-setting workshop, and to my surprise and pleasure, over a hundred people came. There is a hunger for information about how to make teams more effective, both for the project and for the individual.

As an introductory exercise, I asked people to individually think of a team on which they had felt their effectiveness and respect buoyed up, where they felt they were made better and thrived because of the team. But about 10 percent of the room was *unable to think of a single such instance in their lives.* That alone is impetus enough to keep working on improving our teams.

Some teams are ready to work on team culture right away. Others, often tech teams, are more resistant. Along with the financial advantages of success, perhaps the best way to convince a technical or academic team of the criticality of culture—the *how* of working together—is to show team members the evidence from the peer-reviewed cognitive science, organizational science, and social science literatures for the importance of culture for effective work.

When I ran a workshop with the Psyche project, I started by enlisting three of our top leaders (our operations phase project manager, our deputy principal investigator, and our operations manager). I presented them with a strawman outline, and we edited it and took on the leadership and facilitation of different parts of the workshop. Having the three of them working with me on the workshop was critical to showing a united front to the team about the importance of this exercise. Having the three of them willing and eager to do this work was critical to the effectiveness of the workshop with the team.

We started by inviting everyone on the team, from all positions and levels and organizations, to attend the workshop. Because our team is spread over the world, we needed to design the workshop to be hybrid: We'd have perhaps fifty people in person at the Jet Propulsion Lab, and the rest would be joining remotely through Microsoft Teams. We'd be breaking into groups periodically and then bringing ideas back to the whole team, and so we needed to train and prepare facilitators for each breakout group; we also needed some experts in Microsoft Teams to help us form virtual groups and then bring them back to the plenary session. There's always plenty of organizational overhead in a workshop.

We called the workshop the Cruise Kickoff. The spacecraft had launched successfully about six months earlier. The intervening months had been consumed with what's called Initial Checkout, where the team followed a meticulous plan for turning on and testing each subsystem on the spacecraft and working up to uploading sequences of commands that the spacecraft would execute autonomously. Now we were at the point where the spacecraft operated autonomously for a week at a time, with just "all's well" low-data check-ins, and once per week the spacecraft stopped thrusting, turned to Earth, and downloaded and uploaded significant amounts of data.

The team was settling in to both the new routine and a new team organization designed for this phase of the mission. This was the perfect time to hasten recovery from the extreme stress of the launch slip and set the tone for the new phase. The three-hour workshop was organized into these three parts, each starting with a brief lecture providing important scientific data about the topic, and each with its own interactive exercise:

1. Not just what we do but how we do it (and a survey)
2. Challenges for hybrid teams (and a conflict scenario)
3. Cultural norms are critical . . . and inevitable

1. Not Just What We Do but How We Do It

I started this section with another important finding from Ron Friedman, behavioral expert and founder of ignite80. When launching a project, many teams follow a predictable cadence: They assign tasks and start working. High-performing teams, on the other hand, are more than three times as likely to begin by first discussing *how* they will work together, paving the way for fewer misunderstandings and smoother collaboration down the road.

For many technical teams, this is a new paradigm. I then talked about the dichotomy between "task," the work that we do, and "culture," the way we do the work. The cruise phase of a space mission is defined by people working together on data and coding, rather than building hardware, and so setting culture is all the more important and conflict all the more destructive. I talked about the five individual superpowers that I covered in Part I of this book, and then we set our goals for the event:

- Greater understanding of how our actions and words affect others.
- A few norms of process and culture that we create together.
- Uniting as a high-performing team, enabled by the culture that we have chosen for how we work together.

Our operations manager then discussed why this topic was critical for the team's success, and he then surveyed the team, using questions designed to make each of us more aware of the importance of the culture we were hoping to influence. They chose among four responses: *never, seldom, usually, always.*

- How often do you thank or appreciate others for their work?
- How often do you think about who may have the most authentic, firsthand knowledge before jumping in to answer a question?
- How often do you invite quiet team members to contribute in meetings?
- In your meetings, how often do you record action items, the lead person for each action, and the action due date?
- How often do you talk to people in your group, to make sure everyone knows what's going on?
- How about people across the team in other groups?

We ran this survey using an online app and showed the aggregated results in real time and talked about the strengths and weaknesses that emerged.

2. Challenges for Hybrid Teams

After a short break, we went into section 2, "Challenges for Hybrid Teams" and a conflict scenario.[17] I talked about research-based findings regarding the challenges that hybrid teams face when people communicate less and seldom in person, and what can be done to remediate those effects (this topic will be addressed in Chapter 12).

Our deputy principal investigator then took over to run the conflict scenario. The idea is to present the team with a scenario that might actually happen, and to practice the resulting hard conversations in a productive way, before those conversations happen in real life. We divided into breakout groups of five to ten people. Our online people were put into virtual breakouts. Each breakout had a facilitator, either one we pretrained or, if there was no such person in a given group, one they elected. The facilitator's job was to keep the group on task, give everyone time to speak, and record and report the group's output.

We gave the whole group a scenario to read:

> It's 2028, and Psyche team members are in a meeting to discuss orbital ops. We are coming up on the asteroid quickly! But we've just learned that our budget has been cut and we are not going to be able to staff the operations team as fully as we wanted. This change appears to be endangering the science data return and the ability to reach our level 1 requirements. Chris, a scientist, says, "Let's start planning for how we can best perform operations under a reduced budget that ensures no data loss. After devoting my career to this mission for the last seventeen years, I don't want to risk losing any of the precious data I've long been waiting for."
>
> Devan, a young engineer who joined the mission team two years ago, says, "Yes, and I have a bunch of different ideas, each with a different mixture of benefit and risk. I suggest we quickly put together a tiger team to start looking at the trades."

Alex, with deep experience in space missions and who is in a leadership position, says, "I've seen this over and over. Every time we invest a huge effort to figure out how to not lose any data and then eventually NASA comes through and fully funds us. Your proposal to study this complicates things, diverts our attention from other tasks, and so itself creates risk. I think we should just wait."

We gave everyone this prompt: Please list one or more potential risks or costs and one or more potential benefits to the way the leader cut off discussion in this scenario.

In the breakouts, there was an initial quiet period during which each person was asked to think of their own possible responses to the prompt. Then, each group discussed their ideas together and agreed upon a group response to the prompt. The breakouts lasted twenty minutes.

At the end of the breakouts we put a link in the Teams chat to a Google form where the facilitator could enter their group's ideas; after the workshop we sent a complete list of (unattributed) responses to the whole team.

This conflict-scenario exercise was surprisingly fruitful and uniting for the team. There's a magic to saying out loud concerns for the future that people had inside them, to showing they can be talked through and solved, and to seeing that the leadership is dedicated to a transparent, ethical treatment of issues.

3. Cultural Norms Are Critical . . . and Inevitable

Finally, we started the third and final part of the workshop: "Cultural Norms Are Critical." I kicked off the session by talking about bad apples; I told the story of Dr. Riskin and his medical neonatal intensive care unit teams, some with rude leaders and some without, and the devastating patient outcomes from teams that were silenced by rude leaders.

Bad is stronger than good in many areas of human psychology, so we need to emphasize psychological safety and make negative comments gently. I discussed the role of positive culture in minimizing implicit bias and in allowing people from many backgrounds and experiences to show their merits rather than being bullied out. I introduced norms as a concept. Norms can be relational or procedural: how we act, what we do, and more. I gave some examples.

Then Bob, our project manager, spoke about trust: "A team without trust isn't really a team—it's just a group of individuals, working together, often making disappointing progress. Trust means that you rely on someone else to do the right thing. You believe in the person's integrity and strength, to the extent that you're able to put yourself on the line, at some risk to yourself. Trust is essential to an effective team, because it provides a sense of safety. When your team members feel safe with each other, they feel comfortable to open up, take appropriate risks, and expose vulnerabilities."

Next, I asked the group to think about a team they'd been on where they felt *more than* instead of *less than*, where working was a pleasure, where outcomes were good.[18] What was one of the practices that made that team great? What are the key ways people in that team interacted? Beginning with these questions set up guardrails that kept anyone who was feeling disgruntled from starting with specific complaints and, in general, limited people's incentive to suggest norms that forbid actions ("Never interrupt people"). Instead, people were thinking about the pleasures of a great team and positive ideas for improvement.

The breakout groups then talked about their norms and selected one or two to share with the broader team. We kept a complete list of all the norms the groups listed. Then I told the team that I'd be doing an analysis of the norms list and sending information, including the whole list, back to the team after the workshop. We could have done this work together in a variety of ways, but we had no more time that day. I gave a summary and reminded everyone of the actions and outcomes from our workshop: Process, cultural, and relational actions—the *way* we do our work—should be transparent, like the air we breathe, making our days more pleasant and our work more successful.

Here are the actions and outcomes for today:

- Greater understanding of how our actions and words affect others.
- A few norms of process and culture that we create together.
- Uniting as a high-performing team, enabled by the culture that we have chosen for how we work together.

Here are some of the sixty-nine responses (unedited) to what, in their experience, had helped a great team be great:

- Recognition that people may have invisible struggles, being gentle and supportive with everyone at every level, especially in the wake of changes.
- Setting up team culture very early on, and cultivating it at every phase.
- Frequent, open, and safe communication allows us to feel "more than." Reasoning: People should feel safe to ask questions, and having frequent and open discussions builds trust.
- Acknowledgment from colleagues that you had a good idea (rather than always nitpicking and finding issues that can be improved).
- Team lead provided great guidance. And was a human first, ahead of their title. Getting to know people better helps with being able to ask for help.
- Humility—never assume you are completely right.
- Actions delegated broadly, across the team, not to the same certain individuals.
- Assume positive intent in interactions.

I put the sixty-nine responses into a spreadsheet. I then pulled out common themes and counted how many times each theme was included in a suggested norm statement. There were a few themes that rose well above the others, and I wrote them into suggested norms. I circulated all the analysis and the possible final norms to the team, received comments, and edited them.

Here are the top norms chosen by the Psyche team for each of three categories:

- **Behaviors of individuals:** We work to build an environment of mutual trust.
- **Ways we interact:** Each person's opinions and questions matter and are heard and valued.
- **Actions of leadership:** Leaders recognize each team member's professional excellence and their importance on the team.

You might consider doing a similar exercise with your team. We create our own culture, and therefore we can create the culture we most want.

While culture, the topic of this chapter, is certainly all about communication, it's mainly about how two or more people work together. Next, we'll expand this topic into team-wide communications. How do we keep everyone on the same page? How much does everyone need to know, and when should they know it? Does that change when a team is in crisis? The short answer is *communicate, communicate, communicate.*

8

ENABLE CONTINUOUS COMMUNICATIONS TO FLOW

When the Psyche mission missed our 2022 launch date, we began holding all-team meetings over Webex to keep everyone in the loop. In retrospect, we should have started them much earlier, way before COVID, way back, well, right at the beginning—if I had known then what I know now.

I wasn't sure at first whether everyone on the team would want to know everything that was happening. Parts of the science team, for example, had little to do with building the spacecraft and were on light work between the proposal and the arrival of the spacecraft at the asteroid, six years in the future. But two hundred people were consistently showing up to the all-team meetings, so the interest was broad enough.

What I hadn't realized is that some people felt they were out of the loop and wanted to be in the loop, even when they didn't have a lot of active work for their part of the project. These people were feeling disenfranchised, in part because they were the ones most emotionally and intellectually connected to and loyal to the project. Even if there were others on the team who did not come to the all-team meetings and did not feel the need (or have any practical need) to learn the day-to-day work the team was doing, there were others who did, and investing in them is critical for future team cohesion and success.

Nonetheless, I was not certain how well the communications in these meetings were being received, and I kept watching for reactions from the team. One day, a young scientist named Sean left his camera on and I could watch him. I could see the light in his eyes brightening as I briefed the group on what we would be presenting later that week to our program managers at NASA headquarters. Normally, parts of the science team would not get briefed on budget management and the progress of spacecraft integration. But I could see from the interest in his face and that of others, and the questions they asked, that this kind of information made each person feel more connected and helped them make their own decisions within their own part of the team.

Similarly, when we presented the budget management and spacecraft integration material to our manager at NASA headquarters later that week, we received feedback about how nice it was to have both our successes and our challenges laid out.

COMMUNICATING TO THE WHOLE ORGANIZATION OR TEAM

Laying out both successes and challenges is an approach I have insisted upon in our program reviews from the very beginning. We briefly summarize what we have achieved, show where we have challenges and what we have done to meet them so far, and invite ideas and participation. This way we share the challenges with the whole team and with our leadership at NASA, we can work together to solve them, and trust is built up for any harder times ahead.

One Psyche team member described this communications style as radical transparency. Whatever you want to call it, the aim is to respect the intelligence, responsibility, and dedication of your team and all your stakeholders within and outside your organization. Talking openly and unashamedly about challenges we face also models that good practice for the rest of the team and, we hope, helps people feel comfortable to bring forward problems in time to fix them.

But continuous, transparent communication can also be disruptive if it engenders anger, doubt, or misunderstanding. Be honest and also let everyone know the context. If there is bad news, share it. For example, if you've just learned you did not win a key grant or contract, you need to tell the team because they will be wondering anyway. Perhaps share that information along with what you might have learned about why you weren't picked and what the team can do better next time; talk about next steps and the work ahead, so everyone is looking forward and needn't be despondent or think that you are. Your team is strong and capable and smart. In fact, a team that can look at misfortunes and setbacks and simply start fixing them and learning together is a team that, in times of emergency, will feel like the safest place to be, a place where calm, forward progress always happens.

In some cases, such as with especially sensitive information, communications should begin with individuals, then proceed to small groups, and then expand to the larger group; we call this socializing new information. In these cases, communications need to be designed to move upward, downward, and horizontally through organizations, reaching everyone.

Sensitive information is best served in small groups at first, but even then, some people might react strongly, or misunderstand, or want to take precipitate action. Fear of disruption cannot stop you from communicating. Part of the goal of communications is to empower each person to take responsibility for their job—they should not be sheltered from organizational trouble under a managerial welfare state, where the management takes responsibility for everything.

According to Chris Argyris, who, when he did this work, was the James B. Conant Professor at the Harvard graduate schools of business and education, many communications from leadership to teams follow this script: Hide your fears about the other person's likely resistance to change. Cover this fear with persistent positivity. Pretend the two of you agree, especially when you know you don't.[1]

Though this common script may make individual meetings more pleasant, it's fundamentally dishonest. If you want a team of equals who each bring their best and take responsibility, then calmly and impersonally speaking the truth is the best path.

Central to all this effort is the imperative that leadership and team members all adhere to the same norms. This is what Gary Pisano calls "cultural flatness."[2] Everyone has the same positive behaviors, and everyone has responsibility. Further, Pisano suggests, cultural flatness means that all communications channels are open, not only hierarchical channels that cleave to some organizational chart. Everyone has to be able to speak to everyone (in my organizations I just ask people to keep me in the loop when speaking to my boss or my boss's boss, as long as it's possible and appropriate to do so). Thus, in a culturally flat organization, we all treat each other with respect and civility and follow the norms.

No matter your position on the team, you should work on your own clear and transparent communications. Think about your in-team communications as trust conversations in which you state clearly how things really are, showing successes and framing challenges to allow input. These communications are not marketing pieces; people can smell a marketing piece a mile away and are immediately alert that they are receiving a story that has been spun to make its deliverer look better or push its hearer into a particular decision. That's not the kind of posing any team needs. Be an exemplar for your team by laying out both the wins and the challenges, and then the whole team owns them.

On a Friday in April 2022 we discovered our biggest communication miss. To review our team's progress, our project manager brought in a deeply experienced engineer who had overseen the production of flight software before. On that Friday, she sat down with the Psyche project manager and laid out, with data and schedules, the impossibility of our being ready for launch in August. Our manager brought in more experts, and they talked all afternoon.

At dinnertime, the project manager texted me and I put down my glass of wine and stopped making dinner with my husband. I called the manager, and he said simply, "I have sent you a Webex invitation for seven." I said, "This doesn't sound good." He said, "Nope. I'll tell you then."

At 7:00 that Friday night, I learned we were going to miss our launch date, which meant the entire project might be canceled by NASA, everyone would lose their jobs, and the spacecraft would never launch and never orbit that enigmatic metal asteroid. It was not a good day.

How did this happen, this surprise? There should never be a surprise of this magnitude. Over the six months prior to April, the project leadership thought that we were fighting challenges but that launching on time looked likely. We in the top leadership group had been watching the software metrics and hearing the reports from that team. The reports sounded like this: "We're struggling and we're behind in our metrics, but we think we're going to be able to catch up."

But it turns out that was not what the small team that was writing and testing a specific part of the flight software (Guidance, Navigation, and Control) was saying. This small team of intensely dedicated and talented engineers was actually saying, "We need more resources, and we need people on this team with more experience with this exact software application. We are not going to make it otherwise." The team's managers were pushing back, and they were delivering a different message up the line to us. They didn't want to bring us bad news. And so, we did not know the depth of the problem until it was too late to fix it for that launch date.

Ours was a failure of communication and culture, not a failure of engineering, effort, or intention. This failure cuts me to this day. The software engineers were absolutely doing their best, and their rage at having failed had many people on the subsequent review board in tears. It was not their fault. Their leadership was overhopeful and not adhering to the cultural norms we'd tried to set, but then, spreading norms to all corners of a giant, intensely busy team is not an easy task. The managers were also absolutely doing their best.

How can we fail, when every person is actually doing their best and is smart and paying attention? Amazing. We can still fail.

One of the communications efforts we made later was a series of focus group–like discussions about what problems the team was facing and what we should do about them. These were helpful: We gathered a lot of ideas, filled a spreadsheet, and wrote dispositions for each one, and our leadership group enacted changes.

But I realize now that those focus groups could have been so much better. To get complete buy-in when you ask for ideas, discuss the whole evolution of the problem and solution. Invite people to take responsibility for the change and fund them to do so. Without full engagement you'll get disengaged ideas and disengaged answers: Whatever the problem is, it's felt to be fundamentally someone else's problem. Remind people that all problems are everyone's problems, as long as the organization communicates and expects each person to be responsible.

To bring out the best in team members, managers need to give up command and control, and team members then need to accept responsibility. Ownership of decision-making increases job satisfaction in most cases, unless the people are much more comfortable having other people bear all the risk. In that case, you might need new people.

As Chris Argyris, the business professor we met above, has explained, the era of management by physically monitoring employees and conducting employee surveys is over. These are excellent breakthrough communications tools, and we still need to do those things, but to get the best communication from the whole team, we also need to ask the team to reflect upon their own responsibilities and actions.

In fact, that is what this whole book is about. Each of us needs to reflect upon our own actions and behavior and use the continuous self-analysis of metacognition to check on whether we are listening to information and passing pertinent information on to the right people who can benefit from that knowledge—not all they *need* to know but all they can benefit from. Overall, we want to avoid *knowledge hiding.* If team members feel relaxed, safe, and communicative, they will be less likely to hide critical knowledge.

What are some things that help?

- **Confidence in the justice of the organization:** Rational decisions and fair treatment lead to less knowledge hiding.
- **Group understanding of how we relate to each other:** If there is less conflict, there is less knowledge hiding.
- **Confidence in communications:** That's what we are talking about in this chapter.

We need a team that can talk about what we don't know instead of what we already know.

YOUR OPINION CHANGES THE PEOPLE AROUND YOU

Here's a special note on culture for leaders at heart. We are all greatly influenced to not only behave the way those around us behave but also to perform to the expectations of those around us, whether those expectations are high or low.

It's amazing how much we are influenced by the expectations around us. A vast literature exists showing that teachers' expectations of students have a controlling influence over students' performances, whether the teachers' expectations are positive or negative. We can transfer these findings from teacher to leader and from student to team member. The key is the power structure: We perform to the expectations of not only our peers but especially to those with power over us. Back in the 1960s researchers Robert Rosenthal and Lenore Jacobson gave primary school teachers invented test data that showed their students to be exceptional. When teachers had inflated ideas of the students' potential, the students tended to perform better than expected. Decades of intense research on this topic ensued, as you might expect.

Twenty years later, Thomas Good, then a professor of educational psychology at the University of Missouri–Columbia and currently a professor and head of the Department of Educational Psychology at the University of Arizona, summarized the research. Teachers form opinions about students early in the school year, and these opinions influence how the teachers interact with the students. The students (or team members) take in the expectations of the teachers (or leaders), and unless students resist those expectations, the teachers' opinions will affect the students' self-image, level of effort, and outcomes.

Good highlighted two effects:

1. The self-fulfilling prophecy effect, in which an originally erroneous expectation leads to behavior that causes the expectation to become true.
2. The sustaining expectation effect, in which teachers expect students to sustain previously developed behavior patterns, to the point that teachers take these behavior patterns for granted and fail to see and capitalize on changes in student potential.[3]

Christine Porath, professor of business at Georgetown University whom we met above, ran an experiment where researchers belittled college students as a group, and college students who heard this belittling performed 33 percent worse on anagram experiments and came up with 39 percent fewer ideas in a brainstorming exercise. The researchers' personal rudeness actually limited the students' creativity. Even students who witnessed the belittling but did not have it directed at them performed 20 percent worse on the anagram exercise and produced 30 percent fewer brainstorm ideas. Further, Porath found that experiencing rudeness made people three times less likely to help others, and their willingness to share dropped by half.[4]

Clearing initial biases from our minds and believing in the potential of everyone around us is a key skill for every team member. Adopt that growth mind-set on behalf of others, and know that every person can excel.

COMMUNICATING WITH INDIVIDUALS AND SMALL GROUPS

A big team is really a collection of small teams. Like Amazon's two-pizza team size (teams should never be bigger than the number of people fed by two pizzas), whether teams are legislated to be small or not, people work closely only with a certain number of others. The way to make many small teams into one big team, then, is with communication and culture.

Small groups are excellent for productivity, equity, efficiency, and communication. Large size, on the other hand, often brings with it hierarchy, distance from decision-making people, and watered-down communications. Small groups also form their own culture, sometimes different from that of the outer, larger organization, whose goals and practices can seem vague and theoretical in comparison to the immediacy of a small group's everyday experience.

What happened with that small team that was building the Guidance, Navigation, and Control software for the Psyche mission? We in leadership and our review board listened to each person on that team who wanted to talk. We heard the pain. They got more help, better leadership, and the resources they needed to complete the job, and it was a huge success. The flight software on our spacecraft is working extremely well.

None of that, though, makes up for the pain of the experience or for its expense. How could we have known sooner what the problems were, soon enough to fix them? First of all, in the months leading up to the big reveal in April, we heard little or nothing from the individuals on the team, and we heard relatively little from their immediate leadership. I now realize that was a major warning signal. Silent teams are not happy, productive teams; they are teams with hidden problems. Our communications in the larger team—vertical and horizontal—had broken down.

Part of the reason for the breakdown was that we were building the software and the hardware during the COVID pandemic and lockdown. When teams go remote, communications across teams typically almost cease, and individual projects are siloed (more on this in Chapter 12). Had I known that then, I would have worked doubly hard to reach every subteam.

Now, I encourage leadership to conduct more "skip meetings," where we meet with people several layers of the organization removed from us to learn what is really happening across the team. Skip meetings without exception have helped me to understand important concerns and issues throughout the organization. They are invaluable.

COMMUNICATION IN MEETINGS

Meetings can be the key to communication, transparency, buy-in, and motivation, or they can be boring requirements that give you time to catch up on email. You want your meetings to be can't-miss moments, not want-to-miss moments.

So much of the success of a meeting depends upon how each person participates. You can make it clear to everyone beforehand what the specific outcomes of the meeting should be and who the final decision-maker is. Allow everyone interested in the outcome to attend. By holding meetings only when necessary and ensuring they have a purpose, they will be energetic. If you track the action items and their deadlines, people will get in the habit of delivering on time, and the meeting will gain even more momentum. Many things are better hashed out in person; make sure those happen elsewhere and keep meetings strictly for setting goals and deciding specific actions.

Here are a few guidelines for meetings:

- Set goals for the meeting at the beginning. If there are no clear actions or outcomes to be decided, cancel the meeting.
- Comments should be as specific and detailed as possible; generalities don't drive conversation forward effectively.
- Listen to what others say and build off that in conversation. Seek to understand and learn rather than be right.[5]
- If you unintentionally offend or hurt someone, rather than explaining how your comment shouldn't have hurt, let your good intentions show by apologizing.
- Meetings need to avoid both diverging from the topic before it's been completely discussed and being repetitive. Intervene if the meeting is diverging.
- Make people aware of the phenomenon of "piling on"— commenting that they've had the same experience or restating the same point. There's no need for that.
- Revisit the goals of the meeting at the end, noting which ones you have reached, and read over the list of actions to be taken: who is going to do them and what their deadlines are.

At one time I was leading an academic department in revising our course requirements for the bachelor's degree. This was a particularly contentious topic, and I wanted to make fairly big changes but also avoid having the process break down into conflict. I started by talking one-on-one with everyone who had worked on the curriculum in the past, hearing their ideas and their stories of past struggles and attempting to come to agreement with each one on something that they particularly wanted. People told me their thoughts in private, just the two of us. This was my work on dyads.

Building on that background, I first made a strawman: I proposed a new curriculum that included some mostly nonnegotiable new ideas and others set up as choices or with question marks. When there is an important process, document, or action that I need a group of people to work on and decide upon, I like to start with a strawman, a draft of what we need to make. The draft should be clearly editable, even disposable, but presenting a strawman to work from significantly simplifies the process as long as there is a lot of input from everyone before the meeting. By starting from an outline that I had devised, I was in effect putting up guardrails to keep us headed down the road in a certain direction; such a starting point is usually an extremely strong indicator of where the project will go, since people tend not to change the starting point past recognition.

Bringing in a strawman that likely won't get radically changed during the discussion is both a strength and a weakness. Ideally, the strawman will allow the group to make great progress toward a final version without having eliminated options beforehand that would have been better (go through some of the problem-solving processes from Chapter 2 and the strategy work in Chapter 10 first). When I presented my strawman in the meeting, the people I had talked with saw their ideas reflected in it.

Sometimes meetings shouldn't have critical decision points. Consider having "no secrets" meetings, which Paul Axtell, the corporate trainer whom we met above, writes about. Go offsite, maybe have some pizza, and let everyone ask anything they want. Leaders can ask open questions like "What do you think I need to know? What are you thinking that you are not saying?" And team members can likewise ask anything they want. Being given permission to speak completely openly can transform relationships and teams.

What about a bad meeting, when people get bored, nothing really gets decided, and you run out of time? On the one hand, live and learn, think about what you'll do better and differently next time. On the other hand, did you know that a bad meeting can hurt work quality for the rest of the day?

Brent N. Reed, doing research in organizational science at the University of North Carolina at Charlotte, has studied the effects of bad meetings. He and his colleagues found, in a study of five thousand knowledge workers, that over a quarter of meetings were experienced as "bad meetings," and the workers left with a so-called meeting hangover. For hours, sometimes for the rest of the day, people who had bad meetings would experience reduced focus, motivation, and productivity. People with meeting hangovers find themselves replaying the meeting in their minds and sometimes wanting to avoid more interactions with coworkers.

To avoid meeting hangovers, cure these most common issues with these actions:

- **Problem:** Irrelevance of the topics discussed and poor time management.
  - **Solution:** Don't dominate your meeting; facilitate it, which includes keeping others on topic while not being the one talking the most.

- **Problem:** Lack of a clear agenda or objectives.
  - **Solution:** Send an agenda before the meeting, and turn the agenda into an action plan with specific actions, individual responsibilities, and due dates.

If you find yourself or your coworkers in a state of meeting hangover, consider having a walking meeting to discuss what happened and find some positive actions to take. Walking is a great way to work out stress and get back into a rhythm, and finding solutions to problems is the best medicine of all.

IMPROVING YOUR STATUS MEETINGS

Regular status-update meetings can end up on autopilot, with the same agenda and the same people—everyone reporting that everything is normal and they're working on the same issues, with no specific follow-up. But I learned from the Psyche launch slip that status meetings are an absolutely critical touchpoint for communicating outward and upward in an organization.

Consider having "wins and challenges" as a structure. Everyone is invited to announce their wins, which gives everyone a chance to cheer for one another. And then, everyone is expected to discuss challenges they are dealing with. One of the best ways to improve a status meeting is by requiring metacognition. Ask each person to annotate and comment upon their report as they give it. Have them consider these questions:

- What is it about this challenge that worries you?
- What's the biggest point you are making in your report?
- Here's a number that's different from last week. Is that difference important?
- What should we pay attention to?
- This outcome is as expected, but this one worries me. Why? Let's dig in.
- This situation could be important in the future because . . .

Without the speaker's extra commentary, not only the speaker but the hearers themselves may be on autopilot or may not have the context to understand what's important.

One of the constant challenges we all face is consistently reevaluating work to make sure we are noticing when things are going awry, need more attention, or have downstream implications. A problem that's already identified is so much easier to address. But how do we identify problems when they are tiny or just approaching so they might be avoided?

It's a constant zooming in and out. How do you trigger yourself to really assess where you are? Maybe once a month in a review meeting, look at your plans and at the big Gantt charts (charts that show tasks and activities versus time and which activities are dependent upon finishing others first) and ask, "Where are the problems?" Compare what you did do since the last status meeting to what you had planned to do, and explore the differences.

With these two relatively small changes—having each person annotate and comment on their report and interrogating your Gantt chart or schedule for problems—status updates will function as valuable early alarms of trouble.

FIXING PROBLEMS WITH COMMUNICATIONS

Unsurprisingly, communications failures are often the start of conflicts. According to James Herbsleb, a professor researching socio-technical interactions at Carnegie Mellon University, the largest sources of conflict in organizations are assumptions on the part of one person or incorrectly interpreted communications (where, in each case, more discussion could have clarified the situation). Since communication is impaired for hybrid and remote teams, conflict is an even higher risk for them.

Feeling disconnected from remote colleagues can lead to teammates making harsh assumptions and judgments about their collaborators at other locations. And, unfortunately, bad is stronger than good in many areas of human psychology; this is known as negativity bias. There is even a research paper with the brilliant title "Sad, Thus True: Negativity Bias in Judgments of Truth."[6] Since psychological safety is critical for free-flowing communications, and free-flowing communications are critical for conflict avoidance and resolution, we need to go gently with negative comments and make certain that they are perceived to be about a topic or idea and not about a person.

Each time there is a misunderstanding, a failure, or a problem, dig in a little and see if there isn't a communications problem at its root. Work on improving communications in your team and throughout your organization as much as possible. Let people know that giving information to the group is also giving it responsibility, responsibility to use that information to discover and help solve problems and, most importantly, to communicate back with radical transparency. That radical transparency is a form of trust. We trust one another not to overreact, and we give one another responsibility along with that trust.

The next chapter talks about how to take that trust and responsibility to the next level by always delegating some decision authority along with the task.

9

DISTRIBUTE AUTHORITY

When I was about twenty-three years old, I found myself leading the business side of a small magazine that ran professional wine tastings and published the results; each issue was a review of many wines made from the same varietal of grapes. I reported to the publisher and through him to the board, while a team of four or five people reported to me.

All of those reporting to me, save one, had been at the magazine before I came on board, and they each knew, I assumed, a lot more about their jobs than I did. On a scale from my needing to tell them step-by-step how to do their jobs on the low end, to our agreeing on the goal and their independently making all the decisions about the products that were needed and all the steps needed to make them on the high end, I assumed they were on the high end.

I was also new to the world of delegating. At first, I gave too little direction to the people reporting to me, and one or two of them did not get their work done efficiently enough. For them, I took to having an in-depth conversation once a week until we both understood the details of what needed to be done, and we wrote down the tasks for the week as a kind of contract. We'd check on whether they got done the next week. That was a compromise between being too hands-off, which had caused them to flounder a bit, and being so hands-on that they did not have enough leeway to make up their own minds on the method and pace the work needed.

I wasn't managing them too closely, but I felt that the publisher was micromanaging me. He'd check in on every step of my every task and often tell me to change what I was doing or drop it and start something else. I began to think that if I needed to work independently for a little while to make some progress, I needed to hide.

"Micromanager" is never a complement. But never checking in on people who are working with you isn't good practice either. A new person in a job should get the support and oversight they need to learn and then be given more and more leeway to decide how the job is best done.

Together, the publisher and I were making common errors in delegation. On the one hand, I was giving too much freedom for decision-making to people without enough direction to support them in being effective. Decision-making has to be kept close to the work itself, but all of us needed to have a better common understanding of the business and its goals for the way I was doing it then to work. The publisher, on the other hand, was not ceding any authority or decision-making when he assigned work; he needed to determine and critique every step. There are better ways to delegate and to share authority.

HOW TO HELP PEOPLE MOVE FROM NEEDING DIRECTION TO DIRECTING IT THEMSELVES

When a person comes into an organization as a junior member, they are often told exactly how to do their job. Perhaps you have been in that position. I remember well my early days of learning and having very little leeway to bring in my own opinions. For example, the people I worked with in a consulting company wanted their market analyses done and presented a certain way, and I learned and did it that way. As trust is formed between the team and the new person, and as the new person demonstrates their understanding and ingenuity, they get more autonomy to make decisions and act.

Delegation—better called assigning work—sometimes has a bad name when it's thought of as passing the buck on some undesirable job. But what delegation really means is clearly communicating who has responsibility and authority for a task and giving them the respect and confidence that you know they can get it done. What almost everyone wants is to manage themselves and their own project, and to work with people who are also self-managing.

Back in 2016 I and three others founded an education company called Beagle Learning, which, at its heart, was about encouraging self-management. Rather than creating learned helplessness, we wanted to give every person a sense of agency to make changes and take steps to improve their world—to be, in fact, a leader.

Two of my cofounders, Carolyn Bickers and Turner Bohlen, described a continuum: For new people on the job, a manager might need to explain the goal, describe the work and work products needed, and outline the steps the person needs to take. For an employee with some experience, the manager might need to describe only the work products needed, and the person then figures out the steps needed. But what every team leader wishes for, and what each of us wants to be, is someone who needs only to be told the goal of the exercise, and they figure out the rest.

Most everyone in any new situation experiences taking responsibility and making decisions—that is, becoming self-managing—as a growth curve. Therefore, part of the art of assigning work is meeting your colleagues where they are on that curve and supporting them for success. That's what I was trying to do with my colleagues at the magazine. First, I would determine the goal and then discuss the work outputs needed with the team member who would be doing the work. If they were somewhat experienced, they would then go off and decide how to do the work. If they were inexperienced, I would talk about the steps needed to get the work done.

As team members get more experienced and develop more agency, they will be able to do more: suggest changes to the work output and critique and help to improve the goal. That's what we want; that's what almost everyone wants: to be a thought leader. To help people reach higher levels of autonomy, leaders need to delegate tasks that encourage people to grow, so they can move along that growth curve, as shown in the table here. Leaders also need to give support, reviews, and check-ins to ensure that team members are succeeding and advancing in autonomy and responsibility.

PROGRESSING RESPONSIBILITY AND AUTONOMY ON YOUR TEAM			
	When a leader sees a need for a task or project, they . . .	When a senior team member receives the work request, they . . .	When a new team member receives the work request, they . . .
THE GOAL OF THE WORK	Determine or delegate the goal	Discuss and critique the goal	May or may not understand the whole goal
THE OUTPUT NEEDED TO MEET THE GOAL	Determine or delegate the output	Propose and discuss the output needed	Are given the assignment of the output to be made
THE STEPS OF THE WORK TO CREATE THE OUTPUT	Determine or delegate the work process	Determine the work process	Are guided through the work process

Delegating is usually thought of as a job for leadership. But just like in team culture, everyone has a role in assigning work. Anyone who has some responsibility over a task can share their responsibility, and anyone who is adjacent to a task can support it. That's what delegation really is: organizing the tasks within a team.

Sharing responsibility—part of which is delegating or being delegated to—is a prime aspect of successful team behavior. Delegation is part of creating a networked team where each person can support the others in their work. Delegation thrives in an organization where people take responsibility for their actions, where the power to make decisions is a source of joy, and where communications are strong. The following are elements of effective delegation (and I'm including delegating to peers, and even to oneself):

- Includes the authority, along with the responsibility, to do the job
- Increases individual autonomy
- Increases confidence in asking for feedback
- Reduces distance in the power structure and leads to flatter organizations
- Indicates respect for the person doing the work

TRUST AND FLEXIBILITY IN DELEGATION

None of this works without trust. When a task is passed from one person to another—delegated—the person doing the passing has to give the new owner the responsibility for the task and, therefore, must trust them. (You can trust but verify—but you must trust!)

The director of a team I oversee came to meet with me and told me that one of our staff was just not climbing up that learning curve fast enough. That staff member was not improving on tasks that the director had instructed them they needed to improve upon.

"What did you do this last time he didn't meet the mark?" I asked.

"I had to take all his notes and redo them," she answered.

"Did you go over all the changes with him?" I asked.

"I will; that's next," she answered.

She'd felt trapped between the need for the work to be as good as possible and the need to help someone newer to the job learn. In this case, I felt that we needed to lean into helping the staff member learn, rather than focusing 100 percent on perfecting the product. We talked more, and I saw that her push for excellence often led her to taking delegated work and improving it.

We realized two things: Helping someone else improve their work, just like any kind of teaching, requires that the learning person actually do the work, maybe iteratively, maybe right alongside the more experienced person, but the learner needs to do it. And even more importantly, we realized that we need to recognize when work is good enough, even if it's not exactly how you would have done it. Let other people express their excellence, and don't change what doesn't need to be changed.

DELEGATION IS A TWO-WAY STREET

On the other hand, pay attention to the ways people delegate to you. A common problem with weak leadership is delegating a task while (sometimes secretly) withholding the authority to do the task. There's little that's more frustrating than being asked to do something, doing it well, and then having it dropped or even publicly criticized by the leader who asked you to do it. So when you receive a task, immediately take responsibility as the delegee by agreeing on a timeline for completion and milestones for communications and redirection if needed and on understanding the context of the task and who the stakeholders are. Then you can control the process of getting the task done and ensuring everyone involved is kept in the loop and no one is surprised.

I've failed at being a good delegee many times. Some years ago, the head of our organization asked me to prepare a plan for how we would design and use a building he was planning to create for our project. My team and I had a lot of fun with this challenge, and it generated a lot of excitement. I handed in the plan. I never heard a word of feedback, and then the new building was shelved. I don't think the leader ever looked at our plan; the building funds were not available, and the idea was dropped.

A year or so later, the same leader asked me to write a playbook for the future of our discipline across the organization. Did I take my lessons learned about delegation and ask about timelines, or outcomes, or when I might expect feedback and what the next steps would be? I did not. I just went away and spent time and personal capital creating this playbook. I handed it in, and the leader told me, "Oh, don't worry about the playbook now. We're going to go about this a different way." This time, it was my fault. I had not been an active delegee. I had not learned my lesson.

One of the great follow-on effects of delegating with some authority is that the people accepting the tasks are given a chance to practice thinking about the implications of what they do and taking responsibility for those implications. Soon, there's a team of people with insights on the strategic level and not just on their local, tactical level. This is a team that can bring valuable richness of thought to decision-making, and that's what the next chapter is about: bringing the whole team to the table for decision-making and strategy.

10

WORK TOGETHER ON DECISION-MAKING, TACTICS, AND STRATEGY

Angry faces ringed the table at a meeting of a space-mission team building a probe that would be sent to Mars.

"What do you mean, there is no more mass margin?" one person asked. (Mass margin is the extra mass above what the spacecraft is designed to weigh but bookkept or documented in case any parts of the project get heavier than originally designed. It's like a rainy-day fund but for mass.)

"We had an extra 100 kg we could use with heavier design modifications back when we were funded. My team has been so careful up to now, and when I ask for an additional 5 kg, I'm told it's not available? Where did it all go?"

I looked around and saw one or two faces—people on the teams responsible for subsystems that had been extensively redesigned— looking carefully neutral among the sea of angry expressions. That's where the mass went, I thought, to those subsystems in private conversations that were not announced to others on the team. And although this example is one in which leadership was not involving the team as a whole in decision-making, it's also true that the members of the team were avoiding sharing information and decisions with one another. If the team members had communicated transparently, then together they could have made better decisions for the project.

Here's another example that shows how the Mars probe team could have avoided the problems with mass margin: On the Psyche team, like the Mars team, our project manager managed the margin personally rather than handing it out to each subteam at the beginning for them to use at will. But unlike the Mars project manager, he held meetings with all subsystem teams present to show what the current mass budget was, along with any recent changes, and invited each subsystem team to discuss their need for more mass. Each request and the reason for it was heard and either supported or constructively criticized by the other team members. Everyone knew where the mission stood and that decisions were made as fairly and openly as possible.

If the team leader only distributes scarce resources in response to individual requests, then the people who receive the resources may not be the most in need nor the best managers of their work. Instead, they are often the boldest, the most familiar with the leader, or the most convincing (though perhaps not the most correct). And, in this scenario, the leader carries all the responsibility and the stress of problem-solving without the best information or support of the greater team.

Team members play a critical role in enabling the whole team to be included in decision-making. If you or any member of the team don't communicate transparently and include the rest of the team in decision-making, you are hurting the success of your project and the health of your team. When team members overreact, take things personally, or think the worst, then it's going to be very hard for anyone to share freely or ask opinions openly. The team, ultimately, makes it possible for communications to be clear and for their opinions to be heard.

Recall the advice from Part I and use it here as a team to ensure that each of you, and your leadership, can share information completely and ask for input. Don't overreact to news that might be bad. Prepare your input to be heard. Organize your ideas clearly and make sure they are relevant and that their relevance is clearly articulated. It's amazing how the importance of a statement can be entirely missed unless the speaker spells it out.

Involving the team in decision-making, however, is not the same as consensus decision-making, which can be slow and even lead toward mediocrity. I'm an advocate for giving the leader responsibility for decision-making, but also for ensuring that that leader has heard all the relevant opinions and ideas from the team before they make that final decision. Each team member owes it to their team and to their leader to productively express their ideas and opinions and have them heard. And each leader owes no less respect to people on their team: Listen to what they have to say. Then decide.

If you are respected by your team, and your ideas are taken into consideration, you're much more likely to be happier in your job and even more effective as you think more strategically. And your leadership will make more informed decisions. Remember, not every decision will go your way, and when one doesn't, your job as a team member is to *disagree but commit* to the decision that was made. You stay the course and do your part wholeheartedly to support the team in the direction that was decided. In this way you build goodwill and ensure, more than ever, that the next time your input will be sought and the team's communications will continue to be transparent.

A big part of leadership's job is anticipating the future. When will we need to use that mass margin, and how should we hand it out? This chapter will help with future planning with strategy, tactics, mental anticipation, and how to handle uncertainty.

PLANNING AND ANALYZING AT SEVERAL SCALES

Have you seen the movie *Election*? In it, a teacher asks students to define ethics and to define morals. What is the difference? A student begins to answer but is cut off by the film's narration. It happens again later in the film, and we are left never learning the difference. I have felt the same way about the terms *tactics* and *strategy*. What are their definitions? Where do you draw the line between them?

As it turns out, I'm not the only one. There's a vast literature that discusses the terms and attempts to clarify them. So if you, too, are also unsure, you're not alone; if you *are* sure you know the difference, know that your clear understanding is not shared by everyone. Is the strategy of your organization just one of the tactics of a holding company in implementing its even higher-level strategy?

The terms *strategy* and *tactics* originated in ancient Greece and were used for military activities. Strategy was the overarching plan, and tactics, from the word *taktikos*, meant "the art of arrangement." War and sports metaphors are commonly used in business, and so it was natural for business to adopt these terms. There is some agreement today that tactics are a lower-level set of actions that support the more visionary strategy. Without struggling with more specific definitions, that's how I'll use the terms here: Tactics are actions that support a higher-level, longer-term strategy.

STRATEGY AND TACTICS IN BIOLOGICAL SYSTEMS

Are there other systems where strategy and tactics occur that could inform how we use these concepts to plan and execute actions in our organizations? One possibility is the ways strategy and tactics are used in biological systems. Concepts from the field of biology can be used in your life or within your organization as metaphors or in some cases literally, particularly in the ways that organisms manage to survive and thrive in competition with other species. Could thinking of your environment as an ecosystem yield new insights?

Sir Richard Southwood, an entomologist at Oxford University, published an influential paper about tactics and strategy in the natural world. He first described "habitat templets" (using the word *templet* in place of "template"), which are graphical representations of environmental aspects like resource availability, disturbance patterns, and predation activity. He then described tactics, which are short-term responses to the environment, and strategies, which are long-term evolutionary changes to adapt to the environment. Here are Southwood's five main tactics that organisms can use to pursue an optimal strategy for survival:

1. Tolerance of harsh (adverse, stressed) conditions
2. Defense against other organisms (predators, parasites, competitors)
3. Food harvesting
4. Migration or other change of habitat
5. Reproductive effort: number and weight of young[1]

TOOLS FOR STRATEGY AND TACTICS

You may have heard it said that some people are great strategists (they have the vision to look ahead and set more distant goals that guide the team in a clever direction), and that other people are great tacticians (they can figure out the steps needed to reach the goals). A key sign of individual effectiveness is the ability to fairly rapidly cycle between long-term strategic and short-term tactical thinking. I'm advocating for you to become both a strategic and a tactical thinker. If you think at multiple levels, your work will be so much more effective.

We already know that the line between strategy and tactics is a blurry one. Partly that is true because there may be not just one step from a strategy to a tactic but several steps of increasing specificity. One of the challenges of writing a good strategy is making it specific enough to be implemented. Many strategies are too general, whether given to you from above or thought of by you and your team, and need to be broken down into substrategies before tactics can be written.

The highest-level strategy for a company selling educational programs might be "Gain market share." One strategy that can be nested within that one is "Gain market share by offering new microcredentials every month." Then, there might be an additional layer of nested strategies before tactics can be designed: "Gain market share in high schools by offering new physical and biological science microcredentials each month *and* gain market share in primary school by offering new monthly microcredentials for nonmathematicians."

Now there is a strategy of sufficient specificity that we can write some tactics to achieve it. So lesson one of strategy is you may need to drill into the strategy and write substrategies until you get to a point at which they are implementable.

When planning space missions, NASA uses a tool called the science traceability matrix to get from goals to objectives to solutions to implementations. The matrix format starts with a statement of your biggest final goal or purpose, and then breaks it down step-by-step into actionable pieces: What's the specific objective related to this goal that you want to solve? What information do you need to solve it? How will you obtain that information? It's not all spaceflight out there, of course, but the traceability matrix concept can be applied to any problem. In the context of this chapter, I've changed NASA's goals and objectives into strategies and tactics.

The purpose of a traceability matrix is to show both why achieving the goal is important and exactly how the goal is to be achieved. By systematically filling in the matrix from left to right, your solutions are facilitated step-by-step. This is generally a group experience: Bring in all the experts! Invite the team. Invite the stakeholders. Talk about it with everyone, and then everyone feels bought in and a part of the process.

SAMPLE TRACEABILITY MATRIX						
High-Level Strategy	Substrategies: Must be measurable and achievable with tactics.	Measurements: What defines success of this strategy?	Tactics: Actions you will take to achieve the substrategy (you may have several tactics for each substrategy).	Measurements: How will you measure the progress of your tactic?	Data product: What will be the output of this measurement, and who will review it?	Resource requirements: Who is needed to implement this tactic, what money or other resources do they need, and how long will it take?
Gain Market Share	Gain market share in high schools by offering new physical and biological science micro-credentials each month.	Increase market share in science teacher training in our state from 10 percent to 30 percent within one year.	1. Research high school micro-credential needs.	Interview buyers and teachers at fifteen high schools across two states.	Tabulate their greatest pain points on science-teacher education and what resources they now use; to be reviewed in two weeks by whole team.	One interviewer half-time for two weeks; one script writer for one day.
			2. Design minimum viable product for top candidate micro-credential idea.	Need three learning objectives and one teaching unit for each.	Storyboard of micro-credential to be presented to team two weeks after research is complete.	Graphic designer, one to three subject matter experts, one learning designer; each half-time for two weeks.

Starting from the left, the high-level strategy for this traceability matrix is "Gain market share." Next, the team identified one substrategy, "Gain market share in high schools." There is likely to be more than one substrategy, but I'm showing only one here. After defining how success of this strategy would be measured, the team has designed two tactics to address it: "Research high school microcredential needs," and "Design minimum viable product"—to be done in that order.

RUNNING THROUGH SCENARIOS IN YOUR MIND

I was cochairing a committee that was tasked with gathering information and writing a plan to conduct scientific research on the nature of the ocean floor, in a series of six audacious and technologically challenging dives in next-generation submersibles (the nature and destination of this project has been changed in this description for reasons of confidentiality). In our first meetings, my cochair and I set a tone of calmness and openness, encouraging people to listen to others and inviting everyone to speak. We talked a bit about the culture we sought, one in which we could have productive disagreements that lead to rich information and clear decision-making. Conversations were fruitful, and the work of the committee moved ahead. So far, so good.

Soon we would need to prioritize a long list of possible science tasks to help us learn about the deep ocean, and then we would need to arrange however many we could fit into the six dives. I knew this was a process that could go smoothly or be derailed by misunderstandings and needless arguments and diversions into minutiae or personal obsessions. How to keep us on track? I started running through scenarios in my head. We needed to allocate enough time to go through this process so that people had the chance to speak and be heard, to feel relaxed enough to share what they really thought, and to think creatively. I thought that we needed to practice before the deadline loomed and the decisions were final.

I was using a form of metacognition, thinking about the process by playing out scenarios, seeing where things might go wrong, and analyzing why. I imagined destructive arguments and constructive arguments. I decided a key step was getting the whole committee involved in metacognition: discussing *how* we were going to make these decisions long before we actually had to make them. I had realized, by imagining how the committee would work together and what questions would arise, that the key was going to be having everyone try out processes for prioritizing the science and finding their advantages and disadvantages together, so that when the time came to decide on how to proceed, we all agreed, at least, on the path to decision.

I needed, specifically, to avoid what I imagined in my mind to be unproductive off-ramps from the road to decision and completion. We might get into a long discussion about the capabilities of the submersibles, for example, which we had no control over and which were not yet determined by the builders. Therefore, early in the process we had to agree on how to handle unknown hardware capabilities and thus avoid that off-ramp leading to a time-consuming dead-end road. I think of these kinds of early decisions and agreements as the guardrails on my road leading to creating a clear outcome together. Don't go off the road into a swamp.

As a committee, we brainstormed different ways to prioritize the science. We prioritized in part by science themes, ranking which ones we thought were most important according to average scores from everyone on the committee and to the common scientific instruments or samples needed. Then, in two meetings a month or so apart, we practiced using these rankings. This way everyone's ideas of how to do it were executed, we all got to talk about why we ranked things as we did, and we began feeling the happy flush of reaching consensus. All this before the final list of science tasks was assembled and the decision became critical.

Envisioning how tactics can be designed to cumulatively achieve strategy requires a creative mind imagining a future spreading across time (days, weeks, months, years) and including in an optimistic way the results of actions. Most importantly, this creative mind has to imagine the interactions of the people doing this future work: Who has the key skills? What will happen if you ask a specific person to do the task? Will they carry through? Do they work well with the others on the team?

Here are some topics to play through in your imagination ahead of taking action so that your tactics have the greatest chance of success:

- How can your group be guided to a decision, as in the anecdote above?
- What could derail the project in the future (at NASA these are often called death threats)? How might you fail, and how can you prepare to combat these threats?
- Who outside the team might care about what you are doing and be either an ally or a problem? Whom should you gain as an ally before you start? Who might object and what might they say? Who might be doing this already? Consider anyone you report to, other teams in your organization, people outside your organization who might want to know about what you are doing (or whom you might not want in the know!). Strategize about how to best communicate with them and whom to include in the communication process.
- Plan your tactics and steps and run some scenarios. Imagine you are flying up above your project and looking at the whole playing field, the whole forest, the whole nation, whatever your whole landscape is. Are your tactical steps taking you toward the strategic outcome you want? What are the stumbling blocks ahead?
- Imagine time passing. What will the future bring? Imagine how your scenarios will change with time. Will the passing of time bring new death threats to your project, new opportunities, new stakeholders you need to bring in?

AN ENTREPRENEURIAL MIND-SET: ACTING FAST WITHOUT ALL THE FACTS

Wow, do we humans like clarity. We like to know and understand everything around us! Cognitive scientists are even able to measure how uncomfortable we are when we don't know all the answers but still have to make a decision. It turns out that when we are under stress and in a state of indecision, we tend to leap to a decision that may have no basis for it, simply to get relief from the terrible tension of indecision. Being a great entrepreneur in your life or work requires that you develop a tolerance for incomplete information and an ability to make the best possible decision in an uncertain world.

One key result of practicing metacognition is that it gives you more control over your own thinking processes. That control allows you to avoid decisions that are motivated by irrelevant emotions (like panic!) or are made too hastily—that is, before accruing the minimum acceptable amount of information. People who have practiced metacognition are more likely to discover and follow alternative solutions and strategies and are therefore more adaptable under pressure in a changing environment.

Metacognition is therefore critical to being entrepreneurial, which is actually defined by social scientists as the ability to identify, take action upon, and solve challenging problems *in an uncertain landscape*. It's all fine and well to identify and solve problems and strategize, as I've been discussing above, when you have time to sort out all the options, decide on a solution, and figure out how to measure success with certainty. But what about when you need to act fast, and you are not certain of anything, from the source of the problem to the likely effects of the solutions you are considering? A really successful strategist acts fast and doesn't ever let important issues or opportunities lie just to see what will happen. The key to being able to act fast is, of course, metacognition: You need higher-order thinking to assess the landscape, rethink current strategies and tactics, and quickly pivot if needed.

And you need to do it with your team, so that people are not whip-lashed by the decision and do not feel left out—moments of rapid decision-making are risky not just for the outcomes of the decision but also for the stability of the team. If you include the team and get their ideas and thoughts, then it can become a moment of team solidarity instead of stress. Sometimes, the most important step is just finding a structure in which to assess the various ideas and concerns you have.

Previously in this book I presented structures for describing a problem, assessing solutions, and implementing strategies. Now, let's take it up a level. Knowing there is a structure for thinking about strategy and problem-solving in a changing, uncertain, and time-constrained environment can be a great calmer in times of stress. It's all metacognition.

Now that you are a metacognitive expert, let's take a look at a model for metacognition in entrepreneurial, risky, time-constrained, and information-deficient situations, as developed by the vice chancellor and dean of management at Syracuse University, J. Michael Haynie, and his colleagues. Sit down with your team and work through these steps.

First, recognize that the environment you are in influences how you think about your options. Haynie and colleagues use a great example: If you are in a hostile environment, you are more likely to focus on minimizing losses than you would if you were in an environment that feels full of opportunity, in which you would typically think more about making gains. So describe the environment as you perceive it, and describe the decision or problem in front of you.

Then, think about how novel, uncertain, and dynamic the circumstances are. Haynie points out that research shows that the more novel, uncertain, and dynamic the circumstances are, the higher your metacognitive response is likely to be. The more dynamic, the more you will naturally think about the people, tasks, and strategies in front of you with awareness and assessment. If your situation is less dynamic, you'll need to more consciously move your metacognitive skills to the front.[2] Engage your metacognition: overcome your biases, see your whole landscape, assess the skills of your team and the relevance of options in front of you clearly.

Next, form your solution and strategy from your metacognitive information. Haynie uses as an example an experienced entrepreneur faced with choosing the most appropriate avenue through which to secure funding for her venture. In a normal cognitive scenario (rather than a metacognitive one), she might look at some recent data on where the most funding is flowing from within her sector and go there first.

But if she has dialed up her metacognition, she'll think about the pitch skills she has on her team and their past record, recent interactions she's had with all possible sources of funding, news and rumors in the community that might form biases for funders, and ideas she has about which possible sources want to be approached first and which might be open to being a second option. In other words, she puts together all her concrete information (current funding flows in her sector, for example) and nonconcrete information (rumors and how they might influence thinking, for example) and looks at it all as a landscape before deciding.

She knows that there is a lack of perfect understanding and a lack of a perfect way to forecast, but she doesn't let that stop her from arranging all her information in the best way she can, making a decision, and moving forward.

Working and living in an ever-changing team, project, and world makes keeping those dyads and team culture fresh and communicating and making decisions together important. If the playing field is ever-changing, then the only way to move forward with confidence is if the whole team knows how we got where we are and that we have the tools to make progress from here. Next, we'll talk about some of the most critical roles leadership has in facilitating and supporting a great team.

PART III

ABOVE

How Leaders Serve
and Support Great Teams

All this talk about creating thinking, empowered individuals from which to build teams is great, but unfortunately our human brains do seem to require leadership to keep the organizational fiction alive. Without leadership reinforcing the culture and the goals, people can devolve into a me-first, ladder-climbing attitude, which breaks up teams. Without leadership, people's actions can dissolve into tactics that stray away from the higher-level strategies that unite the work toward the vision. Either way, the organization is at risk.

Though this book's concepts work for any discipline, I often show-case scientists and engineers because their teams typically offer clear examples to learn from. Scientists especially, along with engineers and all academics, have worked their way along a career path that rewards a willingness to fight in the face of disagreement from all sides, a deep faith in one's own intellect and abilities, an instant critique of every new idea, a level of comfort with being in charge of one's own decisions, a respect for charisma, and a need to appear as a top expert. None of these characteristics is necessarily the best one for building collaborative teams. In fact, these characteristics are often the opposite of what is needed to make a bonded, collaborative team. For a team to be effective and optimally enable each person to contribute their best, team members need to be able to show concerns, weaknesses, gaps in knowledge, and even failures without being eviscerated by the hero-experts at the table.

The purpose of thoughtful culture building, therefore, is to counteract some of the negative effects of unguided human behavior. We need to think about how to be our best selves. Here is where the leader needs to show up as strong and authentic. The leader needs to model and reinforce the culture and to support the team members who do the same. And the leader is the main person who determines the value of the individual. No wonder each team member thinks often about the state of their individual dyad with the leader.

As we neared launch with the Psyche mission, we had a leadership group that consisted of several project managers and deputy project managers with different skills. One of our leaders mainly looked up and out, spending more time thinking about relations with the top leadership at the Jet Propulsion Laboratory, at partner organizations, and especially at NASA headquarters; one looked inward toward the team and thought about how to organize and motivate the team; one looked down and in at everyday activities to make sure that the work was getting done and that individuals were cared for; and one looked at processes being used to measure progress and whether they were motivating the teams in the right directions and tracking meaningful metrics.

When selecting leaders, including yourself, look for people who have really added to the advancement of the organization. Many people stand out from the crowd because of what they have done to further their own personal success. But to be a good leader, you have to care more about the success of others and of the organization. Fight for your colleagues to win. Some people lead by pointing to themselves, and some people lead by pointing to the other people on the team. I try to be the second kind.

Each chapter of Part III discusses a key leadership skill that enables teams to be at their best:

* Lead by Example
* Keep Teams from Losing the Recipe
* Excel at Margins and Metrics
* Develop Better Ways to Assess and Reward Your Team
* Keep Partner Organizations Energized and Connected

These are skills you can practice even if your position is not defined as a leader. Every member of the team should be a leader. Think like a leader, and act with responsibility. Bring forth ideas and take actions that make your team greater. As a wise person once said, "Problem-solving makes a leader; following directions makes a worker."

11

LEAD BY EXAMPLE

I had arrived early for the Psyche Monday status meeting at the Jet Propulsion Lab. I was the first one in the familiar room, with its whiteboards covered with sketched graphs and numbers, its bulletin boards holding prints of Psyche student art, and a conference table so large that there was only a narrow aisle between the table and the chairs lining the walls. I sat on the long side of the table, about two-thirds of the way back from the screen at the front where slides would be projected, because I knew I would be speaking at this meeting and wanted a microphone so the online people could hear.

The team started filing in, small groups chatting and laughing. Some came to the table and plugged in their laptops and readied presentations; others sat in the chairs along the wall, calling out to our organizer that they had uploaded their slides to a common folder.

This scene is probably pretty familiar to you. Think of the last time you walked into a conference room for a meeting. Normally, as people stream into the room, certain individuals automatically sit at the head or the foot of the conference table, marking themselves as leaders. Or they sit at the conference table because they expect to be recognized by the leaders and have their voices heard. Other people sit along the wall because they are not expecting to be needed. People self-stratify according to whether they expect their voice to be heard and respected; that expectation is produced by the culture of the organization. It should not be that way. Everybody, no matter where they sit, has to be able to speak.

I watched this happen in every Psyche mission meeting. I sit at the table only when I need better access to a microphone because I'll be speaking a lot; otherwise, I sit along the wall where I can see everyone. This way, I can help encourage quiet people to speak up when they seem to have something on their mind, and I can model sitting anywhere in the room.

It's everyone's job, not just that of leadership, to make sure that every person gets heard and that each is heard with the same respect as everyone else. All too commonly, the ideas of a junior person, a disabled person, or a woman are criticized more or passed over more quickly than ideas that come from a senior person.

Leading by example means according the same respect to each comment, using your power to raise up others rather than aggrandize yourself, and urging others to do the same. All the aspects of the culture you are creating must be lived by you first.

Even more importantly, since everyone can be a leader no matter their position, you need to exemplify high-quality thinking and action that will translate into your being seen as a leader. You can improve your personal efficacy, your cultural interactions, your contributions to the team, and your strategic thinking, and thus be seen as a leader.

Attitude also matters. To make a difference, you need practice and drive and grit. Being a strong leader requires, in the words of the psychological profile, "high hedonistic and low fatalistic." Low fatalistic is the confidence that one's actions *can* change the future—that the future is determined at least in part by our choices. High hedonistic describes people who feel and believe in happiness and, in some cases, people with the drive to find ways to make things better. If there is no hope, there is no purpose in movement. And the greatest work is done with the energy that comes from hope and belief in the impact the work will have.

Then, there is ethics. Just do the right thing. Even if it is really tough, if it is the right thing, then you can do it. The rightness removes some of the fear. Believe your stomach when it tells you what is important. Take the high road. Try to do only things you'll be proud of in ten years.

WHAT MAKES A GREAT LEADER?

One of our human implicit biases is to view loud voices, constant self-promotion, and a willingness to stand up first as indicators of leadership. That's so ironic! People with these characteristics and others (including being tall) are often selected for leadership, when in fact some of those characteristics are irrelevant to leadership while others indicate poor leadership.

Many people have listed the characteristics that make a great leader. McKinsey & Company have listed optimism, selfless leadership, continuous learning, resilience, levity, and stewardship (leave everything better because you were a part of it). Others list positive energy and a balanced personal life. At the top of my list are having personal values that benefit others and thinking of others before thinking of oneself.

As Tomas Chamorro-Premuzic, a professor of business psychology at Columbia University and University College London, explains in a *Harvard Business Review* podcast, "[T]here are many competent men who are, ironically or paradoxically, overlooked for leadership roles. This is precisely because they have some of the qualities—empathy, self-awareness, integrity, and humility—that ultimately make them better leaders but don't really make them leaders to begin with. If you succeed at playing within the current rules of the game, you're going to get further, but then you're going to make things worse. And if you don't, you might never be selected." That traditional command-and-control style of leadership just does not work anymore, if it ever really did.

A tech leader recently said to me, "I've always felt being part of a team with a 'strong' leader feels more like being employed than being part of a collaborative effort. This is a hot take, but leadership in our society is slightly overvalued; I much prefer scenarios where all input is considered, more akin to the scientific process than simply implementing past methods to meet a deadline."

The McKinsey consultants Aaron De Smet, Arne Gast, Drew Goldstein, and Richard Steele created and have run for years the Organizational Health Index (OHI).[1] They had always included authoritative leadership—that is, the use of authority and pressure to get things done—in their survey. It's a classic modality, and one they expected to continue to drive leadership.

In a McKinsey quarterly in 2024, they wrote that, to their surprise, authoritative leadership no longer predicts organizational health in any way and no longer therefore appears in their organizational-health model. It simply fell out. According to De Smet and his colleagues, authoritative leadership is obsolete. These are the leadership qualities that remain high indicators of organizational health:

- **Empowering leadership.** Leaders should make sure those closest to the work have the autonomy to make their own decisions. Organizations that emphasize empowering leadership are 2.3 times more likely to use effective leadership to shape the actions of people in the organization and 3.4 times more likely to be healthy.
- **Decisive leadership.** Leaders should make and follow through on decisions and do so at speed. Organizations that emphasize decisive leadership are 2.5 times more likely to use effective leadership to shape the actions of people in the organization and 4.2 times more likely to be healthy.[2]

So here is your challenge, all you leaders. Be the exemplar, help create and live the culture, see and value every individual, guide the strategy, find a way to help every team member perform their best. But don't be heavy-handed. Be a part of the team.

BE THE KEEPER OF YOUR CULTURE: FOCUS ON THE TEAM, NOT YOURSELF

"The only thing of real importance that leaders do is to create and manage culture," commented Ed Schein, an early expert in corporate culture. As leader, you should be working constantly to embody the team's norms. A good way to practice this is to select just one of your team's norms to carefully embody on any given day. If you are concentrating on listening respectfully to every voice, encourage a quiet person in your meeting to speak. Know that person's name and why they might have a good perspective on the topic under discussion. Listening is the most important oral communication skill for producing success in a team—more important than talking and more important than presenting.

Your embodying the team's norms is critical to making the team culture a living entity. It's a statement of ethics and equity, and it will lead to a more successful team. Simply stating that we are great communicators or that we are constantly innovating is not a great way to set culture. These statements seem too abstract. Erin Meyer, who is a professor at the INSEAD business school in Fontainebleau, France, has studied the effectiveness of using case studies to embed and reinforce culture. She recommends presenting the team with "dilemmas" with two possible solutions for discussion, such as this one.[3]

> **Dilemma:** You are an electrical engineer in a creative burst, and
> you are working on solving a long-standing issue with a piece
> of equipment. As you work, you discover a serious problem
> with another part of the hardware, and you think it could

pose a significant schedule delay and cost increase for the project, but you are not yet sure of the problem's cause and so don't know its effects.

Option A: Bring the problem to the team immediately, even though you don't know the root cause of the problem yet and you haven't finished your own work on the original issue either.

Option B: Keep working for another twenty-four hours and try to both learn more about the root cause of the problem and move closer to your own solution before you bring information to the team.

Either one is a reasonable choice. Which aligns better with the culture you are working to encourage? Bring this or other dilemmas to your team and discuss them. How do the options align or fail to align with your culture? This will bring the culture to life in a meaningful way.

While celebrating wins is critical for the team, when leaders think of their own personal successes, the appropriate level of celebration is different. The combination of transparency and humility (or any similar nonnarcissistic inclination) means leaders should, as Reed Hastings writes in *No Rules Rules*, "whisper wins and shout mistakes" when it comes to your own actions. Be vulnerable and transparent, and thus raise trust and point the spotlight on the team, not yourself. (A note on timing: When the whole team is going through a crisis, that is not the time to shout mistakes. That is the time to remind everyone of the team's resilience.)

When we finally accepted that the Psyche spacecraft was not going to launch on time, I fell into a state of stress and even despair, interspersed with moments of rage. Not a desirable state. I was furious that my plans for the last stage of my formal working life had been crushed by the years of extra work needed: We would slip fourteen months to launch, and the trajectory to the asteroid would now take over five years, not just over three years as our original mission plan had called for. Even the time in orbit at the asteroid would need to be longer to achieve the same science. In all, about four years had been added to the length of the project.

I hated that some decisions made by organizations associated with the project had helped push us to this slip, despite all our efforts to stay on time, and I felt it personally: People in those organizations had made decisions that deeply affected *my* career. I had done everything I could, identified and fought all the fights, to help us succeed. If the mission was canceled by NASA, I would own that responsibility entirely, as the leader—all the failure and all the shame. I was furious.

And then one day I woke up and said to myself, "I can't believe I am so distraught about this." "My spacecraft is late" is probably the definition of a first-world problem. I immediately felt like an idiot. We had saved the mission; hundreds of people would retain their jobs and in fact would have them for longer. We would come to understand vastly more about our solar system, and the taxpayer dollars would be well spent. My family was fine; we would still have a house to live in and food to eat. I had to get over myself.

And in that moment, I largely did. I was my better self by far when I thought of the team and the project, and my worst self when I thought only of myself.

Each of us is generally thinking of the world relative to ourselves— what is nice for us, what advances us, how things reflect upon us. Instead, work on this improv precept: Help the team have success.

In his book *The Culture Code*, Daniel Coyle writes about the coaching strategies of Gregg Popovich with the basketball team the San Antonio Spurs. Popovich uses three belonging cues: You are part of this group, this group is special, and we have high standards that I believe you can reach. Popovich knew everything is personal. And he knew how to let people know they mattered and *also* that they could achieve at the highest level. Sometimes you may think people mattering is *dependent* upon their achieving at the highest level. But no, every person matters, period. And, separately, they can achieve.

In school we are rewarded for being self-serving—for watching our schoolmates with a critical eye, for jockeying for position in the grade curve, for viewing one another as competitors and trying to get ahead. Abandoning, to the best of our ability, both the self-centeredness and the competitiveness within our teams has an astonishingly positive effect. As soon as you put others forward and support them and stop shining the light on yourself, everything works better, everyone performs better, and everyone gets along better. Work on reciprocity. Find meaning in something outside yourself.

Those leaders who lead by pointing to themselves are missing a world of effectiveness and success. Joseph Folkman, cofounder of Zenger Folkman consulting, has the research to prove it. He analyzed the effectiveness and leadership style of 3,800 leaders based on 360-degree evaluations from managers, peers, direct reports, and others. He found that by carefully apportioning credit among all those who deserve it, the apportioner attains higher status than they would by claiming the win. Those who took credit were rated as the most ineffectual, and those who gave all credit away were rated as the most effective.[4] The apportioner attains the status of leader, of a person powerful enough that they can afford to share the credit, and one who knows so much about everyone on the team that they can identify who actually did the work. Apportioning credit is the act of a leader.

A Checklist for Leading by Example

1. Embody your team's norms. You are never the exception. All the aspects of the culture you are creating must be lived by you first. Pick one norm to consciously embody during each week.

2. Pay attention to who is speaking, and whether just a couple of voices are controlling the direction of the team. A team's success is created by benefiting from the knowledge of every team member. Encourage quiet people to participate.
3. Accord respect to each speaker on your team.
4. Use your power to raise up others rather than aggrandize yourself, and urge others to do the same.
5. Believe in your team; have a realistic but optimistic view of the path forward and the future.
6. Know, and express, that each person on the team can achieve the high standards you all hold together.
7. Apportion credit among all those who deserve it. Don't lead by pointing to yourself.

A WARNING TO HELP YOU REMAIN A GOOD EXAMPLE FOR YOUR TEAM

Have you ever thought that your leader was out of touch? That they were making poor decisions, that they didn't listen to you, that they didn't seem to care? You know what? You might not have been imagining it.[5]

Hubris. Sometimes, when a leader displays this combination of bold self-confidence, vision, and risk-taking, hubris can be inspiring and describe a person with the thick skin and determination to succeed in leadership.

But there is another side to hubris: a refusal to take advice, inattention to detail, unwillingness to look at evidence and change their mind, exaggerated pride, contempt for others, a lack of inhibition, and a distancing from reality.

As Lord David Owen, a physician, neuroscientist, and former British foreign secretary, and Jonathan Davidson, a professor of psychiatry and behavioral sciences at Duke University, wrote in 2009, the dark side of hubris can make a strong, inspiring leader into someone who causes people to worry about their mental health and, more importantly, someone who makes terrible decisions for the world.

Owen and Davidson stress that a leader need not be considered a success for hubris syndrome to develop. Power is the key influencer: The greater the power and the longer it is wielded, the more likely hubris syndrome is to develop.

By studying the records of US presidents and UK prime ministers over a one-hundred-year period, Owen and Davidson found that over time, otherwise high-achieving leaders cut themselves off from critics and overestimated their chances of success. They coined the term *hubris syndrome* to describe this combination.[6]

In other words, power does corrupt. The longer leaders lead, the higher the likelihood that they will develop hubris syndrome. Over time, power causes personality changes. Owen and Davidson defined fourteen symptoms of hubris syndrome and then identified five of fourteen presidents and prime ministers during their study period as having the syndrome.

British Prime Minister Neville Chamberlain believed that he could appease Hitler. The later PM Tony Blair supported the 2003 invasion of Iraq despite his advisers telling him there was no basis for the invasion whatsoever. US President George W. Bush wore flight gear and stood on the deck of the aircraft carrier *Abraham Lincoln* with the message "Mission Accomplished" hanging from the ship's tower behind him.

Later, Peter Garrard from St. George's University of London and colleagues tied linguistic markers to the symptoms of hubris syndrome and were able to track the increase in hubris in Margaret Thatcher and Tony Blair over time, based only on the words they used when speaking.[7] Hubris syndrome may eventually be an officially diagnosable mental problem; Jean-Paul Selten, from the School of Mental Health and Neuroscience at the University of Maastricht, argues for its inclusion, and links it to exaggerated pride, contempt for others, and a diminished sense of reality.[8]

And get this. Holding power for a lengthy time actually changes our brains.

The Berkeley psychologist Dacher Keltner has studied power for decades and concluded that people with long-standing power positions "acted as if they had suffered a traumatic brain injury—becoming more impulsive, less risk aware, and, crucially, less adept at seeing things from other people's point of view."[9] Measuring the link between hubris and actual changes to the brain became a question.

That link has now been documented by Jeremy Hogeveen of Canada's Wilfrid Laurier University and his colleagues. They put people holding more- and less-powerful positions into a magnetic brain scanner and found that those holding more power had considerably diminished ability to "mirror" other people's experiences. Mirroring is wincing when you see someone stub their toe, or laughing when you see them laugh. Mirroring is a critical part of empathy; can you walk a mile in the other person's shoes? Turns out, these long-term power-holding leaders could not.

Sukhvinder Obhi, one of Hogeveen's colleagues, found that even when he explained to the powerful what mirroring was and asked them to do more of it, they could not. Their ability to empathize was, at least temporarily, *gone.* It's not just national leaders who succumb to hubris syndrome. It's leaders at our institutions and, as we rise in leadership, ourselves. David Owen said in 2008 that hubris syndrome is less likely to develop in a leader who retains personal modesty while in power, keeps their previous lifestyle, and has humor, cynicism, and humility. Having confidants such a partners, friends, or colleagues who are unafraid to criticize the leader can also help that leader avoid hubris syndrome. And one of the best ways to curb hubris syndrome from the outside is by holding leaders accountable for their statements, actions, and decisions. Start with yourself.

TOXIC LEADERS

Leaders should not lie or be passive-aggressive, or take digs at people. Leaders should not be in the business of driving the weak out. Some more truisms: Leaders should never be arrogant, spiteful, or condescending, nor should they engage in gossip. Oh my gosh. Have you done some of these things? Well, we all have. Time to get better.

Lieutenant General Hal Moore is a legend in the military and a legend in leadership. In his book *Hal Moore on Leadership,* he presents a beautiful summary of the good leader: "[A leader] . . . should always act with humility and treat his subordinates with respect and dignity."[10]

We all underestimate the impact our words have, as Moore points out. Sometimes we are tempted to indulge in anger or otherwise fail to control ourselves, when we feel our status allows us to behave in ways a less powerful person could not get away with. But contrary to popular belief, yelling and ordering will not speed up the result but will make people hate you. Some people think toxic leadership is acceptable as long as the mission is accomplished. But completing the mission should never come at the cost of trampling your subordinates' dignity or betraying their trust.

Look for any echo or vestige of yourself in this compilation of types of toxic leaders:

- **Bully** leaders inflict emotional pain by shouting and force.
- **Narcissistic** leaders are arrogant and self-congratulatory.
- **Divisive** leaders are like narcissistic leaders, but channel wrath and arrogance toward only those they perceive as weak; may use public humiliation as a tool.
- **Exclusive** leaders form cliques and shield those who are in them.
- **Hypocritical** leaders seldom practice what they preach; this is a deeply unethical leader (and this is why you need to embody your team's norms).

- **Sycophantic** leaders exclusively seek approval from their own leaders and can lack courage to make decisions that benefit their own team due to their desire to always say yes to their own management.
- **Teflon** leaders find others to blame rather than taking responsibility.

HOW CAN A GOOD LEADER FIX A BAD CULTURE?

My friend Jake was wooed by a Silicon Valley education company startup and came on board as a product manager. He had a team of five, and together they were prototyping new products for high school classrooms. The team completed their first prototype and excitedly sent it to the CEO. Most of the team was working remotely, and constant communication came through their Slack channels. After delivering the product, the team's channel exploded with happy emojis, everyone congratulating each other. The next day, however, the CEO responded to the prototype.

"This prototype is a piece of shit," he wrote, "and it makes me hate what we are doing." I wish I was making this up. That was the totality of his response. Nothing specific, nothing actionable, and no encouragement to do more or gratitude for effort. The team was devastated and went silent. Remember about silent teams? It's not a good sign.

Jake tried to get more feedback from the CEO on what was wrong, but the CEO added nothing specific, and Jake was not sure how to press for more. He was new and didn't know how the CEO would react. Instead, Jake decided to change the culture within his own part of the team. Jake and his team conducted a norm-setting exercise together, something similar to the one I described in Chapter 7. They agreed on norms of civility and communication. They wrote up their ideas and posted them on the company Slack channel, only suggesting how things might be done, without any specific stories from the company or names.

Just ideas for how teams might work, and how this particular team intended to move forward.

Jake and his team were working pretty smoothly and cheerfully on their next prototype and revisions to the first one. People in the company were coming to Jake to share ideas. You can imagine just what happened next: The CEO began to make it clear he now thought Jake was the enemy. Jake was threatening the CEO's power. By making a safer haven within the company where people were happier and by creating trust, Jake was now getting a lot more authentic information than the CEO was, and he was now becoming a little power center of his own, effectively weakening the CEO and making him look bad. Uh-oh.

The CEO reorganized the company and put Jake's team under the management of someone else. There was no discussion leading up to this change; a new org chart was simply posted on the internal website. Then, people who spent a lot of time talking to Jake started to get fired (again, I am not making up this story). After the third firing, everyone understood that talking with Jake was a fast route out of a job. The CEO won in the sense that he did in fact destroy the culture Jake had set, and he did isolate Jake. Jake suffered anger and hurt, and then he went off and found another job.

What are the lessons here? First, if you are a CEO and you're feeling threatened, think hard about how you can be a better CEO and cleave to your best ethical standards while you rerationalize the corporate authority and communications pathways. And if you are Jake, make sure you include your CEO in your culture efforts. The real lesson is culture has to be an effort of everyone. A good culture requires the leadership to sign on and to live the culture, and it requires the team to sign on too.

A lot of the bad culture I've seen in academia stems from a feeling of status, that the status of a senior professor means they can misbehave at will and not be punished in any way. Unfortunately, that's often been true. Faculty members who achieve tenure and then bring in big grants or are constantly interviewed on CNN are often forgiven the most awful of transgressions (nonconsensual sex with students being an outstanding example I know of) by leadership who both value the money and prestige and fear the reprisals.

I've occasionally invited faculty members to imagine their mother or their grandmother or both standing behind their chair as they spoke in faculty meetings. Would you be saying that if she were there? The people who laughed out loud were generally those who were not misbehaving, and the others did tone it down.

That toxic status behavior is often, of course, directed against staff rather than other faculty members. I had to have a stern conversation with one faculty member to enforce the rule that he was not allowed to swear at the staff. The most incredible part of the whole incident was that he was surprised I would say this to him. I suppose he had done it before with no repercussions.

The first thing to take in is that culture is contagious, and behavior is contagious. I've heard people say, "This will be a great place to work once so-and-so retires." And perhaps sometimes a single person really can make that big a difference, but more often they have helped create a pervasive set of behaviors that have become ingrained and will persist after the toxic person leaves. If one person swears at the staff, another person is likely to do that next time they are in a conflict.

Culture change often requires some people to leave, some new people to come in; changes can also be driven both from the grass roots and the leadership. Because we carry culture unconsciously within us the way a sponge carries water, changing culture requires change on the organizational level and on the individual level.

Courage. All these stories—Jake's taking control of his team's culture, my insisting on civility from a bunch of senior faculty members—are stories of small acts of courage. Leaders need to have the courage of their convictions and take action when needed. A classic failing of courage is when a leader is unwilling to work with team members on their own mistakes and issues. When a team member is truly bad at their job, the leader has to communicate with them about the problem and set up a plan for improvement. If improvement does not happen, that team member needs to move to another job.

Some degree of acceptance of wrong actions and poor performance has existed everywhere I have worked, and it used to surprise me when problematic people were just shuffled to another team without putting a plan in place to help them fix their problems. That kind of trading people happens as a function of cowardice and conflict avoidance, two things that all leaders need to overcome.

A toxic culture affects not just the work product and the contentment of the team members but also their very health. A study by Joel Goh, a Harvard professor, and his colleagues found that people experiencing a toxic work culture were 35–55 percent more likely to be diagnosed with a serious physical disease.[11] A toxic work culture is ten times more likely than low compensation to create a resignation rate higher than industry average, according to an MIT study. In other words, a good culture keeps team members on the team, and does so more effectively than higher pay.

Fixing a bad culture requires commitment by leadership, work within each team to set norms of behavior, and analysis to see if people are in their optimal roles and whether they suffer from overwork. This is the work of many months.

Fixing, setting, and maintaining culture all start with the leadership. A leader who is uncivil, or passive, or defensive will encourage that behavior in the team as surely as adding salt to milk changes its flavor. Don't underestimate the power of your actions as a leader. Whether you are a chairman, a department head, a group leader, or a meeting facilitator, your leadership style influences everyone around you. When changing culture, start with specific actions and back them up with words.

A LIST OF ACTIONS FOR CHANGING A BAD CULTURE[12]

1. **Leaders:** Talk about civil behavior, collegiality, and the problems of harassment and your intolerance of it. Talk publicly. Talk frequently.

2. **Leaders:** Check that your organization's processes and structures reinforce the culture you are creating. Culture can be a topic in people's job evaluations and in training programs. The structure of the organization may need to be adjusted to reflect the culture that's wanted.

3. **Leaders:** Be willing to sit down with people who misbehave and compel them to behave. Be committed to this. If your faculty member swears at your business office manager, sit down with the faculty member and explain that such behavior is not acceptable. By constantly emphasizing good manners, some harassment will be stopped before it begins. And, we hope, more serious harassers will be surrounded by a community who will help stop them.

4. **Everyone:** Be a good bystander. Speak up when something is wrong.

5. **Everyone:** If you experience harassment: report, report, report. Without reports, leaders cannot take action; what we do not know about, we cannot fix. So, leaders and peers, support those who report. Support their courage.

6. **Leaders:** Protect those reporting. If a graduate student who reported bullying by their adviser, for instance, finds that their adviser is no longer supporting them, be willing to write letters for the student. Get on the phone with possible employers and support their employment. Discuss with all parties that retaliation is illegal and will not be tolerated. The responsibility of a department chair to protect the career of a graduate student who has had to report against an adviser is not discussed enough—it should be.

7. **Everyone:** Reporting should be confidential, both for the accuser and the accused. Allow the necessarily private due process to occur. Avoid sharing thirdhand rumors. These weaken the confidentiality of the case, and they weaken any ensuing legal case

against a harasser (multiple overlapping rumors, when shown by a lawyer to be just one event, already reported, make the case against the harasser much weaker).

8. **Everyone:** Please treat everyone else with the same respect. Senior faculty members should not feel free to be dismissive to staff and students, for example.

9. **Leaders:** Communicate. Remember that every year new students and staff arrive who have not experienced the norms of your culture; they need to hear that your organization is actively trying to create a positive, supportive culture where each team member has a sense of belonging, that you will not tolerate harassment—and that if it occurs, they will be fully supported in their reporting of it.

10. **Leaders:** If you need to convince your upper management of the importance of correctly following through on a harassment case, remember that you can use three arguments:

   - *Ethics:* Allowing harassment to go unpunished is simply unethical.
   - *Productivity:* Allowing harassment to go unpunished harms the culture and lowers the value and quantity of work being done.
   - *Legal:* Allowing harassment to go unpunished places your organization at risk for damaging legal action.

BEING A LEADER IN CRISIS

Here's the easier way: Come in as the new leader of an organization already in crisis. Problems have been partly identified, and you bring fresh eyes, fresh determination, and fresh energy—and whatever happened in the past to cause the crisis, it wasn't your fault; you weren't even there. However, that honeymoon period doesn't last for too long, and pretty soon you are just an ordinary leader in crisis.

By definition, as leader you are responsible for fixing crises. The buck stops with you. But what does that mean, in practice? No one can know everything, and no one can fix everything, and fixing always takes time.

What does it mean, in practice, not to be able to fix everything? How much failure is acceptable?

I was sitting in the conference room with the NASA board reviewing the Psyche team's performance during the year of our launch slip, breathing in hot stale air, every chair occupied, listening to the first conclusions of the board. One board member after another was talking about the suffering of the people on Psyche's Guidance, Navigation, and Control software team. My head started to feel light, and my skin started tingling up my back and down my arms. I had a feeling of floating, and I thought I might throw up. I was having an extreme physical reaction (well, extreme for me) to the horrible knowledge that I had utterly failed.

I had talked a lot about culture with the Psyche team. "Listen to every voice," I had said. "If something is wrong, speak up. We want to know." The Guidance, Navigation, and Control subteam *had* spoken up, but they had not been listened to sufficiently, and each member had suffered high stress as a result. If we had acted earlier, we might have been able to fix the problem and launch on time.

Maybe. Maybe not. But that didn't matter anymore. Now we were not launching on time, and it was my fault. When there came a moment when I could reply, I said that I had stressed this kind of culture from the beginning, and the fact that this part of the team had not been heard was my fault. I said, "I think this team might be better off if I resigned the leadership and a new person came in for a fresh start." This was both the correct and honorable thing to do, in my mind. When a corporation makes a big mistake and the share price plummets, the CEO often steps down.

To my surprise and confusion, the reaction from the review board members and from NASA headquarters leadership was immediate and strong: Please do not step down. We need you to make this happen. One person even said to me, "I don't think this team will make it to launch without you." I don't believe that, but I was reassured that at least people had seen and appreciated my efforts, even if they had not been enough.

At the same time, I was not really being held accountable for what happened. If I was so involved, how did I miss the problems? Either I am responsible, and I failed, or I could not have found and fixed the problems and am therefore extraneous and not a proper leader. I still struggle with this, as much as I love leading Psyche and am thrilled to be working with this team.

What does it mean to be responsible and accountable? How many problems can any one person be expected to be able to detect? No one can detect every problem. So it's the fixing of the problems that's the test.

WHAT KIND OF CRISIS LEADER SHOULD YOU BE?

The kind that is most authentic to you, of course. No matter your leadership style, however, you have to have grit. Grit, as Angela Duckworth, a developmental psychologist at the University of Pennsylvania, says, consists of interest, practice, purpose, and hope, and you can't take away that last one. You have to believe a solution will be found and progress will be made. (If you need a pep talk, see Chapter 3: Do Not Give Up.)

Sometimes leaders in crisis are expected to act like old-style military leaders—all command and control, no listening and consensus building. Don't you believe it.

"They were supposed to be physically tough, technically infallible, and emotionally detached. And that closedness, it actually got in the way of staying safe in an environment with thousands of moving parts." This quote, which is from Hanna Rosin, a host of the podcast *Invisibilia*, refers to the old culture on oil rigs. That old culture worked reasonably well when there were only twenty people on the rig, but once the rigs were drilling at a mile deep with hundreds of people on the rig, people had to be able to ask questions, admit they needed help, and communicate clearly.[13]

While that culture is an extreme one, all of us probably see echoes of it in our workplace. Some people still think that being tough, distant, and domineering, to use the words of Georgetown University business professor Christine Porath, is the way to be respected as a leader. Studies show repeatedly, however, that leaders who are civil and respectful score 40–80 percent higher in social status, 23 percent higher in competence, and even 16 percent higher in power than do gruff, domineering leaders.[14] Be civil and respectful, and when the going gets tough, be even more civil and respectful.

Take a note from Hal Moore. There is always something you can do to influence the situation toward success. And after that, there is one more thing. And after that, one more. Always be thinking, "What should I be doing, or what should I stop doing, to maximize our chances of success?"

Be versatile in changing between enabling and hard-decision modes. Enable your team to weigh in with their knowledge and opinions, and then when speed and definitiveness are needed, make those hard decisions yourself.

Daniel Coyle, the author of *The Culture Code* whom we met before, reminds us to embrace the messenger. "One of the most vital moments for creating safety is when a group shares bad news or gives tough feedback," he writes. That news, that feedback, needs to be embraced. If it's just tolerated, as Coyle says or, worse, passed over or rejected, the message is that it is not safe to bring real information. Greet the messenger's information not with "How did this happen?" but with "What have you learned so far?" That wording respects and encourages the messenger, rather than making them defensive.

The ability of a team to accept that they need to adjust, and perhaps to adjust rapidly, is one of the biggest indicators of a healthy, optimistic team, even in times of crisis. People who have had too many failures or who have lost trust will be slow to change because they will not trust the new direction.

Notice how long it takes your team to adjust to a change, whether they are synchronized in their adjustment, and whether they "fibrillate" (in the words of David Noble from Evidence Based Research and Michael Letsky from the Naval Research Lab). They define *fibrillation* as when a large proportion of work being done by team members ends up being unusable. Watch for the symptoms Noble and Letsky see in misfunctioning teams, including the following:

- Extra time required for the team to recognize a problem in teamwork or product development (agility).
- Larger fraction of tasks delayed because needed precursors were late (synchronization).
- Larger fraction of preliminary individual products never used (fibrillation).
- More occurrence of individual products that cannot be assembled because they are incompatible (friction).[15]

Research shows that in volatile and ambiguous circumstances, being a versatile leader with flexibility in changing viewpoints and behaviors is critical for results. In fact, Rob Kaiser, a leadership coach and CEO, describes versatility as a "meta-competency," similar to my metacognition in this book. Being a versatile leader requires assessing the needs of the situation from a high-level view and then deploying a suite of behaviors and actions suited to the situation.

The suite of behaviors to choose from can be imagined as lying along an axis from forceful to enabling and another axis from operational to strategic. This second axis is a key to leadership. In technological projects in particular, people who rise to leadership tend to be tacticians buried in the technology and the process in which they have thus far spent their careers. Look for those special people who can toggle from tactical to strategic thinking and who bring along the attendant skills of negotiation, planning, and diplomacy. Stretch those skills by reading and practicing the skills described in Chapter 10: Work Together on Decision-Making, Tactics, and Strategy.

A Checklist for Leading During a Crisis

- Be civil, respectful, and full of grit. You and your team can do this.
- This is the time for complete honesty and the most truth and ethics you can manage.
- Don't do anything just for the optics of it. Sometimes people change leadership or start new programs just so others can see movement. Do what's really needed.
- Super overcommunicate when in crisis. You won't be able to perceive how much extra communication is needed by the people on your team; they will need more than you can imagine.
- Listen to people at all levels.
- When something goes wrong, sometimes people need to talk about their trauma several times before they feel fully heard, but you also need to move on and separate their personal pain from the project goals. Say that out loud and do it.
- Think of any team that has been quiet for some time (such as happened with the Guidance, Navigation, and Control sub-team in Psyche). Now, look at your org chart. Where do you *think* you know everything that's happening but maybe you don't? Where has it been too quiet recently?
- Act immediately. Waiting is never better. When you first spot a danger in the distance, you don't know whether it's running toward you or away from you, so act fast, and you'll be able to deal with it even if it's running right at you.
- If something is wrong or needs adjustment, adjust immediately, put metrics into place, and begin to measure improvement or

the lack of it immediately. Do not wait. Expect the same of your people.

Throughout this chapter we've talked about being an exemplar of the culture, never letting go of humility, and ways to handle change and crisis. The emphasis has been on the culture: the culture of leading, of change, of crisis. Now, let's talk about tasks. How do you, as a leader, help your team do their best at their tasks?

12

KEEP TEAMS FROM LOSING THE RECIPE

The email explained unemotionally that a part of the Psyche space-craft's communications system would arrive a few weeks later than planned. No explanation. Maybe not a huge problem, except this was not this subcontractor's first slip. We'd already implemented regular virtual meetings with some of their leadership, but the issues that were causing problems were neither getting resolved nor becoming clearer to us through virtual conversations.

Face-to-face, we learned that they had not been successful in "tuning" the part we needed for our communications system—so it wasn't useable. But why? All our videocon meetings had yielded nothing other than we're starting over with this unit and we're going to be submitting a new invoice to you for our additional costs. So we increased the pressure by planning a "boarding party," where some of our team would visit and make the real human connections (dyads!) and find out what was really going on.

When the boarding party visited—all smiles and good-to-meet-yous—they learned what was really happening. The company's one tuning expert, a woman named Helen, had retired. To get the part made, they ended up having to bring Helen back from retirement. We worried all the while that she was going to say, "No, I've had enough" or, awfully, that she would get COVID as a result, but thankfully she carried through.

A year later, across the country, a different company's delivery schedule was slipping. This problem was even more serious because the company was not sure why the parts were not working. It wasn't a missing process, like tuning; it was something more complex. We put together an expert team, called a Tiger Team, and eventually they CAT-scanned one of the complex parts and performed a destructive analysis on it. They found multiple issues, including wrong bolts, epoxy blobs where they should not be, and some shaving-like foreign matter in areas with moving parts. To my astonishment, we learned that this company also had to bring an expert back from retirement to make a proper part, and again, *her name was Helen*! Different company, different part, same story. Why were these companies forgetting the recipe?

Suddenly this problem, the problem of humans learning how to do or make something important and precious and then forgetting that knowledge, both obsessed me and appeared everywhere I looked. Why hadn't I wondered about this before? Looking around me, I thought, human progress is like a sieve, knowledge constantly dropping through to be left behind forever.

Here's an example of a lost recipe, an example that completely shocked me when I learned of it. Modern-day concrete wears away rapidly under seawater. Piers built of concrete weather and crumble and need replacement. Cracks form, and seemingly naturally enough, they just widen over time. We've all seen that over and over.

But the Romans had a kind of concrete that actually strengthened under salt water; cracks, once water seeped into them, repaired themselves. The Romans had better concrete than we have today. The dome in Rome's Pantheon, at 142 feet in diameter, is still the world's largest unreinforced concrete dome!

Roman concrete contains a particular group of minerals (calcium-aluminum-silica hydrates) that strengthens and even heals broken concrete. It's now thought that these minerals were introduced into the concrete by adding volcanic ash. Lime, a standard ingredient in concrete, and the volcanic ash reacted immediately when mixed to create those hydrates, which continue forming and reacting over time, filling cracks and strengthening the concrete. At one time it was thought to be a happy accident, the result of adding trash materials, such as ash. But Admir Masic, an MIT chemist, says that Roman engineers were too clever to be that sloppy or casual: "Our hypothesis is it's not part of bad processing; it's part of the technology."[1]

How can we have forgotten how to make this concrete? When the Roman Empire fell, large civic projects requiring significant amounts of concrete similarly declined, written documentation did not sufficiently describe the key processes, and the information was lost. Except for the fall of the empire part, the rest is exactly like the story of the Helens.

DOES WRITING IT DOWN REALLY HELP?

I thought about procedure manuals, which are one of the resources people think of when they worry about losing knowledge. But written procedures and training manuals, as it happens, are inefficient transmitters of knowledge.

First of all, people seldom read carefully. And second, people seldom think about what they've read. In fact, written procedures actually act to *stop* people thinking on their own. As Chris Argyris, professor of business who warned us above against blanket positivism in conversations, has written, "Genuine learning in organizations is inhibited by a second universal phenomenon that I call *organizational defensive routines*. These consist of all the policies, practices, and actions that prevent human beings from having to experience embarrassment or threat and, at the same time, prevent them from examining the nature and causes of that embarrassment or threat."[2]

Reading instructions regarding a step in a process inspires us to carry out that step without thinking about it more deeply or criticizing it. We mainly try to understand it enough to simply follow it. Finally, writing can never capture every step in a process or convey all the knowledge about a process.

Here's an example. I searched online and found a recipe for frying potatoes.

1. Put the butter in a pan (I use a stick-free pan, the butter is for taste) and melt.
2. Add potatoes and turn over every few minutes until brown. Not all need to be brown, but make sure they are cooked through. Usually takes about fifteen minutes.
3. Add salt and pepper sometime during frying time, to taste.

But I have some questions. How hot should the pan be? How could I tell whether it was hot enough? How can I tell if the potatoes are cooked through? What if my potatoes never get brown? This used to happen to me, and eventually, I learned that I needed to put in fewer potatoes at a time so that the pan remained very hot and the potatoes would brown. Otherwise, they just steamed. That's information that the recipe writer knew but did not transmit.

But if I followed the recipe exactly, and it didn't work, who could blame me? I'm doing exactly as told. Writing can't contain enough of the tacit knowledge, those unspoken, perhaps not even conscious, practices that give experienced people their success.

Remember when we were discussing metacognition back in Chapter 5? Deanna Kuhn, the Columbia University faculty member, points out that cognitive psychologists differentiate between declarative knowing (knowing *that*) and procedural knowing (knowing *how*). These are often separate in the human mind. Procedural knowing, knowing *how*, can sometimes be wordless and unexamined—it's tacit knowledge. The owner of tacit knowledge can do the thing, but they might not even know what they are doing, specifically, that gives them success.

Some examples of tacit knowledge are unconscious but effective communications strategies, like a chef understanding what the right texture of dough looks like when light glistens on it, or a lab technician knowing to warm up adhesive so it never fails. Unlike "information" in its usual use, tacit knowledge generally cannot be communicated with words, often because the knowledge or actions involved are not conscious for the person who knows the technique.

LEARNING IN PERSON IS THE HUMAN WAY TO LEARN

Tacit knowledge is one of the reasons why training others in your processes is difficult. What does the expert mean when they say, "Stir the solution until it is well mixed"? What does the expert do if the solution doesn't fully mix? What is the tacit knowledge of how to handle that? Does the expert always leave the solution to cool a bit before moving it, or make sure to do it on a humid day, or wait for the train to stop running on the track outside so the building doesn't shake? Those are kinds of tacit knowledge that make just following the instructions in a procedure manual unlikely to be successful.

Shoulder-by-shoulder apprenticeship is the ideal way for new people to learn. Turner Bohlen, my son and the cofounder of Beagle Learning, and I call this the Helen Principle. As in the examples from the Psyche mission, individuals may possess a unit of knowledge that is critical to the success of your project, and it may well be a unit of knowledge that only they have. Thought of in this way, any project can be measured in Helens: How many Helens' worth of knowledge does your project require? (In fact, we looked up how frequently the name Helen has been used and found it was particularly popular between 1880 and 1960.

Around 2020, when the Psyche team was experiencing a lack of Helens, the tail end of the Helens from the war years and just after would have been retiring.)

We each hear at some point in our careers that everyone is replaceable. It's a good curb on ego. But are we really? Experience would say no. We are only replaceable if we have trained people to do the specialized things we are best at, and ironically, protecting that information so that we are irreplaceable simply ensures it dies with us. Training others, sharing your knowledge, is a special form of showing community and responsibility, and your colleagues will respect you all the more.

One morning at a conference I sat at a table with some people I had not previously met. One turned out to be a senior leader at Sony Corporation. Fantastic, I thought: He must have thought deeply about how to bring the apprenticeship model into the tech sector.

After some introductions and small talk about the conference, I told him about our Helen experience on the mission and my ensuing deep interest in how information can truly be preserved and my thought that apprenticeship—standing right there beside the expert, looking and learning—was the only real way. I thought he might have great ideas about how to do this because of his position of leadership in a country with an intense and ancient tradition of apprenticeship.

He laughed and, rather than talking about Sony, asked me, "Have you heard of the Ise Shrine?"

No, I had not.

The Ise Shrine is one of the oldest in Japan. It has operated continually for around two thousand years. Its origins go back to the Emperor Sujin, who reigned from 97 to 30 BCE. He declared that the Sun goddess was too powerful for her worship to be encompassed by the court and that a dedicated site was needed for her. In the reign of the subsequent emperor, a site was selected, and the goddess herself approved, and so the Ise Shrine was founded.

The Grand Ise Shrine (Ise Dai Jingū) is in fact a collection of many shrines. There are two main shrines, the central of which is in service to the Sun goddess, and over a hundred smaller shrines in service to the Shinto religion. Shintoism's roots in Japan date to before 600 BCE—that is, a mind-boggling 2,600 years ago. (For a beautiful view of the shrines, search for images of the Ise sankei mandara, which are a series of maps of the shrines meant in part to guide pilgrims.)

How does a religion continue largely unchanged for all that time? That is the question my friend from Sony posed to me that morning.

Beginning around the year 690 CE, the keepers of the shrine began rebuilding the entire main building from the ground up, every twenty years, every person participating, side by side. The builders are mainly sawyers, carpenters, laborers, and thatchers, and each learns their discipline from other monks as part of a continuous, 1,300-year stream of knowledge. The stated goal of rebuilding is to reproduce the old version as closely as possible. A new shrine identical to the old rises on the site, and when it is ready, the old one is completed deconstructed. Some sacred objects are transferred to the new shrine, and others are made anew every twenty years. Most recently, the shrine was rebuilt in 2013, its sixty-second edition.

By rebuilding the main shrine twice in the average working lifetime of each monk, interspersed with rebuilding the many smaller shrines, every monk is immersed in a stream of education in how to build, furnish, staff, and run the shrine. The knowledge is continuous.

TAKING THE APPRENTICESHIP MODEL TO HEART

Often, we think of writing books as a great way to record and save knowledge for the ages. Compared to a written tradition, the continuous learning tradition of the Ise Shrine is like a living garden as opposed to a lost tablet. Just as languages that have no living speakers are called sleeping languages (a term preferred by many Indigenous people to "dead languages"), so I now think about knowledge that is not practiced but just written in books: The knowledge in books is more of a dream, an object of reverence but often not of practicality.

If you are learning in person, as an apprentice, you can use the same "Why, why, why, why, why?" technique that we talked about in Chapter 5 in the context of metacognition. Apprenticeship is a great way to learn—far more deeply than from any procedures manual—how a person does their job. Imagine you were learning to fry potatoes. When the expert melts the butter and says, "It's time to put the potatoes in," you can ask, "How do you know? Why is this hot enough? What would happen if you made it hotter before cooking?" And so forth.

Shoulder-to-shoulder apprenticeship to avoid losing the recipe is only one part of the importance of being together: Being in the same place physically not only allows people to enjoy communication but also encourages that communication to bloom into innovation. The economists David B. Audretsch and Maryann P. Feldman have spent much of their careers studying innovation in industry. Sometimes we think that innovation is a phase in an organization's timeline: Innovation happens at the beginning, when the organization is developing its products and processes. Audretsch and Feldman have shown, however, that innovation can happen throughout an organization's life, and that it depends on a dedication not just to research and development but also to the communication of tacit knowledge.[3] Tacit knowledge actually encourages innovation, and its transmission is enhanced by, and possibly cannot happen without, physical proximity. This is partly why geographical regions become hotbeds of innovation: Many people with their own reservoirs of hard-won tacit knowledge meet, talk, and create an atmosphere of high-level achievement and information. Think Silicon Valley.

These "knowledge spillovers" thrive on proximity. The idea of knowledge spillovers dates back to 1890, when the English economist Alfred

Marshall coined the term. Expanded over time to the Marshall-Arrow-Romer spillover, the idea has come to explain how information travels among firms and spurs innovation. The closer together the firms are physically, the better the transfer of tacit knowledge. The economist Edward Glaeser and his colleagues researched and wrote about knowledge spillovers and concluded that "intellectual breakthroughs cross hallways and streets more easily than oceans."[4]

Know that both quality (not losing the recipe) and innovation are dependent upon the transmission of tacit knowledge and that transmission of tacit knowledge is dependent upon physical proximity. Think about this: What happens to knowledge and understanding when teams work remotely?

REMOTE TEAMS

The concerns came back loud and clear when I read the responses to our Psyche team survey. People wrote, "I don't know what is happening in other parts of the team. I've stopped getting information from the development side. The Florida team doesn't talk to us anymore."

Had the whole team culture collapsed? Well, no. The problem was COVID. The team had gotten siloed, and members had stopped seeing one another face-to-face. Feeling isolated led to people thinking they had been devalued in some way, or that their work wasn't recognized, or that leadership had become insular. The lack of communication led to feelings of insecurity.[5]

Almost all of us are now in teams that allow some or all of us to work from home part or all of the time, according to data from Gallup and Meta for Work. Before COVID, some of this hybrid work existed, but of course the pandemic is what made it ubiquitous. How we work together and our need to shore up process and relational activity is even more critical when work is hybrid because the culture of working together is diminished and degraded when communication is remote.

In 2022 a research team from Microsoft, University of California, Berkeley, and MIT, led by Longqi Yang, studied what happened when 61,182 Microsoft employees were sent home to work in 2020 because of the COVID-19 outbreak. The researchers analyzed six months of emails, calendars, instant messages, video and audio calls, and workweek hours and found that the Microsoft teams became increasingly siloed, the same effect that our Psyche team's survey had revealed.[6] The most direct and constant work relationships, which I'll call degree-one relationships, remained intact and communication and decision-making proceeded. But *every* other work relationship—those of people spoken to less often, or in other parts of the organization, or of the newly hired—either dwindled or fell away completely. The loss of these second- and higher-degree relationships left each core team isolated from the others. In isolation, the teams were less effective and also lost some of the feeling of belonging to a larger organization with a larger purpose.

As soon as humans draw a circle around their village and stop communicating with other villages—or, in this case, stop communicating with adjacent teams—the adjacent villages and teams become "other" rather than "us." For example, in one survey, 41 percent of remote workers thought their coworkers were saying things behind their backs, as opposed to only 31 percent of in-person workers, according to research done by Zoltán Lippényi and Tanja van der Lippe from Utrecht University in 2020.[7]

Along with the dangers of siloing, hybrid work brings the challenges of communicating via telephone, text, and video.

The Degraded Communications of Remote Work Can Break Teams

We all know about the fatigue of looking straight into other people's faces on your screen all day during meetings or classes. But besides energy, what else gets lost in virtual communications? Gestures aid in communicating emphasis, priority, emotionality, confidence level, and other critical enhancements to understanding. Gestures, of course, are almost completely lost in asynchronous and audio-only communications and are partially lost in video communication.

Midair hand gestures during speaking have been divided into two categories: deictic and iconic. Deictic gestures (pointing gestures) can check or repair team understanding by calling attention to shared objects or words. Iconic gestures are used to communicate ideas, objects, or actions in the absence of descriptive vocabulary for them. For example, waving your hand in the air in a motion like fluid flowing into a tank and then out a pipe in its bottom, while simply saying "the water is routed to the house." These gestures can give watchers a more nuanced understanding or even create understanding where there was none.

Studies by Lawrence Domingo and his colleagues at Stanford University have shown that deictic gestures do not work in remote communications.[8] The complete or partial loss of gestures in remote communications means a level of ambiguity about meaning and direction occurs that might have been resolved in person. Awareness of this loss may inspire speakers to be more verbal, or even to gesture more in front of their faces where video callers can see them. Empathy is often elicited by body language and subtle facial expressions that we miss partially on video conferences and miss entirely through telephone and text communication. Lack of empathy can lead to lack of trust, or increased rudeness, and in general to even poorer communications.

Connection between people is created by *feeling* seen rather than literally being seen in person. Talking about this with the team and having people work on listening, showing they are hearing, and connecting personally with remote teammates can make all the difference.

When some members of a team are in the same office and see each other with some regularity, while others are either fully remote or in other colocated offices, a special kind of siloing happens. People who share an office feel more like a team, and the presence of the remote team members fades. The colocated people form their own silo. This in-group, out-group behavior quickly extends to language, with those who are colocated using "we" to describe the people colocated but not their remote team members.

Watch those pronouns. *We* should refer to the whole team. We had a situation on Psyche where someone in leadership was also on a specific subteam, and whenever he used the word *we*, it was clear he was referencing the subteam. People in leadership and on other parts of the team began to connect with and trust him less because his language showed he didn't feel a primary sense of belonging and loyalty to the whole team.

Islands Together in a Sea of Remoteness

Of course, the challenges of remote and hybrid work are balanced by the advantages to the employer (for example, access to a broader workforce and less turnover) and to the team member (for example, more time with family because commuting is eliminated and lower stress from the comforts of home). This kind of work is here to stay, so let's work on fixing the challenges.

Unsurprisingly, the remedy for the problems with remote and hybrid work is more time face-to-face. Multiple social science studies show that in-person communication creates higher levels of consensus, more communication, higher trust levels, and greater efficiency.

Remote and hybrid teams need "islands" of time in person to reconnect. These reconnections can create lasting bridges across the time apart. The frequency and activities of these in-person islands depends upon the team: How long have they known each other? Do new relationships need to be built? Has the nature of the work changed?

And by the way, virtual happy hour does not count as an island. We need to be together in three dimensions, working but also sharing what the organizational scientists call contextual information: vacation schedules, office politics, and so forth. This practice builds familiarity and friendship.

The consulting company McKinsey tracks team performance and culture constantly and through data analysis recently found that their own optimal individual schedule is about 50 percent together or with clients and 50 percent work at home. At 50 percent colocated, they keep their teams intact and enable closely knit relationships even for new team members and give each person the freedom of 50 percent remote work. It's nice to know that traveling to work in person is not a luxury or a junket (unless you happen to pick the Mariana Islands). Meeting in person from time to time is a necessity for our success at work.

Improving knowledge transfer is founded in good teamwork: establishing clear communications, knowing one another's roles and responsibilities; working on ways to first record what is recordable; and then using an apprentice system for learning the rest. The importance of knowledge transfer is one of the many ways I am reminded that humans work naturally in villages—or, as we say in business, teams—and that being apart is a big challenge for quality and a sense of belonging.

The biggest part of never losing the recipe is working side by side. The apprentice model is the classical model of human experience, throughout the millennia, and just because some of us like to sit alone in our offices in front of our monitors doesn't change that fact. You can protect the critical tacit knowledge of your team with time together, and that's especially important for remote teams. Now that the team is running along with a good cadence of in-person work and training, it's time to measure and monitor the project as it progresses.

13

EXCEL AT MARGINS AND METRICS

What is the easiest way to know when a project is heading into trouble? When you are tracking progress in a clear, quantitative way and you see that progress is slowing or has stopped. Leadership, and in fact everyone on the team, needs tools to measure progress and know when interventions are needed to reach the goals the team is after. These are your metrics: the things you measure, track, and examine to see if progress is being made.

Before you go down that long road of tracking and watching and working, set yourself and your team up for success by adding margins into what you expect to achieve. If you think the project will take a year, build in an extra two months (or more!) of schedule margin, in case something goes wrong. If you think the spacecraft you are building will need the power of 15 kW solar arrays, either work on building a spacecraft that will only need 10 kW of the 15 kW arrays you bought, or buy 20 kW arrays. Have some margin in your power needs.

Margins and metrics, the two *m*'s, are two key ways to achieve this kind of clarity.

MARGINS

Margins are the headroom, the space for error and growth, that is available to be used above the planned amount. You expect to finish by June 1, but you have four weeks of schedule margin in case of problems; it'll still be fine if the project is complete by July 1. You give yourself extra time in your schedule for unknowns, and if your funding group will allow it, extra money in your budget as well. On NASA space missions, we build in margin to our mass (how much weight the rocket will launch and the thrusters will push) to our propellant budget, even to the schedule of electrical connectors between parts of the spacecraft.

In NASA's *Systems Engineering Handbook* Revision 2, *margin* is defined as "the allowances carried in budget, projected schedules, and technical performance parameters (e.g., weight, power, or memory) to account for uncertainties and risks. Margins are allocated in the formulation process based on assessments of risks and are typically consumed as the program/project proceeds through the life cycle." In other words, unexpected issues arise and need to be dealt with. And sometimes that means things like the cost, mass, or power requirements will increase. The set margin allows the project to accommodate increase in cost, mass, and time during the planning and building phases. In every space-flight project—indeed, in every complex project—the costs tend to go up over time from the first estimates at the beginning of formulation. And the mass goes up. And the power requirements. And . . . you name it. Seldom do any metrics go down.

After decades of experiencing this growth, the aerospace industry has created systems for anticipating where the budget, the mass, the power requirements, and all the other metrics will end up by the time a new system is built. We need to plan ahead for these changes and have the resources to accommodate them from the beginning. The way we do this is by setting margins, or growth reserves, into every metric we can.

Part of the issue is history. If what you are doing has been done many times, you can use that history to guide your own process. But if that history is different from your own project in any one of many possible ways, it will not actually be pertinent. And in any project that involves development of something new—whether a product, presentation, or analysis—more often than not the project's planned margins are not enough. Why are we bad at setting margins?

With new things, we don't know how long it will take to do the thing, and in fact, how long will depend upon the person doing it. Try it yourself. Estimate how long it will take you to do each thing on your list and then track the time. If we can't assess our own time requirements, how can we assess those of others? Humans are both overoptimistic and poor at estimating the impact of what we don't yet know.

Bent Flyvbjerg and Dan Gardner in their book *How Big Things Get Done: The Surprising Factors That Determine the Fate of Every Project* describe how they created a database of sixteen thousand megaprojects in over twenty fields and from 136 countries and found that 91.5 percent of the megaprojects were either over budget or behind schedule or both. At the top of the list for overruns are the Olympic Games.[1]

One of the reasons running the Olympic Games has the highest cost overruns of any category except nuclear waste storage is that every Olympics is different. New host, new city, some new sports, newly designed buildings. Flyvbjerg and Gardner call this "eternal beginner syndrome." There is no relevant history to use. It's the same with planetary exploration: Every spacecraft is a bespoke design for a new science target with new science to do. Anytime you hear "never been done before," alarm bells should go off. How many technology miracles can you afford? If it hasn't been done before, plan with extra care and give larger margins.

Defining, tracking, and managing margins is a powerful way to understand the progress of your project and for everyone on the team to understand where the project stands. These margins and the team's progress against them should be posted where everyone can access them, and they should be presented and discussed at team meetings. The Jet Propulsion Lab, NASA Goddard Space Flight Center, and the other big spacecraft builders have learned a lot from prior flight projects and teams. The lessons learned have been codified into principles and practices. JPL has the JPL Design Principles, for example, and Goddard has its Gold Rules. They are not all the same.

For Psyche, we keep a lot of margins. A lot. The big ones are cost (overall for the mission but broken down into every tiny subsystem), power (again in total but also broken into the power required by every subsystem to function), and mass—but there are so many more:

- Performance margins (for example, timing, throughput, storage size, latency, accuracy, and precision)
- Hardware margins (for example, switches: current capability, voltage level, protected or not, arm-and-disable circuitry, fused or nonfused)
- Science margins (for example, the cameras need to be able to take images at a higher resolution than we need to reach conclusions about our science hypotheses)
- Telecom system margins (for example, the link parameters to the Deep Space Network)

If anyone on the team sees a possible change needed that would affect cost, they follow a standard procedure so we can track and decide carefully on these issues. The team member brings the issue (for example, the need to replace a part that we planned for but is now no longer being made) to a committee on threats and liens, which meets every few weeks. We discuss the issue, the actions needed, and the likelihood and size of the impact. We accept it as a "threat" against our margin. And if the decision to spend the extra money is the right one, we make that decision and move the change to the official "lien" against the cost margin. Sometimes changes are in our favor and save money. But more often they are not.

I've been wondering: Why is the need for a 30 percent margin in the preliminary design phase so universal? Why do we all underestimate so

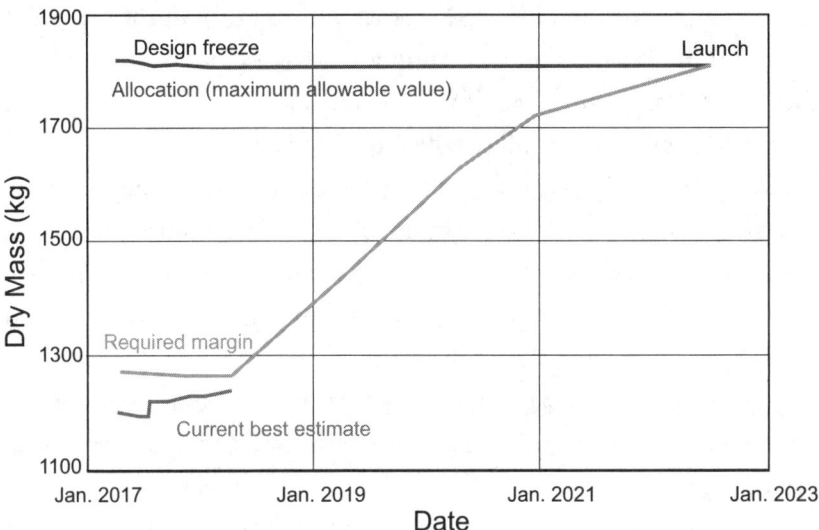

Starting in 2018 the Psyche mission tracked the total dry mass (mass without propellant) for the spacecraft. The required margin follows the guidelines agreed upon by the project: the current best estimate and the maximum expected value tracked month by month during the build of the spacecraft. As the plan matures, the possible needed margin decreases. (Note that this graph shows the original launch date, not the final launch on October 13, 2023.)

dramatically and, in a way, so predictably? In a discussion with a group of scientists and engineers, we wondered whether human evolution favored the optimistic risk-taker. Perhaps we are wired to be optimistic underestimators.

But a systems engineer offered another opinion. We can know only so much about a complex system in the beginning. We budget based on what we know. And as time goes by and we dig deeper and deeper into subsystems, writing requirements as we go, we learn about interactions among subsystems that we had not anticipated. He suggests that interactions among subsystems account for the margin. For example, as we dig into subsystems and learn about interactions, we might learn that some piece of hardware needs additional switches, a new card, a new cable, or a bigger model. There goes some of the cost and mass margin.

One day I was talking about this issue with Psyche's project manager. "Why can't we anticipate, when we are planning a project, more of the complexities and interactions that will come up in the future?" I asked. He said, "Think of the planning stage as a series of swimmers in their lanes in an Olympic pool. We have one subsystem in each lane, and they start out swimming all parallel, separated only by the floating lane markers, completely in contact with each other's work. At the end of the planning phase when we start to build, it's like the swimming pool opens out into the ocean, and the lanes splay out, and suddenly there is open water between the subsystems, unexplored topics and interactions and parts replacements and things that just didn't exist when we were planning. What you need is a team where every person is looking out over the lane markers, owning that wild area between topics, looking for ways to make it all work."

METRICS

The second tool is metrics. What measurements of progress should you be tracking to understand your project best? Which metrics are specific enough and which are too general to give good guidance? There's a tendency to measure what I might call vanity metrics: the metrics you want to show off in your marketing materials. There's a huge problem with these. First, the pressure to inflate them is even greater than with other metrics, and second, they often do not measure what really matters to the success of the team and project.

Ironically, some of the first metrics you should track are the margins themselves. The JPL Design Principles codify, from experience, which key metrics to identify, track, and report on and how much margin each should have as a function of the life cycle of the project. As in the Psyche mass-margin chart above, you need a lot of margin when you are just beginning, but when the thing is almost completed, there's not much more mass that could possibly be added, so the margin is small. There are dozens—hundreds—of books and articles in which you can read about KPIs (key performance indicators) and how to set and measure them.

Here, I want to share a story about metrics that shows how to think about your project holistically and identify where the vulnerable parts of your project might be.

On the Psyche team, we had a period of time when we were tracking the number of units of flight-software code that were completed and sent to the test bed for checking out. We watched as, week by week, code was passed for testing, but the number completed was never as high as the planned number. The team was never able to complete as much code as the plan called for. After a month went by, the team was falling behind by a similar number of uncompleted tasks every week, so the leadership couldn't say performance slip was simply due to someone being on vacation or because the tasks that week were particularly hard. The team leader had to take some action.

He replanned the whole project from where we were in the schedule out to the end. And the team immediately started falling behind again. Eventually, that team lead was replaced with a new team lead, who began to look into the problem. The team lead, once it was clear the team was regularly failing to hit their goals, needed to ask why. The problem was not the programmers, who were phenomenal, and it was not the scope of the project, which was reasonable. The problem was the metrics. We were tracking the wrong thing, or I should say, we needed to be tracking additional things in order to understand what was happening.

Despite our efforts to track the right metrics for software development, we discovered that we were missing a key part of the work. The team was testing the software in many necessary ways—another key metric and one we were tracking—but that metric did not then track the work the *same* team needed to do to fix the problems that emerged in testing. All the work fixing problems was unpredictable and, in some cases, took up so much time that the code production team and test team were brought to a standstill—and that specific work, fixing problems, was untracked in our metric system. To be useful, metrics need to be carefully planned: Is this measurement a true assessment of the work being done or of the outcome that's really wanted for the team? And then, the metric needs to be both highly specific and transparent to everyone.

For the software team on Psyche, the metrics were pretty depressing and disheartening; the team members all knew they were working as hard as they could and, despite all that work, were falling behind, week after week. Metrics, when made well and communicated clearly, motivate and bond a team rather than threaten it.

Think about what the needed outcomes are. Not just when will the project be done, but what can we measure from each key step in the process so that we can identify bottlenecks and issues. For the software project, we certainly needed it done by a given date. But more, we needed to track all the steps of its cycle: How much code is being written? How is it being tested? How long does the testing take? What is the error rate? How long does fixing errors take? And, most critically of all for us, how much of this can be parallelized by having teams working simultaneously instead of sequentially?

We had made the mistake of not including the whole team in planning how to measure their progress. If the team takes part in creating the metric (transparent communication, delegation, respect), then the metric can help the team perform better (recognize problems, take action, and develop quality). The team could have reasoned through the process together and identified what steps needed to be measured and monitored.

THE SPECIAL CHALLENGES OF MEGAPROJECTS

Megaprojects—temporary projects that have a budget over $1 billion, last more than a year, are often governed by committee, and have multiple stakeholders, changing requirements, multiple new technology developments, and large virtual teams, or some combination of these— have special challenges in setting margins, tracking metrics, and also in maintaining positive morale, motivation, and culture. Examples of megaprojects include skyscrapers, dams, nuclear reactors, Hollywood superproductions, and space probes like Psyche. Compared to smaller projects, margins in megaprojects are even more important, and more often wrong. Humans are bad enough at predicting the future for smaller projects, but for these big ones, particularly without exactly similar projects to compare to, it's even harder.

In megaprojects, the margins need to be increased proportionately with the number of new inventions needed for success. Sometimes in spaceflight these are called technology miracles. For example, let's plan a mission to pick up rock samples on Mars and bring them back to Earth. Rocket sends spacecraft into space: check. Spacecraft arrives at Mars and executes the famous seven minutes of terror as it enters the atmosphere, and then the Skycrane fires its retro-rockets and comes to hover over the Martian surface, lowering the rover on cables: check. Sound crazy? Yeah, but so far, so good, because *we have done all this before*, and we know how it goes.

Now the rover drives autonomously over the surface to the rocks we want back on Earth for analysis—we want to see if there are any signs of microbial life on Mars, and we need the samples to do that. Uh-oh. We don't have a technology to pick up the samples from all their various locations and attitudes and depths buried in the dust. In our planning document, here a miracle needs to occur, and we invent a reliable, affordable way to pick up samples on Mars. This is new, and it will be expensive.

These novel technologies—unknowns—have the biggest potential cost increases and schedule demands. Therefore, deciding when to release schedule or cost margins and when to hold those parts of the project strictly to their original plans is critical. A standard process in flight missions is the Technical, Schedule, and Cost Board (TSC Board). If anyone on the team needs to request more money than their budget allows or more time, then they need to write up a case on why they need it and what will happen without it, and they need to work this out with their subteam and then present it to the TSC Board for consideration.

The presentation and questioning are transparent to the team, impersonal, and completely documented.

Bringing together decades of his research and experience, Edward Merrow, founder and executive chairman of Independent Project Analysis, published a comprehensive book including analysis of over three hundred industrial megaprojects. He showed that according to the normal project criteria of cost, schedule, and quality, most would be considered failures on the basis of cost and schedule overruns.[2] Another study of transportation projects, largely roads, which one might think we know how to budget for, showed they were over budget on average from around 20–45 percent.[3] A third study of over two hundred large dams built in sixty-five countries found three out of four were over budget: On average, costs were 95 percent above budget, with no significant difference between regions. Even more telling, these dams were built between 1934 and 2007, and there was no improvement of budgeting over that period of time![4]

In a wonderful review article on this topic by Giorgio Locatelli at the University of Leeds, the author states that there are two schools of thought about cost overruns of megaprojects: (1) "evolution theorists," who believe that overruns are caused by scope changes in the project, and (2) "psycho strategists," who combine psychological contributors such as deception, planning fallacy, and unjustifiable optimism with business strategy to explain overruns.[5]

These categories can be written out in more detail. Flyvbjerg and Gardner conclude that there are four categories of reasons for cost overruns in megaprojects:

1. Technical drivers for cost increases include vendor price increases, bad project design that requires rework, and, especially, scope changes. Requiring more of the project after the planning stage is over is a classic way to increase cost.

2. Psychological drivers of cost increases include overoptimism about completion speed and an unwillingness to accept risk.

3. Deliberate underestimation of costs by vendors to increase the likelihood of selling their product to the project and by politicians to look better to their constituencies.

4. Poor financing and contract management can also drive cost up by awarding subcontracts to the lowest-priced option, often a group unable to handle the challenges coming up.

Edward Merrow, the megaproject expert from Independent Project Analysis, cuts to the chase and says the number one reason for cost overruns is greed. People bid too low just so they can win. Project planners cut corners and create plans with incomplete or wrong details and unrealistic cost estimation, but by the time those come to pass, the planner is long gone onto other projects. The politician who gets the project underway with rosy anticipation is on to higher office elsewhere by the time the project falls apart.

What, statistically, does it mean to be over budget? Flyvbjerg and Gardner found that on average, building projects are 62 percent over budget. That means that a large number of projects are much more than 62 percent over budget. In fact, they found that the distribution of final costs was not a beautiful bell curve, but that the high end of costs was "fat-tailed," that is, that an inordinate number of projects came in way, way above the average overrun. For building projects, 39 percent of projects costed in at higher than the average overrun, and of this 39 percent, the *average* overage above the mean was 206 percent. That means that costs doubled and that a large number of projects were even above that value.

For aerospace projects, the average overrun is 60 percent; 42 percent of projects were above the average overrun, and their own average overrun was 119 percent. IT projects average a 73 percent overrun, with

28 percent of projects being above the average overrun, and their own average overrun of 447 percent was more than four times the original estimated cost.

One of the key ways costs get distorted is by what Flyvbjerg and Gardner call *strategic misrepresentation*, the deliberate misstatement or distortion of information for strategic purposes. This is a common issue in deep-space projects, where subcontractors need to keep selling their expensive, specialized subsystems to stay in business. Strategically, they need to win the contract to keep building at all, since these subsystems are generally not production line items. Every contract really counts. The system dictates that the proposer write the most convincing proposal possible and then work out the higher cost and change orders and longer schedule later. First, you just need to win.

Then we need optimism to attempt these big projects, and optimism can work against the needed realism in our budgets and schedules. A great example came when the Psyche team hit a snag with a software system. We knew we needed to replan the work ahead to add in some more software capabilities, and we needed it done by a certain date. We all gathered in a conference room to hear how the replanning was going.

"We figured out we can parallelize all these activities," said our software lead, Brian, pointing at a schedule he was projecting onto a screen, "but there's little margin. It's a very success-oriented schedule." Success oriented. This is how we describe a schedule that will work if, well, if everything works. It's possible it'll end up all fine, but if anything goes wrong, we may be in trouble.

Ian Newby-Clark, a professor of psychology at Guelph University, has studied people's tendency to be optimistic while making schedules. He and his research group found that people consistently rate pessimistic scenarios as less plausible than optimistic scenarios. When people are asked for the most likely scenario, they consistently settle on the same scenario they had previously described as the best-case scenario: They are success oriented by nature.

Is there a solution? Maybe. Newby-Clark also found that people *did* take pessimistic scenarios into account when predicting someone else's completion times.[6] Right there is a great reason to have a review board.

THE STRENGTH OF THE PEOPLE MAKE
THE STRENGTH OF THE PROJECT

Why, then, does a discussion of cost overruns on megaprojects belong in a team's book? Because of the outsize stress and fractures in a team that cost overruns, schedule overruns, and quality failures cause and because a high-functioning team can overcome these issues and reach success.

Throughout this book we've been talking about the importance of one-on-one relationships and communication in the present day for future project progress and outcomes. David Whitmore, the head of energy for Pcubed in London, and a team of three faculty members from project management and construction units at universities studied the landscape of cost overruns and concluded that the fundamental error was people using tools and mind-sets from one hundred years ago.[7] Surprise: It's the people!

For current projects that will be completed in the relatively near future, the standard metrics are cost, schedule, and quality, and the products themselves as agreed upon. But what if the eventual recipients of a project's outcomes are several generations of workforce turnover in the future? Will the third person in the leadership of the customer's organization or, for that matter, the third project manager of the project itself agree with the decisions and actions of the earlier people? How can we keep everyone on the same page over a long span of time?

The variety of stakeholders in a project increases this complexity, since each will likely turn over during the course of a long project. In the case of the Psyche mission, some subcontractors might value the project for its ability to create follow-on space exploration projects. The scientists

225

involved want not just new knowledge on behalf of humanity but also spectacular new results that will be published under their own and their students' names, to the enduring glory of their careers. NASA wants to meet the cost, schedule, and quality metrics, along with the strictly negotiated success criteria of the mission so that Congress smiles upon them. NASA also wants photogenic and mind-expanding discoveries to keep the American people enthralled.

Here's a small checklist of considerations for your team, if you are a leader within a megaproject:

- A normal project might consist of a planning phase followed by work and a sprint to the finish. A megaproject, in comparison, consists of many marathons, and the win at the end of each marathon is the opportunity to run another marathon. Contain stress, make sure people take vacations, pace yourselves.
- Say you are a team, even a family, and mean it. Stay in touch, invite people back, honor them.
- Consider many restarts of the team culture and process, with workshops and norm setting, each time the nature of the project changes.
- Think about the swim-lane metaphor and make sure your subteams aren't too isolated from each other.
- Involve the team in solving challenges, setting metrics, and tracking margins. Give the team the respect of knowing they can make this happen.

Margins and metrics sound so dull, but they are really the purified essence of the whole complex job you are doing. They are the indicators and the magnifiers that let you and your team know whether you are making it or not. With those indicators in hand, it's time to get much better at rewarding the team for their successes.

14

DEVELOP BETTER WAYS
TO ASSESS AND REWARD
YOUR TEAM

When we realized that we were not going to make the Psyche mission's initial launch date, the entire team was affected. During the hardest part of our launch slip, we worried a lot about how much stress the team was feeling, how loud the negative voices of a few unhappy team members and a few people outside the team were, and whether people were willing to keep pushing for another year. We worked with a social scientist to create a survey, which we sent out three times over that year, to see if our efforts at team culture and communication improvement were working. We called the survey effort the Psyche Weather Report.

Up front in the survey, we asked enough demographic data to know which part of the team the person was on and whether they were new to flight projects. Because there were about 250 people at JPL being surveyed (we did not survey partner organizations) and because I solely handled the data, the team members were fairly well assured of anonymity.

Then, we asked team members to rank ten statements on what is called a Likert scale, a subjective scale with five intervals from strongly disagree to strongly agree. The ten statements were listed in random order in the survey, but they fell into four categories of inquiry: vertical communications in the team, horizontal communications across the team, team leadership strengths, and belonging and appreciation:

PSYCHE WEATHER REPORT

Communications vertically

My team leader listens to my thoughts and concerns.

My team leader accurately communicates my thoughts and concerns outward.

My team leader is responsive to the issues that I raise.

Communications horizontally

I have strong working relationships with my counterparts on other parts of the Psyche team.

Psyche team members from other parts of the team communicate well with me.

Team leadership strengths

My immediate team has sufficient experience to know we can achieve the work at hand.

My team leader organizes schedules and work plans reasonably.

Belonging and appreciation

I know my work is valued by the project and my coworkers.

I feel a sense of belonging to the Psyche community.

I feel like all members of Psyche are on the same team.

Over the three surveys, we saw the ratings improve, and we also saw how certain parts of the team were less happy and more resistant to improvement than others. I'll share some strategies to help teams recover and improve.

Not every leader can survey their team as often as we did on Psyche, so how do you know how your team is feeling? Relying on the comments from your closest colleagues is not an accurate measure. But if there are deep concerns—issues that team members are sharing and asking their colleagues about so that they have become clearly articulated and are clearly in need of fixing—you need to know. These concerns may threaten both individual and group success.

At the same time as you strive to hear the concerns—and the joys—of all parts of your team, leaders can start by assessing the clearest rewards: You can analyze and repair broken salary structures—that is, those that are based not on merit but on the loudest voices, on friendships, and on implicit bias. In many industries, these drivers for salary are so common that you could consider it the standard, unfortunately.

Your goal as a leader, then, is to assess the state of your team and find ways to reward them. Though I just mentioned salaries, we know that most people seek, first and foremost, respect and autonomy and a sense of mission in their work. That's your key task, articulating that and providing the respect and autonomy to the extent that makes sense.

All of this requires that you judge people on their merits and make sure that no matter how quiet and unself-promoting they may be, their accomplishments and contributions are judged objectively and rewarded accordingly.

LEADERS, LEADERS IN TRAINING, AND NOT LEADERS: REWARD THEM ALL

Julia came to us one morning at work and let us know that she was putting in her notice. She had another position waiting and was giving us two weeks' warning of her departure. I was surprised and saddened: I had thought the job was going really well for her, and she seemed fairly happy.

Later in the day, when the two of us were alone, I had a chance to talk to her more. Was there anything about the job that was not working for her, anything I could learn from and improve with? She said no: The education work she was doing for us was exactly what she was most interested in, and the work challenged her and changed all the time and was never boring. "But," she added, "as much as I do love this job, I have a son at home with special needs, and every day there is a new challenge and a new problem to solve to help him thrive better. And so, I've found," she continued, "that I do not also want to have a new challenge and a new problem, and especially I do not want a new surprise, every day at work. As much as I enjoy this job and this team, I need a job that's going to be easier and more repetitive, since I get enough challenges and surprises at home."

This was not the first time that I found someone who did not want what I wanted in a job: something that is giving me continuous growth, challenge, and advancement, something that surprises me and gives me new questions to answer. I used to think that everyone wanted that and that I could support the people I worked with in not having to put up with repetitive jobs. Carter was the first to show me that what I assumed was a fundamental human wish and human right was not so fundamental. He had an assistant job position that consisted mainly of scheduling. As I do with most everyone who works with me, I asked him what his aspirations and wishes were for the job. Would he like, for example, for us to develop some projects that he could add to his scheduling, to stretch his skill set and give him other things to think about? No, he replied, after some thought. He didn't want more challenge. He wanted to be great at scheduling and call it a day. As hard as that was for me to accept, his continuing happiness in the job showed me he certainly knew his mind. And I found other ways to reward him.

Both Julia and Carter were quite good at their jobs—smart, pleasant, and communicative team members. But they were not leaders and innovators. I think of them as steady producers. Often steady producers don't want to participate in brainstorming or strategy exercises; they see these exercises as destabilizing, as challenges at which they might fail. That's another place where I stumbled as I learned: I kept trying to get a happy team of steady producers to participate in deciding the future direction of the team, thinking that everyone would naturally want to join in, add their ideas, and think about change. What fun! But no, change can be frightening, and perhaps not having great ideas can feel like failure.

Think about what you need in your team, what mix of leaders, innovators, and steady producers. Watch out for steady producers who get into leadership positions. They can keep a team functioning beautifully as long as their leadership position does not require them to innovate, create change, or compete. If you need those things, you might need to discover whether your steady-producer leader wants to have training and develop, or whether a sideways move into a less demanding position might be in order.

On the other hand, you might end up with a team that's all thinkers and leaders and innovators! In my world, that's a kind of ideal as long as the culture can be kept collaborative.

POWER OF REWARDS VERSUS PUNISHMENTS

Positive reinforcement is so much more powerful in changing behavior and gaining commitment for a team than is punishment. What is the behavior, and what are the outcomes you want most from your personnel? Communicate them clearly and reward them regularly.

A Gallup survey found that 67 percent of people whose leaders focused on their strengths were fully engaged in their work, while only 31 percent of those with leaders who focused on their weaknesses were fully engaged with their work. This outcome aligns with the striking work of Karen Pryor, a behavioral psychologist and marine mammal biologist, as described in her book *Don't Shoot the Dog*. Any sentient being can be trained to do anything, using purely positive rewards.

Sometimes the creature—or human—doesn't even consciously know they are being trained. (See the season 3, episode 3 of *Big Bang Theory*, "The Gothowitz Deviation," in which Sheldon trains Penny using chocolates!)

Sometimes, of course, it's necessary to focus on a problem or a weakness. You can decouple your affect—that is, the body language, expressions, and tone you use to deliver the criticism—from the criticism itself. Of course, you want the criticism to help the person learn and grow, and you can use that good intention in your affect. Nod, smile, and lean forward while you talk. People feel better about negative feedback delivered that way, and they may take it in more completely and act on it more thoroughly.

When your feedback needs to address behavior, follow the feedback loop established by management and leadership experts Marshall Goldsmith and Mark Reiter. Start with *evidence* of the misbehavior and explain the *relevance* of it. Is the person's behavior affecting their own effectiveness in their work? Is it markedly different from that of others in similar positions? Is it breaking the team or driving people away? Then provide *consequences*. Goldsmith and Reiter cite evidence that shows people will only change if change can be shown to be strongly to their own advantage and that people respond more strongly to potential losses than gains, so decide what the person will lose if they don't change.

Next, develop an action plan with the person. The plan should explain what needs to change and offer specific, detailed, trackable actions the person will take. The person needs to discover what triggers cause them to respond with the unwanted behavior. Then, they must go to the people who have endured the misbehavior and apologize to them (not explain or qualify the behavior, just apologize), and then ask for the teammates' help in improving. Finally, the person needs to check in with the teammates on their progress, perhaps every month for six months or a year. That way no one forgets that the person is trying to change.[1]

SOMETIMES EXCELLENCE IS PUNISHED

What happens when someone on your team is reliably excellent? How do you reward a person who identifies important problems and consistently collaborates effectively with others to solve them, while supporting others and helping them learn?

Lindsay McGregor and Neel Doshi, from the company Vega Factor, point out that people like your high achiever are usually rewarded with more and more stressful goals and demanding meetings, while receiving very little mentorship.[2] Not much of a reward, when you think about it, for being great at their job!

Here is your homework: Think about the best people on your teams and see how you can give them an appropriate set of goals, the minimum possible meetings, and more of your time and attention.

DIVERSE TEAMS PRODUCE BETTER OUTCOMES

Teams with a range of unique perspectives, experiences, and backgrounds produce greater innovation, provide a far greater range of possible solutions, and identify problems that go unnoticed by a more uniform team. Think about the sections on task conflict in Chapter 7: When team members bring forth more and different ideas, the team can come up with better solutions. Sameness of opinion and a lack of choices in decisions are symptoms of groupthink (or a situation where the people with other ideas don't share them, perhaps because of a lack of psychological safety).

One example of the positive effects of a diverse team was shown by business professors Cristian Deszö of the University of Maryland and David Ross of Columbia University. They studied the top firms in Standard & Poor's Composite 1500 list, looking at the financial performance and the size and gender composition of the management teams of these companies from 1992 to 2006. They found that, on average, "female representation in top management leads to an increase of $42 million in firm value."[3]

Other studies have linked both gender and racial diversity in leadership positions to increased innovation and better financial performance. One such global study, by the Credit Suisse Research Institute, examined over two thousand companies from 2005 to 2011, looking for a relationship between gender diversity on corporate management boards and financial performance. Companies with one or more women on the board delivered higher average returns on equity, lower net debt to equity, and better average growth. Though the positive causality of diversity on organizational outcomes is not completely understood, part of the reason may be a diversity in opinions brought to the table to solve problems.

Katherine Phillips, who was an American business theorist and the Reuben Mark Professor of Organizational Character at Columbia University's Business School, and colleagues Margaret Neale of Stanford University and Gregory Northcraft of the University of Illinois at Urbana-Champaign researched the impact of racial diversity on small decision-making groups. The research team assembled three-person groups of undergraduates at the University of Illinois. Some groups consisted of all white students, and some with two white and one non-white member.

The student teams then performed a murder-mystery exercise. Some information was shared among all the group members, and then each member also had important clues that only they knew. To find out who committed the murder, the group members had to share all the information they collectively possessed during discussion. The groups with racial diversity significantly outperformed the groups with no racial diversity. The all-white groups converged on a solution too quickly, without fully examining all the options. Being with similar others leads us to think we all hold the same information and share the same perspective. This perspective, which stopped the all-white groups from effectively processing the information, is what hinders creativity and innovation.[4]

Other studies have shown that listeners in a group of similar people (all white, for example) perceive the information coming from someone not in the group as more novel and innovative. The same results have been found in other groups perceiving themselves as different, for example, Republicans and Democrats.[5] These studies show that hearing an idea from someone we perceive as different inspires more thought than when we hear it from someone we think of as like us.

Simply having participants in your team whom you perceive as different from yourself will cause you, and everyone else in the team, to be more cognitively active and therefore produce a broader range of ideas and options. Members of diverse teams realize that there are likely to be diverse viewpoints on the team and that more work is going to be needed to reach consensus, and so everyone thinks more deeply and carefully. This is true for all types of diversity, including inherent diversity, such as age or place of birth, and acquired diversity, such as expertise or education.

Diversity at all levels is critical. Diversity in leadership, perhaps unsurprisingly, leads to preserving diversity on the team and therefore increasing opportunities for growth into leadership for team members. Without diverse leadership, reports Sylvia Ann Hewlett and her colleagues from the Center for Talent Innovation, women are 20 percent less likely than straight white men to win endorsement for their ideas, and people of color are 24 percent less likely.[6] That is why you, as a leader, need to represent the team in every way, sharing the culture and sharing the diversity.

Traditional Diversity Efforts Sometimes Do More Harm Than Good

A fundamental belief of mine when it comes to building diverse teams is do not divide in order to unite. For example, on the Psyche team we invited everyone to our team meetings, rather than breaking up the team meetings into science team meetings and engineering team meetings.

Does that seem normal? It's not, actually, the standard practice in space missions. Most have regular meetings for the science team only (this is so common that people reflexively call team meetings science team meetings). The engineering team meets only as required to do the job, and the business office, communications, outreach, scheduling, and other functions don't have group meetings at all.

My goal on the Psyche team, however, was to enable every person to speak with and understand every other person and to make dyad connections across all the subcontractors so that when problems arise the team will be maximally prepared to address them. Thus, we had All-Team Meetings, and everyone was invited. Everyone got the same information, and everyone who presented attempted to explain at a level that people in other fields could understand. We even mixed up the agenda, so talks from different disciplines followed each other rather than being in discipline-specific blocks of time.

Inviting everyone to participate signals that everyone is valued and that every job is valued. We want each person to know they are important and to feel respected and take pride in their work. We are all dedicated to having each person be able to rise on their merits. This is a strong Western value and true in many parts of the rest of the world.

Though deeply well-intentioned, some targeted programs to improve diversity and inclusion have, unfortunately, been shown to have unintended consequences. Even to use the words *diversity initiative* is to risk creating an immediate political uproar. For some years there was intense pressure to create these initiatives, and then an intense pressure to dismantle them. Maybe neither of those pressures was right. Both were certainly extreme.

Diversity initiatives affect how people detect discrimination and how people perceive the fairness or lack of it in their organization. Brenda Major, a distinguished professor emerita in the Department of Psychological and Brain Sciences at the University of California, Santa Barbara, has for many years studied diversity initiatives and collated the work of others on the topic. She discusses how the intended message of diversity initiatives is one of fairness: The organization is attempting to express that "this is a fair organization in which people will be treated fairly, without bias, prejudice, or discrimination." But the unintended message that reaches overrepresented groups is that they will be treated unfairly. A further unintended consequence is creating the message that underrepresented groups need help to succeed and are less capable and less qualified. This can lead the underrepresented group members to doubt their own competence, feel that positive outcomes are unearned, and believe that everyone in that underrepresented group is viewed as the same.

I experienced this on the lovely occasion of being elected to the American National Academy of Sciences, a high honor and one I had not anticipated getting. In a way that surprised me, I felt more of a scientist then than I had ever before. Soon after, I went out to dinner with a friend, another woman who was also elected to the academy that year. She said, "You know, you were only elected because you are a woman. You'd never get in otherwise." And she added, "It's true for me, too, and for most every woman." She had internalized the idea that women's science would never be valued as highly as men's, simply because of our gender and not related to what we did and discovered.

I had an overwhelming emotional response: rage. I felt as if her words erased all I had worked on. I remember replying, "If that is true, I'd rather quit everything and walk out today and never do another moment of science. I absolutely reject that." I think, somewhere in my deepest heart, I have never forgiven her for internalizing the idea that women in science can never be as valued as men and for pouring her idea all over me too.

Here's a case where talking about it is doing more harm than good—more harm than good in individual organizations and politically. Don't talk about it; just do it. Treat everyone the same, judge people on their objective contributions, and listen respectfully to everyone. Create opportunity by empowering everyone, rather than by disempowering any individuals or groups. To work together in a team and produce great work, we need to respect each other, listen to each other, receive training as needed, and be rewarded based on what we produce—all this no matter what we look like, where we came from, or what our accent is. Every team needs unique perspectives and to promote trust, respect, and dignity for everyone.

Anne Dagg, a Canadian zoologist, traveled alone in South Africa during the 1950s to become one of the very first scientists to study wild giraffes. As shown in the documentary film *The Woman Who Loves Giraffes*, an interviewer asked her once, "That was something unusual, being there as a woman. Did you think about that?"

"Well, no," replied Dagg, "because I just thought of myself as a person."

Bias Can Prevent Us from Judging People on Their Merits

That's it: Let's just be people together, as Dagg said. Here's the problem. Our implicit bias, unconscious bias, stands like a screen between ourselves and every other person, causing us to judge them and their output unfairly. To create and maintain teams where every unique person is respected and heard and can rise on their merits, we need to remove implicit bias and judge everyone's contributions objectively. There's your challenge: Remove as much implicit bias in your team as possible and find the best ways to assess performance objectively.

Jessica Nordell, who wrote the book *The End of Bias: A Beginning*, wanted to understand the cumulative career-long effects of bias on a person's career. Many studies have shown persistent and pervasive bias in specific situations (women receive less effusive letters of reference than men for the same work, women are offered lower initial salaries than men when coming into the same job with the same qualifications, and so on), but there was little clear data on the cumulative effects of these myriad moments of bias over a career. Nordell teamed up with two researchers from the University of Buffalo, Yuhao Du and Kenneth Joseph, to create a computer model to show career-long effects of bias.

In their imaginary organization, NormCorp, employees do projects alone or in pairs. The projects can succeed or fail, and the employees receive scores for their performance. Twice a year, the employees are assessed for promotion, and the top two employees are promoted. The model penalizes women by a small amount, for example, 5 percent, compared to men, to approximate the many small biases in the real world. When women do a project by themselves, they are scored a little lower than men doing projects alone. When women do projects with men, men receive a little more credit, and so forth. These cumulative deficits in scoring due to gender bias mean that the women have to do more successful projects than men do to be promoted.

There are eight levels of promotion, and women and men are evenly split at 50 percent each at Level 1, the starting level. With a 5 percent devaluation of women's work, only half as many women as men have been promoted to Level 7, and at Level 8, the C-suite, there are only 2 percent women. With just a 5 percent deficit in valuation—an A instead of an A+ for the same work a man does—promotions are continually eroded until, with no difference in the actual quality of the work or qualification of the person, 98 percent of executives are men and only 2 percent women.[7]

This math model example allows us to ignore the everyday mechanics of bias, which are complicated indeed. And of course, the model is equally valid for any target of bias: Here I talk about men and women, but the model works for bias against skin color, disability, regional accent, or immigration status.

Overcoming Unconscious Bias About Who Is Valuable
If your team listens to and respects every member, then you have taken a big step toward minimizing the surprisingly damaging effects of unconscious bias. Examples of these unconscious biases include a pervasive sense that women's work is not as good as men's, or Black people's work is not as good as white people's.

My friend Kate led the team building the power system for a big Earth-orbiting communications satellite. The whole project was behind schedule, and the usual steps were being taken: meetings with the customer, cost-saving efforts, rebudgeting, negotiations for additional payment, experts brought in to assess where the problems were. The software team was behind, but they were making progress against their metrics. The thermal team had some problems with their models, which were showing some parts of the spacecraft getting colder than allowable limits. Kate's team was struggling with a slow-delivering solar panel provider. When the expert reviewers came through, they criticized Kate's management of the subcontractor particularly harshly. And after launch, when bonuses were awarded, the leads of the other subsystems, all men, received more than Kate did, and Kate got a lateral job move rather than an advancement.

Was Kate the victim of gender bias, either explicit or implicit? Understanding the role of gender bias in individual cases can be really difficult. It's not always possible to compare one person's achievements to another person's, nor one person's shortcomings to another's. Understanding, however, how deeply and completely bias affects the whole trajectory of a person's career from a statistical point of view motivates me, at least, to work even harder to allow people to rise on their merits and to work to eliminate bias from our system.

When a team's culture is positive, it allows individuals to rise on their merits, enabling equity and diversity. But if the team's culture is not positive, then your team is not likely to stay diverse. As we learned in Chapter 7, if a person feels as if they don't have a peer support group on the team (and sociologists say it takes about 30 percent of the team to be like you before you stop feeling alone), then they are likely to cut their losses and leave in the face of harassment, thinking they will have a better chance of success elsewhere. Start by talking about bullying and harassment, and then stop such behaviors as they begin rather than waiting until they become severe.

A positive team culture is critical from an ethical and legal point of view, as well as for maximizing financial success and improving the fundamental pleasure and success of each person's work life. Team culture is at the heart of everything that makes a team work.

HIRING ON MERIT AND MERIT ALONE

Don't we always hire on merit? Don't we try to find the most qualified person with the best fit for the team? Absolutely we do. But as with all human activities, our emotions and unconscious ideas and biases can overwhelm the process and make us feel great about picking the wrong person.

When I was being considered for my first big management job, I asked my uncle, who had a lifetime of experience in hiring, management, and entrepreneurship, what I should be thinking about and how I should be preparing for my first big interview.[8] This interview consisted of me and a search committee of five or six, meeting at a big national conference in San Francisco so the committee could schedule the maximum number of candidates.

My uncle said to me that people like to hire people who remind them of themselves. He told me that it's usually unconscious but that I could use it to my advantage. He advised me to research every person on the committee and learn as much as I could about them and then bring up common experiences, such as schools and the like. This was a revelation to me: The interview would be as much about them as about me. Of course, I thought, everyone is bored if the whole conversation is about the other person! I did those things, and I also investigated the public information about the budget and finances and asked questions. I don't know if that's what got me the job in the end, but I surely did learn that people like to hire people who remind them of themselves.

So great intel *if you have something in common with the interviewers.* What if you didn't go to their schools and grew up in a different part of the world and with a different culture? What if you don't dress according to their practices? Well, frankly, you would be at a disadvantage. And it wouldn't be at all fair because where you went to school and how you dress are not strong indicators of how you could contribute to the organization.

How do we make this fairer? If you are going for interviews, you can try this game. You can pay attention to how you dress and how you shake hands and how you laugh, and you can investigate your interviewers and look for commonality. But please, only do this to the extent that you are still being true to yourself. And if you are hiring, or if you are in a group that is hiring, you can think about how the process is done and whether the relevant aspects of the candidates are really being judged.

Hence, the need for hiring rubrics to make sure people get a chance based on their merits rather than the bias of the interviewers and file readers. Write careful interview questions and use the same questions for every person you interview. Write a rubric on which to score interviewees that matches the requirements of the job as laid out in the ad. Listen to yourself when you discuss the applicants: Make sure your responses to their answers are not affected by their appearance or accent.

And once they are hired, assess their work objectively and in the same way you assess everyone else's work. Don't give them a pass on something questionable just because you like them. And reward them exactly as you would reward anyone else who did the same.

Building a Reward System

Now that we've worked through the pitfalls of bias and really made an effort to put in place ways to assess people on their merits, it's time to reward them. Joris Lammers, a professor of political psychology at the University of Cologne, and his colleagues have studied why people strive for power. They discovered that often the motivation was to have autonomy, the power to make decisions for themselves, as opposed to the power to make decisions over other people.[9]

Many studies over the years have shown that people try to move up in organizations not primarily for pay or better titles but to better control their own experience. Here are some key aspects of autonomy that can be worked into your reward system:

- Flexibility of where and when to work, as long as the outcomes are achieved.
- Both responsibility for and authority over their work products, outcomes, and goals.
- Respect in its many forms: Ask for their opinion, let them present their own work, call them out publicly for what they have done.

Work on putting vision and purpose into the work. Articulate why what you and the team do matters and what each person's key part in it is. We all care that our work means something.

McKinsey consultants Aaron De Smet, Arne Gast, Drew Goldstein, and Richard Steele, whom we met earlier in the book, have created a long-running metric called the Organizational Health Index. They say the newly intense need of most organizations now, post-COVID, is a shared purpose. They recommend discussing the *why* of your work to create a common purpose that connects team members to the project. They report that organizations that emphasize common purpose are 2.4 times more likely to effectively set a clear direction and 4.1 times more likely to be healthy than those that do not emphasize purpose.

And then, add in salary and benefits. We often think of this reward first, but people hard at work often think of autonomy, respect, and purpose before they think of money.

Social Events and Their Perils for Teams

We know it's important to celebrate the team and its successes. I was surprised, and then completely understanding, when I learned that some common ways to celebrate—for example, happy hours together—can be alienating for some people and thus have the opposite effect intended. People who feel marginalized at work often feel entirely at sea in a social arena with the team, where familiar structure is gone. At work, each of us knows, more or less, our place in the social structure, how to communicate, and what is expected of us. In a social setting, all those helpful rules can disappear.

Follow these rules in your team social events:

- Err toward the "professional" side of the professional-personal spectrum.
- Have events where mixed breakout groups address work-related challenges and the norm is everyone speaks. This will bond people more safely than a happy hour, and it'll be useful in practical ways as well.
- Try giving the team a dilemma to solve.
- Set up the event around a game everyone knows (but make sure everyone does!).
- Spend a little extra time with the quiet people.

A NOTE ON SALARIES

Whether we are new on the job or we've been there a while, we'd like to know if we're getting what our peers are getting.[10] We're particularly curious if we are women or in another underrepresented group because we know that nationally women and minorities are underpaid for the same work compared to white men. Inequities desperately erode any sense of being valued or having a future in the organization.

To make progress toward salary equity, every one of us with the power to do so needs to analyze the salaries in our organization, look for signs of bias, and find ways to make progress toward equality.

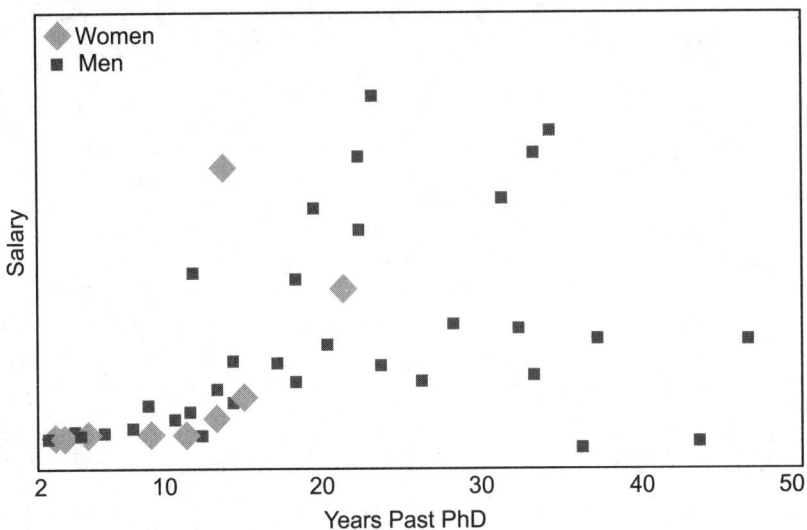

Here are salaries for a typical university department's cohort of professors. (This is data I made up; it is not real data for any organization.) Your organization might use a different discriminator than "years past PhD," and you might have different kinds of issues that push salaries up or down than those I discuss here. But this analysis might form the basis for the one that is right for your organization, and this is a conversation you can start.

One of the first things we see in the data is that all the faculty over twenty years past their PhDs are men. In this dataset, only one or two full professors are women. Think of the ramifications: It is impossible to reach gender equity on any committees that require seniority. There will only be the same one or two women on hiring committees. The same issue comes up for internal candidates for department chair.

Starting at the left-hand side of the graph, the new-faculty data looks like recent hiring practices have been good. Hires in the last few years have all been brought in at the same starting salary. At first glance the gender balance in junior faculty looks reasonable. Let's dig into the dataset a little more.

A few years out, to the right of the dashed line in the graph below, the salaries of women look like they are lagging behind the men's. Why

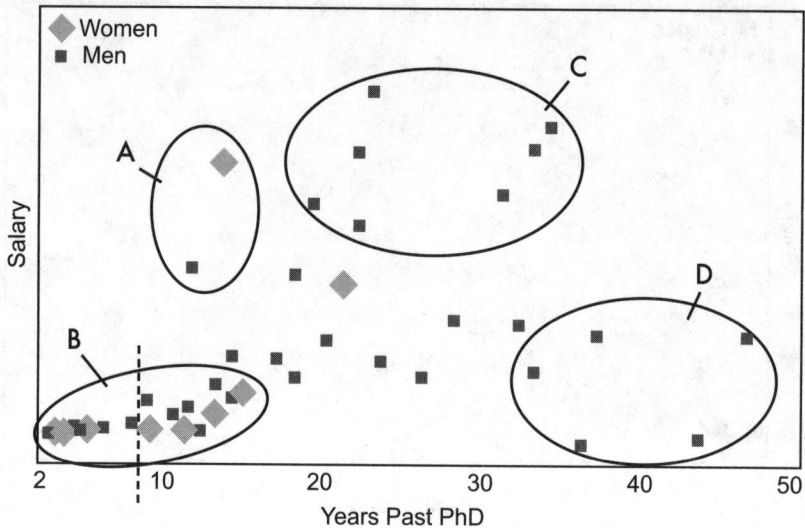

A: A couple of midcareer targeted hires put a new upper limit on the range of salaries. Need to think about how these evolve as years go by, and what they mean to people who do not move to other institutions and thus get large salary raises.

B: Recent hires are coming in at the same salary, which is good. Data looks different to the right of the dashed line. Is this the time of a promotion? Are women receiving lower raises? Only looking at the specifics of the data will answer.

C: These stars have either come in as targeted hires, or received generous retention packages to keep them at this institution, or—best of all—been rewarded generously for exceptional performance without having to threaten to leave.

D: Some rock-solid senior faculty missed the escalation of academic salaries, and never cashed in on retention offers. How can you help moderate the cumulative income deficit?

The groupings of faculty salaries are annotated with some of the possible reasons for salary movement shown. Understanding—and addressing, if necessary—the reasons for salary patterns in the newest hires and the highest-paid people is most important for fairness and morale.

would that be? Different hiring practices, faster promotions, better raises? Do these differences exist for a good reason, or are they the result of implicit or explicit bias? Only looking at the specifics of the data can tease out the reasons; though it's tempting to cry foul just by looking at this data, the organization would have to dig in to understand the pattern.

The biggest spread in salaries happens past the critical full professor promotion, typically fifteen years after PhD. Here we see a few people who have very high salaries (group C) and some others with very low salaries, in some cases lower than new hires of the last few years (group D). This is a common pattern in academia. This looks wildly unfair. What is happening?

In the words of a wise university president I know, academia often runs on the pirate model. Some faculty members receive outside offers and then retention packages to stay where they are, or they jump institutions in order to get better labs, better salaries, and better administrative support when they can't get those things from their own university.

All organizations should value and reward their faculty internally. People should be evaluated on the factors that the organization values and wants to reward. Thus, we should link excellence in any valued area to merit raises. Often, even this simple step is overlooked.

Showy research tends to grab the spotlight. The research superstar gets a big raise while the teaching stalwart does not. But is teaching truly less important? Absolutely never, I would argue. To be valued, though, an activity needs to be highlighted by the administration, and it needs to be measured. Teaching is seldom evaluated in a rigorous way. And similarly, research is sometimes valued in dollars, when its real value is in thought leadership and inspiration. Think back to the discussion about metrics: We need to measure what we want to achieve, and it's the same with people. Thus, the people with big reputations and the hubris to ask for big retention packages rise stratospherically in salary. The people who labor more at less valued activities, or who just don't think it's right to play the retention game, can end up unfairly at the bottom right of the dataset.

Once the data is analyzed, people who are deserving of significant raises will be found. Some people are being left behind because of implicit or explicit bias. In this dataset, the lowest-paid woman, at about twelve years after PhD, might be one of these. Is she actually less meritorious than her nearby peers? That's the question. For the people left behind in the pay game, only regular and, in some cases, exceptional raises will help remedy the gap.

A step in the right direction is a special fund for equity raises. Doing as much as you can, every year, for underpaid people makes a difference in lifetime earnings in the long run. And it makes an even bigger difference in morale. My mother used to say, "There's no such thing as fair." My work in salary equity tends to confirm that for me: so many complexities, so few solutions. But taking the steps you can *right now* is what we all need to do. Here are some actions you can pursue at your own institution:

- Ask your administration to do a salary analysis and look at gender and racial equity.
- Work on creating annual evaluations that use metrics and categories that are aligned with the real values of the institution and that are clearly communicated to everyone.
- Ask about a special account for equity raises.

Bring your most supportive, collaborative self to the table. Believe in your administration and help them live up to what they can be. Good luck, and keep up the effort.

Here is a summary of some of the ideas I've developed over time to help organizations gain diversity via a culture that is nonbullying and nonharassing.

- Do not divide in order to unite. Work on fairness and transparency together and for everyone. Keep your team as one whole team, and don't draw any unnecessary internal borders. Every border is a trigger to perceive status and treat the other side differently.
- Think of local solutions to systemic problems. If, for example, the members of a team with a bad manager fear retribution from that manager, have the director of the whole group write their recommendation or evaluation letters.

- Listening is necessary, but it is not a solution. Listen, and then both take action toward a solution and move on from the bad experience.
- Bring in a diverse cohort through carefully equitable hiring, and then create the culture that allows them to succeed via objective assessment of each person's contribution.
- Reward success with autonomy in many forms: flexibility of hours and working at home, less oversight and more authority, and, especially, more respect. Then add in salary and benefit rewards as well.

Beyond the immediate team, there are usually other teams within the same organization, along with partner organizations, subcontractors, and subcontractors of the subcontractors. Our teams never work in a vacuum. You may not be able to give the same intense attention to these other organizations, but they form an ecosystem that your success depends upon. Next, some ideas on how to keep cultivating that ecosystem.

15

KEEP PARTNER ORGANIZATIONS ENERGIZED AND CONNECTED

A small group of us from the Psyche project trooped into the office of the president of one of our subcontractors. We had taken the extreme step of flying to their offices during the peak of COVID because they were just not delivering the equipment they were under contract for, and we couldn't quite figure out why over Zoom.

After our friendly greetings, our project manager spoke about our concerns and I gave a little science pep talk. This is primary human exploration, going to a place humans have never visited before. It's a big mission, and we are under big scrutiny from NASA headquarters. And we have what's called a planetary launch, I stressed: If we don't launch in our designated period, we may not have another chance for a year or more. It's not like launching into Earth orbit. Earth's orbits are always right there with us, accessible. If we miss our launch window, we may well be canceled entirely.

"What?" he exclaimed. "You can't just launch anytime?" And there it was. He did not understand that our deadlines were real.

I realized in that moment that the president of this subcontracting company had, of course, been running his own calculations of how to best spend his resources and his team's time. I think his bonus structure did not have Psyche as a line item, since the contract had been signed with his predecessor.

Some of the biggest issues we had on the Psyche project during the building of the spacecraft stemmed from working with outside organizations that had motivations and behaviors that were completely logical for their organization but disastrous for the Psyche project. This chapter will show how to set expectations clearly from the beginning, how to align processes across organizations, and, most importantly, the need to visit and spend time with your partners and subcontractors in person. Communicating—in fact, overcommunicating—is key to having your partner organizations think of you first and communicate clearly with you.

WITH BEST INTENTIONS, SUBCONTRACTOR RELATIONS CAN STILL GO WRONG

When we started writing the first proposal to NASA for the Psyche project, back in 2013, I had the luxury of thinking of the proposal in the purest terms. Since we were not likely to win, I felt free of some of the Machiavellian strategizing that other teams were putting in to get one inch ahead at the finish line.

Why were we not likely to win? Usually, mission proposals are won by PIs (principal investigators—in other words, the leaders of the project) who have been through the process before, with proposals that have been refined by going through the whole process and not winning and trying again, and by prime contractors who are not new to NASA. This was my first time, the Psyche proposal's first time, and Maxar's first try at being a prime contractor for deep space.

Feeling free of the scrutiny that comes with being the expected contender, I pushed for writing exactly the proposal we thought was right, including the most important science questions to address, the best instruments to answer those questions, and exactly how the spacecraft should be built. We were doing less mental politicking—not second-guessing what a hypothetical reviewer might think are the science questions we should ask or whose gamma-ray spectrometer we should choose. We were thinking more about an ideal situation where we got to choose the best answers, not the most political or expedient.

We've ended up, more than a decade later, building almost exactly what we planned—except in two key areas, both of which cost us dearly in schedule and budget and overran their margins.

One was a subsystem built entirely in-house by one partner organization. We'll call it Sensor A. As soon as the Psyche mission was selected for flight, we heard from the Sensor A team: We've learned so much from the last time we built Sensor A that now we know we need to make a number of changes in our proposal. Whaaat?!, we on the leadership team reacted. What about our oft-stated principle that we are proposing exactly what we need to build?

The team's only answer was to ask us to review the twenty key changes and see if we didn't agree that we needed them: Among the changes were a particular part no longer made by the vendor and a design that had proven unreliable in previous tests. Indeed, the Sensor A team was exactly right about the changes, and we ended up agreeing. The need for each change was irrefutable.

The problem was each change led to cost increases and time delays. Why did this happen? Because the subcontractor of Sensor A wrote a bit of a marketing piece to increase the chance of winning, rather than the most strictly complete proposal they could. If they had written the strict version, the number of changes needed would have made it appear, in the proposal, that this was not really a completely flight-tested and proven instrument but, rather, a little more of a new design-and-test situation. That would have added risk to the proposal and lessened our chance of selection.

Of course, I understood why. The subcontractor was a small shop, and its continued existence requires a constant stream of customers for its specialized product, and with that pressure, the subcontractor had to make every proposal look as good as possible and then bring in the changes later, no matter the cost.

How to prevent this kind of margin-busting build? Not so easy. Your subs probably will not tell you about their cost, mass and power, and schedule-margin performance on previous contracts. But perhaps you can build in performance incentives and disincentives; this would have been a breach of common practice in our case, but I surely would push for that in the future.

The second key area where our project broke through the cost and schedule margins was quite a different case. Here the subcontractor, whom we'll call Subcontractor B, simply had much bigger fish to fry. Their institutional priorities were not focused on our project. They changed a key product line that we had proposed right after our proposal was selected by NASA, necessitating a lot of changes in what we had expected to build.

So in one case, the Sensor A builders were too small a shop to risk not winning the proposal and thus they oversold, and in the other case, Subcontractor B was too big a shop to care about our proposal as they should have. We also had a third problematic area: One team simply did not have the personnel who knew how to bid correctly (see Chapter 12 on how to keep your team from losing the recipe). We received a bid from them and put it in the proposal, not knowing that it was not feasible.

All the subcontractors, and their subcontractors, had a critical role in the Psyche mission. We could not launch without all their parts and subsystems installed and working correctly. But they did not all receive the full communications blast of our vision and drive all the time. They were not inducted fully into the thrill and the vision and importance of what we were doing. They worked in their own separate organizations.

In fact, most everyone connected to the Psyche mission reported up some other chain in some other organization, and that organization had other priorities than those of our project. Sure, the mission was the contract holder and customer for our subcontractors, but did their future depend upon us, and did they know it? All our subcontractors had other customers and most likely other priorities, and more importantly, other managers with other priorities. Clearly, I had responsibility without authority—I was not the boss of all these teams.

Responsibility without authority is extremely common in any organization. You may lead a team, but in order to get your work done, you need input and deliverables from your colleague's team or an outside vendor or partner. No matter whether you are leading the project, have been assigned responsibility for an output, or are naturally responsible, you need to figure out how to get things done without the power of being a dictator.

ALIGN PROCESSES AND EXPECTATION ACROSS ORGANIZATIONS

I'm talking with a subcontractor about a contract we've just signed. It's so easy to imagine that our expectations are the same, in the flush of happiness at closing the deal. They seem like the right choice: eager, responsive, full of yeses. But that is today. What happens tomorrow?

Tomorrow, it's business as usual; I'm working and assume they are working. Both organizations, mine and the subcontractor's, have a process called acceptance review, in which we check a newly built part to make sure it is exactly as it should be. But weeks go by before I realize how different the two acceptance reviews are. My organization has processes so tight that the project cannot proceed until each acceptance review is completed and double-checked. It's slow and procedural, but by God, every part is checked. Their organization has a form with a box labeled "accept" to tick—but maybe the part was checked and maybe it wasn't. You can imagine the issues this could cause: Not knowing a part was wrong until it is installed—at which point it's too late to replace or repair the part without delaying the whole project.

A remedy for some of the problems of this kind are to sort through, in the contract phase, the specifics of how everything will be done. Here are some questions to ask:

- Exactly how does your organization hire for the project, and can we rely on keeping key people through the whole project, not having them moved to other new projects?
- What are the metrics you use to track progress, and how often shall we look at them together?
- If our personnel will be working together, what are your protocols for training, preparation, and work, and do they align with ours?
- How do you do your quality assurance? Who does it, and when in the process does it happen?

These questions should spark a half-dozen or more questions, appropriate for your specific area and project. Talk these through before there is a crisis.

WHAT IF THOSE EXPECTATIONS AREN'T BEING MET?

You need to have strategies to accelerate pressure on partners and subcontractors when schedules are slipping. The first of these is to make sure that expectations are clear enough that both sides know when problems are occurring—and here you will draw upon the margins and metrics discussion in Chapter 13.

Aerospace talks about the twenty-four-hour rule: If there is some new crisis or problem, work on it for twenty-four hours before reporting upward, in case you are wrong about it and it turns out not to be a problem or it can be easily solved. I'm not a big fan of this rule; I think clear and immediate communication is the key to building trust. Everyone agrees not to panic and overreact (speak calmly and clearly when in crisis!), and then everyone gets to know when anything happens.

However, the *minute* the subcontractor's schedule slips, follow the following five steps.

A Checklist for Managing Late Subcontractors

1. Meet with the subcontractor, either in person or on a video call. Always meet tough information with calm, help, and support.

2. Have the subcontractor produce an initial schedule granular enough that it can be replanned if needed. You have to know enough about the options to figure out how to fix a problem and what the margins are. You have to know enough detail that you can see what can be done in parallel instead of in sequence.

3. Set weekly milestones and hold weekly meetings. The key people—those actually doing the work and those with the authority to make decisions—have to be in the meeting. Focus on progress and milestones, and don't let any slips go undiagnosed. Find out why they happened.

4. Add more management to those meetings as needed. In the end, the heat goes onto the top management, and so they need to be in the loop when things are not going well. Keep them involved with communications between meetings, but don't create any artificial urgency—the need has to be real, the dates real, the fragility of the project accurately communicated. Don't lose your credibility by hoping that some strategic inflation of issues will cause faster movement.

5. Add brief daily meetings ("stand-ups"), if they don't exist already. These are about the usual engineering things: What did we do yesterday, and what are we doing today? Consider having a daily fifteen-minute stand-up just for the problem issue, and fifteen minutes every single day until it's done or solved.

On the Psyche mission, we got to this point on quite a few subsystems, especially during COVID. On one, we were having weeklies that included the senior manager of the subcontractor as well as their project manager and the engineers, along with Psyche project leadership. The subcontractor had already brought on a special expert senior engineer to review the project and coach the subcontractor's team. But progress was still slow, and the reasons for its slowness were not clear.

Then one day the subcontractors had a mishap. A piece of equipment broke, the quality assurance team was not in the room, and there was the fear for a day, until testing was completed, that the flight subsystem itself had been damaged. It had not. That was a big relief!

But the next meeting with the subcontractor, including their top management, was tense. We were all on a Webex video call, discussing the test results and the path forward. The special expert engineer wasn't adding much, which was unusual. And then a chat message came through to everyone, from the subcontractor manager to the special expert engineer: "I guess you're going to have to start spending some time on this project now."

The manager had not meant to send this message to everyone; it was just for the expert engineer. But in that moment we learned that the subcontractor had not prioritized our project, and the expert who was supposed to be on it had not in fact been involved yet. This was my first opportunity to learn the lesson that quiet people are likely covering up a problem, but I didn't learn it until years later when the Guidance, Navigation, and Control subteam issue caused our launch delay (as we saw in Chapter 8). Shame on me.

GET PERSONAL

Every kind of success working across teams and organizations starts with personal, communicative partnerships. As one partner once said to me, "Yes, technically we are a subcontractor. I know we literally have a contract that says that. But we don't like to be called, or made to feel like, a subcontractor. We want the same respect as anyone." This statement makes it clearer than ever why your greatest powers are the powers of personal relationships (your dyads!) and of vision (why do we all care about this project?).

- Travel to meet with the subcontractors and their teams.
- Set up special calls to let them know what is happening on the project, especially when it might be new, internal information that will make it clear the subcontractor is a privileged partner.
- Have lunch with the whole subcontractor team or take the whole team to dinner. Eating together makes people friends in a way nothing else does (but heed the warning about social events from Chapter 14).

Though throughout this book I stress that every person has the ability to perform and think like a leader, there are certain things that anointed leaders especially have to do to create successful projects. In all ways, you need to lead by example. Live the culture of your organization, and do not give in to the temptations of power (to be rude, to require others to do things you wouldn't do, to make decisions without communicating, for example). And then, use your power for the good of the team. Help people work together and share information so it is not lost (keep teams from losing the recipe). Track what the team is doing with metrics, give confidence of success with metrics, and then reward your team for their efforts. Finally, bring those same values and practices into your relationships with subcontractors and other teams. Keep building that culture of success, even beyond your own team's boundaries.

CONCLUSION

The Psyche mission launched successfully on lucky Friday, October 13, 2023, and at the time of writing, it is cruising through space toward its asteroid target. Every week we communicate with the spacecraft using the Deep Space Network of radio dishes, downloading data on where the spacecraft is and how it is functioning, and we work on plans and explicitly on the team dynamic, preparing for the intense work to come when we reach the asteroid in 2029.

The team and all its attendant organizations (NASA, JPL, Maxar, the universities, and on and on) are still learning from the challenges we faced before launch. Every day I see the ways our bigger team, our subteams, and I myself have grown and how we still need to improve. The time spent thinking about these improvements is never wasted.

Every moment you spend thinking about how to make your own performance better, your communications clearer, and your success based on your merits rather than on biases is worth the time and the energy. Not only will your team be more successful, but the improvements will also benefit every individual, every dyad, and the team and project as a whole.

In Part I of *Mission Ready* we started with just you as the irreducible unit with which every team starts. Part I described five attributes that would help you to be more effective, which are how to communicate clearly and calmly even in the most difficult circumstances, how to recognize problems and act, how to not give up, how to develop a strong sense of quality, and how to recognize the importance of process through strategic thinking and metacognition. In the age of AI, these are robot-proofing, success-creating, even happiness-creating attributes.

Next, you need to connect with others until together you form a team. In Part II, we looked at how dyads are networked into a team and how the team sets its culture, deciding on the ways people will interact and get the work done. The team becomes mature and responsible enough for the practices of continuous, transparent communications, delegating authority, and structuring decision-making and follow-through so that everyone understands what will happen next.

Finally, because every person is at least partly a leader and can always improve those skills, Part III of *Mission Ready* looked at teams from above. In successful teams, both leaders and team members understand and practice culture building, communications, delegation, respect, and clear decision-making. Looking at a team from above, each of us can lead by example, keep teams from losing the recipe, set up and use margins and metrics, help develop better assessments and rewards, and build our partner ecosystem. We can work to keep both performance and happiness strong.

In this postpandemic world with its uncertain future, the factionalization of society, the move to working at home, and the failed promise of the internet to bring people together, the importance of human-to-human connection is greater than ever. Change begins on the scale of one human to another. Everyone has the opportunity to build the kind of culture in our work teams that benefits each of us individually as well as the project as a whole. It's on this scale, human to human, that we have the greatest ability to achieve our goals, invent what should be, and build the world we want to live in.

Problem-solving and innovation aren't just code words for making a better-selling product. They are what we need to move forward as individuals, communities, nations, and as a species. Innovation and problem-solving are not done only by geniuses and heroes. They're done by humans and by teams. Let's set up our teams so that each person's contribution is maximized and, therefore, their personal growth is also maximized.

You can become your best and most effective self, the most valuable person on your team, and you as an individual can raise the game of your whole team. The success of a project should also be the success of each person on the project. We can all be mission ready.

ACKNOWLEDGMENTS

To all the teams and close communities I've been privileged to be a part of, these in chronological order and any others I have mistakenly omitted, my deepest gratitude for all I have learned by your sides, for the joys and sorrows and inspirations and insights: the Asbury Hill Stables community; the First Presbyterian Church of Ithaca, New York; the Cornell Wild Roses Ultimate Frisbee team; the community of Third East in the East Campus dorm at MIT; Professor Tim Grove's lab at MIT; Professor Nafi Toksöz's Earth Resources Laboratory team; the Touche Ross management consulting group, Philadelphia; the Brown University planetary and geophysics groups; the Acton, Massachusetts, Friends Meeting; Beagle Learning; and the teams with whom I have held leadership positions, including *The International Wine Review Magazine*; my MIT lab group; the Department of Terrestrial Magnetism at the Carnegie Institution for Science; the School of Earth and Space Exploration; Team Magrathea and the Interplanetary Initiative at Arizona State University; the Space Sciences Laboratory at University of California, Berkeley; and, of course, the NASA Psyche mission team.

Jane von Mehren, my agent, friend, and patient encourager and editor, your gentle but clear words have helped all my projects improve immeasurably from poor, dim reflections of what I meant in my heart and mind to expressions of ideas that were worthy of the light of day. Thank you for your support and belief and uplift.

Acknowledgments

To Emily Taber, executive editor at Basic Books, and her team, all my thanks for your enthusiasm in taking on this project and creating a team with me while we made it real. Though I always, embarrassingly, greet an edited manuscript with trepidation, you and your team's comments have greatly improved the manuscript and were so kindly presented that I never had to cover my eyes with my fingers while I was reading. What a gift it is to have readers with such insight.

So much of the energy and nuance in this book comes from my husband, James Tanton, who is always willing to read and comment on a passage and never stopped encouraging me with "I am so excited about your team's book!"; my son, Turner Bohlen, who is always willing to think deeply and talk with me about the challenges of teams and who has a preternatural gift for working out the knots in a new idea; and my daughter-in-law, Liz Casey, for the humanizing, reassuring conversations where we share all our team challenges and successes together.

I am deeply blessed to share the world with each of these people.

NOTES

PART I: INWARD

1. An earlier version of these five practices appeared here: Lindy Elkins-Tanton, "Start with Yourself," Medium, July 29, 2024, https://medium.com/@ltelkins/start-with-yourself-8c9bd87756c1.

CHAPTER 1: SPEAK CLEARLY, CALMLY, AND ON TOPIC

1. Linda Elkins-Tanton et al., "How to Talk So Your Organization Will Listen," Medium, February 19, 2019, https://medium.com/@ltelkins/how-to-talk-so-your-organization-will-listen-5b9f317cf8cb.

2. Veronika Job et al., "Ego Depletion—Is It All in Your Head? Implicit Theories About Willpower Affect Self-Regulation," *Psychological Science* 21, no. 11 (2010): 1686–1693.

3. Oliver Sacks, *The River of Consciousness* (Picador, 2017).

CHAPTER 2: RECOGNIZE PROBLEMS AND TAKE ACTION

1. Jon Bostock, *The Elephant's Dilemma: Break Free and Reimagine Your Future at Work* (Lioncrest, 2020).

2. Brian J. Lucas and Loran F. Nordgren, "The Creative Cliff Illusion," *Proceedings of the National Academy of Sciences* 117, no. 33 (2020): 19830–19836.

3. Ut Na Sio and Thomas C. Ormerod, "Does Incubation Enhance Problem Solving? A Meta-Analytic Review," *Psychological Bulletin* 135, no. 1 (2009): 94.

4. Kenneth J. Gilhooly, *Incubation in Problem Solving and Creativity: Unconscious Processes* (Routledge, 2019).

5. Joseph Biederman et al., "Clinical Correlates of Mind Wandering in Adults with ADHD," *Journal of Psychiatric Research* 117 (2019): 15–23.

6. Claire M. Zedelius and Jonathan W. Schooler, "Capturing the Dynamics of Creative Daydreaming," in *Creativity and the Wandering Mind* (Academic Press, 2020), 55–72.

7. Marily Oppezzo and Daniel L. Schwartz, "Give Your Ideas Some Legs: The Positive Effect of Walking on Creative Thinking," *Journal of Experimental Psychology: Learning, Memory, and Cognition* 40, no. 4 (2014): 1142.

CHAPTER 3: DO NOT GIVE UP

1. Brad Stuhlberg, "Forget Medals: This Is the Real Power of the Olympics," *New York Times*, August 11, 2024, Section SR, 4.

2. Carol S. Dweck, *Mindset: The New Psychology of Success* (Random House, 2006).

CHAPTER 4: CREATE QUALITY IN ALL YOU DO

1. Robert M. Pirsig, *Zen and the Art of Motorcycle Maintenance: An Inquiry into Values* (William Morrow, 1974).

2. Gary P. Pisano, "The Hard Truth About Innovative Cultures," *Harvard Business Review*, January–February 2019, https://hbr.org/2019/01/the-hard-truth-about-innovative-cultures.

CHAPTER 5: BECOME AN EXPERT THINKER: METACOGNITION

1. Deanna Kuhn, "Metacognitive Development," *Current Directions in Psychological Science* 9, no. 5 (2000): 178–181.

2. David N. Perkins, *Smart Schools: Better Thinking and Learning for Every Child* (Free Press, 1995).

3. Daniel Kahneman and Amos Tversky, "Choices, Values, and Frames," *American Psychologist* 39, no. 4 (1984): 341.

4. "Project Implicit," Harvard University, 2011, https://implicit.harvard.edu/implicit.

CHAPTER 6: BUILD YOUR DYADS

1. Reed Hastings and Erin Meyer, *No Rules Rules: Netflix and the Culture of Reinvention* (Random House, 2020).

2. Gordon L. Flett et al., "The Anti-Mattering Scale: Development, Psychometric Properties and Associations with Well-Being and Distress Measures in Adolescents and Emerging Adults," *Journal of Psychoeducational Assessment* 40, no. 1 (2022): 37–59.

3. Zach Mercurio, "The Power of Mattering at Work," *Harvard Business Review*, May–June 2025, 86.

CHAPTER 7: DISCUSS CULTURE TOGETHER AND PRACTICE IT CONSCIOUSLY

1. Google, "Understand Team Effectiveness," Google re:Work, accessed June 28, 2025, https://rework.withgoogle.com/en/guides/understanding-team-effectiveness.

2. Adam Grant, *Give and Take: A Revolutionary Approach to Success* (Penguin, 2013).

3. Erin Meyer, "Build a Corporate Culture That Works," *Harvard Business Review*, July–August 2024, https://hbr.org/2024/07/build-a-corporate-culture-that-works.

4. An early version of this anecdote appeared in Lindy Elkins-Tanton, "It's Not Just What We Do but How We Do It," Medium, July 8, 2024, https://medium.com/@ltelkins/i-its-not-just-what-we-do-but-how-we-do-it-20751e35bbdd; and "Start with Yourself," Medium, July 29, 2024, https://medium.com/@ltelkins/start-with-yourself-8c9bd87756c1.

5. Rosabeth Moss Kanter, *Men and Women of the Corporation: New Edition* (Basic Books, 2008).

6. Benjamin M. Walsh et al., "Assessing Workgroup Norms for Civility: The Development of the Civility Norms Questionnaire-Brief," *Journal of Business and Psychology* 27 (2012): 407–420.

7. Arieh Riskin et al., "The Impact of Rudeness on Medical Team Performance: A Randomized Trial," *Pediatrics* 136, no. 3 (2015): 487–495; an early version of this section appeared

in Lindy Elkins-Tanton, "The Astonishing, Long-Lasting Damage of Rudeness," Medium, July 22, 2024, https://medium.com/@ltelkins/the-astonishing-long-lasting-damage-of-rudeness-6c0e4d1c918d.

8. Daniel Coyle, *The Culture Code: The Secrets of Highly Successful Groups* (Bantam, 2018).

9. Will Felps et al., "How, When, and Why Bad Apples Spoil the Barrel: Negative Group Members and Dysfunctional Groups," *Research in Organizational Behavior* 27 (2006): 175–222.

10. Carl R. Rogers, "Toward a Theory of Creativity," *ETC: A Review of General Semantics* (1954): 249–260.

11. Amy C. Edmondson and Zhike Lei, "Psychological Safety: The History, Renaissance, and Future of an Interpersonal Construct," *Annual Review of Organizational Psychology and Organizational Behavior* 1, no. 1 (2014): 23–43.

12. Paul Axtell, "Make Your Meetings a Safe Space for Honest Conversation," *Harvard Business Review*, April 11, 2019, https://hbr.org/2019/04/make-your-meetings-a-safe-space-for-honest-conversation.

13. W. P. Rogers et al., *Report to the President on the Space Shuttle Challenger Accident, Volume 1*, No. AD-A171402 (Presidential Commission on the Space Shuttle Challenger Accident, 1986).

14. An early version of parts of this chapter appeared in Lindy Elkins-Tanton, "Make Conflict Safe, Because Without It We'll Never Get Anywhere," Medium, August 5, 2024, https://medium.com/@ltelkins/make-conflict-safe-because-without-it-well-never-get-anywhere-549e780a6369.

15. Karen A. Jehn, "A Qualitative Analysis of Conflict Types and Dimensions in Organizational Groups," *Administrative Science Quarterly* (1997): 530–557.

16. Ron Friedman, "How High-Performing Teams Build Trust," *Harvard Business Review*, January 10, 2024, https://hbr.org/2024/01/how-high-performing-teams-build-trust.

17. Some of the material in this section first appeared in Lindy Elkins-Tanton, "Avoid, Compete, Compromise . . . or Collaborate at Work," Medium, August 12, 2024, https://medium.com/@ltelkins/avoid-compete-compromise-or-collaborate-at-work-e8988a210a8f.

18. Some of the material in this subsection first appeared in Lindy Elkins-Tanton, "Whether You Discuss Them or Not, You Have Them: Cultural Norms at Work," Medium, August 19, 2024, https://medium.com/@ltelkins/whether-you-discuss-them-or-not-you-have-them-cultural-norms-at-work-bf1e1218d985.

CHAPTER 8: ENABLE CONTINUOUS COMMUNICATIONS TO FLOW

1. Chris Argyris, "Good Communication That Blocks Learning," *Harvard Business Review*, July–August 1994, https://hbr.org/1994/07/good-communication-that-blocks-learning.

2. Gary P. Pisano, "The Hard Truth About Innovative Cultures," *Harvard Business Review*, January–February 2019, https://hbr.org/2019/01/the-hard-truth-about-innovative-cultures.

3. Thomas L. Good, "Two Decades of Research on Teacher Expectations: Findings and Future Directions," *Journal of Teacher Education* 38, no. 4 (1987): 32–47.

4. Christine L. Porath and Amir Erez, "Overlooked but Not Untouched: How Rudeness Reduces Onlookers' Performance on Routine and Creative Tasks," *Organizational Behavior and Human Decision Processes* 109, no. 1 (2009): 29–44.

5. This phrase is a version of "Seek first to understand, and then to be understood," from Stephen R. Covey, *The 7 Habits of Highly Effective People* (Simon & Schuster, 1989).

6. Benjamin E. Hilbig, "Sad, Thus True: Negativity Bias in Judgments of Truth," *Journal of Experimental Social Psychology* 45, no. 4 (2009): 983–986.

CHAPTER 10: WORK TOGETHER ON DECISION-MAKING, TACTICS, AND STRATEGY

1. Thomas R. E. Southwood, "Habitat, the Templet for Ecological Strategies?," *Journal of Animal Ecology* 46, no. 2 (1977): 337–365.

2. J. Michael Haynie et al., "A Situated Metacognitive Model of the Entrepreneurial Mindset," *Journal of Business Venturing* 25, no. 2 (2010): 217–229.

CHAPTER 11: LEAD BY EXAMPLE

1. McKinsey & Company, "Organizational Health Index," accessed June 28, 2025, www.mckinsey.com/solutions/orgsolutions/overview/organizational-health-index.

2. Aaron De Smet et al., "Healthy Organizations Keep Winning, but the Rules Are Changing Fast," McKinsey & Company, August 2, 2024, www.mckinsey.com/capabilities/people-and-organizational-performance/our-insights/healthy-organizations-keep-winning-but-the-rules-are-changing-fast.

3. Erin Meyer, "Build a Corporate Culture That Works," *Harvard Business Review*, July–August 2024, https://hbr.org/2024/07/build-a-corporate-culture-that-works.

4. Joseph Folkman, "It's All About Me! What Happens When a Leader Takes All the Credit?," *Forbes*, November 10, 2017, www.forbes.com/sites/joefolkman/2017/11/10/its-all-about-me-what-happens-when-a-leader-takes-all-the-credit.

5. A version of this subsection first appeared in Lindy Elkins-Tanton, "Hubris Syndrome, the Dark Side of Power," Medium, November 12, 2024, https://medium.com/@ltelkins/hubris-syndrome-the-dark-side-of-power-102a346155fc.

6. David Owen and Jonathan Davidson, "Hubris Syndrome: An Acquired Personality Disorder? A Study of US Presidents and UK Prime Ministers over the Last 100 Years," *Brain* 132, no. 5 (2009): 1396–1406.

7. Peter Garrard et al., "Linguistic Biomarkers of Hubris Syndrome," *Cortex* 55 (2014): 167–181.

8. Jean-Paul Selten, "Consider the Hubris Syndrome for Inclusion in Our Classification Systems," *Psychological Medicine* 53, no. 13 (2023): 5889–5891.

9. Jerry Useem, "Power Causes Brain Damage," *Atlantic*, July–August 2017.

10. Harold G. Moore, Mike Guardia, and Johnny Heller, *Hal Moore on Leadership: Winning When Outgunned and Outmanned* (Blackstone, 2018).

11. Joel Goh et al., "The Relationship Between Workplace Stressors and Mortality and Health Costs in the United States," *Management Science* 62, no. 2 (2016): 608–628.

12. A version of this box first appeared in Lindy Elkins-Tanton, "Some Things an Academic Community Can Do About Harassment," Medium, April 16, 2018, https://medium.com/@ltelkins/some-things-an-academic-community-can-do-about-harassment-859abe713946.

13. Yowei Shaw and Kia Miakka Natisse, "The New Norm," *Invisibilia*, NPR, June 17, 2016, www.npr.org/programs/invisibilia/481887848/the-new-norm.

14. Christine L. Porath et al., "The Effects of Civility on Advice, Leadership, and Performance," *Journal of Applied Psychology* 100, no. 5 (2015): 1527; R. Douglas Parker and Amanda S. Marcy, "The Value of Civility," *Strategic Finance* 104, no. 9 (2023): 30–38; and Charlie L. Hardy and Mark Van Vugt, "Nice Guys Finish First: The Competitive Altruism Hypothesis," *Personality and Social Psychology Bulletin* 32, no. 10 (2006): 1402–1413.

15. David Noble and Michael Letsky, "Cognitive-Based Metrics to Evaluate Collaboration Effectiveness," April 2002, paper presented at RTO SAS symposium, "Analysis of the Military Effectives of Future C2 Concepts and Systems," The Hague, Netherlands, https://apps.dtic.mil/sti/tr/pdf/ADA425450.pdf.

CHAPTER 12: KEEP TEAMS FROM LOSING THE RECIPE

1. Amos Zeeberg, "Reinventing Concrete, the Ancient Roman Way," *New York Times* October 19, 2024.

2. Chris Argyris, "Good Communication That Blocks Learning," *Harvard Business Review*, July–August 1994, https://hbr.org/1994/07/good-communication-that-blocks-learning.

3. David B. Audretsch and Maryann P. Feldman, "Innovative Clusters and the Industry Life Cycle," *Review of Industrial Organization* 11 (1996): 253–273.

4. Edward L. Glaeser et al., "Growth in Cities," *Journal of Political Economy* 100, no. 6 (1992): 1126–1152.

5. A version of the remote-teams discussion first appeared in Lindy Elkins-Tanton, "Remote Work Breaks Teams Apart, but We Know How to Fix That," Medium, July 15, 2024, https://medium.com/@ltelkins/remote-work-breaks-teams-apart-but-we-know-how-to-fix-that-390777008080.

6. Longqi Yang et al., "The Effects of Remote Work on Collaboration Among Information Workers," *Nature Human Behaviour* 6, no. 1 (2022): 43–54.

7. Zoltán Lippényi and Tanja van der Lippe, "Co-Workers Working from Home and Individual and Team Performance," *New Technology, Work and Employment* 35, no. 1 (2020): 60–79.

8. Lawrence Domingo et al., "Let Me Finish My Thought: Process Interventions to Change Team Behavior During Remote Design Collaboration," *Proceedings of the Design Society* 3 (2023): 2425–2434.

CHAPTER 13: EXCEL AT MARGINS AND METRICS

1. Bent Flyvbjerg and Dan Gardner, *How Big Things Get Done: The Surprising Factors That Determine the Fate of Every Project, from Home Renovations to Space Exploration and Everything in Between* (Signal, 2023).

2. Edward W. Merrow, *Industrial Megaprojects: Concepts, Strategies, and Practices for Success* (Wiley, 2024).

3. Bent Flyvbjerg et al., "How Common and How Large Are Cost Overruns in Transport Infrastructure Projects?," *Transport Reviews* 23, no. 1 (2003): 71–88.

4. Atif Ansar et al., "Should We Build More Large Dams? The Actual Costs of Hydropower Megaproject Development," *Energy Policy* 69 (2014): 43–56.

5. Giorgio Locatelli, "Why Are Megaprojects, Including Nuclear Power Plants, Delivered Overbudget and Late? Reasons and Remedies," February 2018, arXiv.org, https://doi.org/10.48550/arXiv.1802.07312.

6. Ian R. Newby-Clark et al., "People Focus on Optimistic Scenarios and Disregard Pessimistic Scenarios While Predicting Task Completion Times," *Journal of Experimental Psychology: Applied* 6, no. 3 (2000): 171.

7. David Whitmore et al., "Are Megaprojects Ready for the Fourth Industrial Revolution?," *Proceedings of the Institution of Civil Engineers-Management, Procurement and Law* 174, no. 2 (2020): 49–58.

CHAPTER 14: DEVELOP BETTER WAYS TO ASSESS AND REWARD YOUR TEAM

1. Marshall Goldsmith and Mark Reiter, *Triggers: Creating Behavior That Lasts—Becoming the Person You Want to Be* (Crown Currency, 2015).

2. Lindsay McGregor and Neel Doshi, "3 Ways to Build a Culture That Lets High Performers Thrive," *Harvard Business Review*, June 28, 2024, https://hbr.org/2024/06/3-ways-to-build-a-culture-that-lets-high-performers-thrive.

3. Katherine Phillips, "How Diversity Makes Us Smarter," *Scientific American* 311, no. 4 (2014).

4. Katherine W. Phillips et al., "Surface-Level Diversity and Decision-Making in Groups: When Does Deep-Level Similarity Help?," *Group Processes & Intergroup Relations* 9, no. 4 (2006): 467–482.

5. Richard B. Evans et al., "Identity, Diversity, and Team Performance: Evidence from US Mutual Funds," *Management Science* 71, no. 4 (2025): 3026–3051.

6. Sylvia Ann Hewlett et al., "How Diversity Can Drive Innovation," *Harvard Business Review*, December 2013, https://hbr.org/2013/12/how-diversity-can-drive-innovation.

7. Yuhao Du et al., "Insidious Nonetheless: How Small Effects and Hierarchical Norms Create and Maintain Gender Disparities in Organizations," *Socius* 8 (2022), https://doi.org/10.1177/23780231221117.

8. This anecdote first appeared in Lindy Elkins-Tanton, "News Flash: People Tend to Hire People Like Themselves," Medium, March 2, 2019, https://medium.com/@ltelkins/news-flash-people-tend-to-hire-people-like-themselves-61afd132b3fd.

9. Joris Lammers et al., "To Have Control over or to Be Free from Others? The Desire for Power Reflects a Need for Autonomy," *Personality and Social Psychology Bulletin* 42, no. 4 (2016): 498–512.

10. A version of this salary discussion first appeared in Lindy Elkins-Tanton, "Difficult, Personal, and Hard to Fix . . ." Medium, February 26, 2019, https://medium.com/@ltelkins/difficult-personal-and-hard-to-fix-a669e9543472.

INDEX

Index

Lindy Elkins-Tanton is a professor at UC Berkeley, director of the Berkeley Space Sciences Laboratory, and lead of the NASA Psyche mission. She is the author of *A Portrait of the Scientist as a Young Woman*. She lives in Richmond, California.

RAISING READERS
Books Build Bright Futures

Thank you for reading this book and for being a reader of books in general. We are so grateful to share being part of a community of readers with you, and we hope you will join us in passing our love of books on to the next generation of readers.

Did you know that reading for enjoyment is the single biggest predictor of a child's future happiness and success?

More than family circumstances, parents' educational background, or income, reading impacts a child's future academic performance, emotional well-being, communication skills, economic security, ambition, and happiness.

Studies show that kids reading for enjoyment in the US is in rapid decline:

- In 2012, 53% of 9-year-olds read almost every day. Just 10 years later, in 2022, the number had fallen to 39%.
- In 2012, 27% of 13-year-olds read for fun daily. By 2023, that number was just 14%.

TOGETHER, WE CAN COMMIT TO RAISING READERS AND CHANGE THIS TREND. HOW?

- Read to children in your life daily.
- Model reading as a fun activity.
- Reduce screen time.
- Start a family, school, or community book club.
- Visit bookstores and libraries regularly.
- Listen to audiobooks.
- Read the book before you see the movie.
- Encourage your child to read aloud to a pet or stuffed animal.
- Give books as gifts.
- Donate books to families and communities in need.

Books build bright futures, and **Raising Readers** is our shared responsibility.

For more information, visit JoinRaisingReaders.com

Sources: National Endowment for the Arts, National Assessment of Educational Progress, WorldBookDay.com, Nielsen BookData's 2023 "Understanding the Children's Book Consumer"